456
1/24

THE USE OF BODIES

MERIDIAN

Crossing Aesthetics

Werner Hamacher

Editor

*Stanford
University
Press*

———————

*Stanford
California
2016*

THE USE OF BODIES

Homo Sacer IV, 2

Giorgio Agamben

Translated by Adam Kotsko

Stanford University Press
Stanford, California

The Use of Bodies was originally published in Italian in 2014
under the title *L'uso dei corpi* © 2014,
Neri Pozza Editore, Vicenza.

Printed in the United States of America
on acid-free, archival-quality paper

Library of Congress Cataloging-in-Publication Data

Agamben, Giorgio, 1942– author.
[Uso dei corpi. English]
The use of bodies : Homo sacer IV, 2 / Giorgio Agamben ;
translated by Adam Kotsko.
pages cm. — (Meridian : crossing aesthetics)
"Originally published in Italian in 2014 under the title
L'uso dei corpi."
Includes bibliographical references.
ISBN 978-0-8047-9234-9 (cloth : alk. paper)
ISBN 978-0-8047-9840-2 (pbk. : alk. paper)
ISBN 978-0-8047-9861-7 (ebook)
1. Human body (Philosophy)
2. Philosophical anthropology. I. Kotsko, Adam,
translator. II. Title. III. Series: Meridian (Stanford, Calif.)
B3611.A43U8613 2016
195—dc23
2015032891

A boy from Sparta stole a fox and hid it under his cloak, and because his people, in their foolishness, were more ashamed of a botched robbery than we fear punishment, he let it gnaw through his belly rather than be discovered.

  —Montaigne, *Essais*, I, XIV

. . . it's the fox that boy stole
and it hid in his clothes and it ripped his thigh . . .

  —V. Sereni, "Appointment at an Unusual Hour"

The free use of the proper is the most difficult thing.

  —F. Hölderlin

Contents

Translator's Note

To the extent possible, I have used consistent renderings for technical terms. This is above all the case for the by-now classical distinction between *potere* and *potenza*, which I have translated as "power" and "potential," respectively, even in cases where the latter is somewhat awkward and unidiomatic. The most notable example is in the epilogue's discussion of "destituent potential," which previous translators have sometimes rendered as "destituent power." I have rendered the verb *destituire* sometimes as "to render destitute" and sometimes as "to depose," as the latter often seemed unavoidable. With regard to the two terms that can be translated as "law," *legge* and *diritto*, the latter is always translated as "juridical order" unless it clearly means "right" in context.

Uso is almost always translated as "use," except where the context of linguistics demands the more technical "usage." The verb *esigere* and the noun *esigenza* have been rendered as "to demand" and "demand," respectively, despite the fact that the latter has sometimes been translated as "exigency." It seemed to me that there was no clear benefit to using the Latinate form, especially at the cost of obscuring the connection between the noun and verb. (Relatedly, the term *domanda* is always translated as "question," except in a brief discussion of Marx where the economic context requires the translation "demand.")

A variety of reflexive constructions modeled on Spinoza's use of the Ladino term *pasearse* have been rendered "[verb]-oneself" or "[noun]-of-oneself." My model here was David Heller-Roazen's elegant solution of this translation problem in *Potentialities*. I follow Agamben in translating the Heideggerian *Eigentlich* and *Uneigentlich*, customarily translated as "authentic" and "inauthentic," as "proper" and "improper," and I have altered quotations from the English translation accordingly. The term *presupposato* is translated sometimes as "presupposed" and sometimes as "presupposition," depending on which is most idiomatic. Neither English term represents any other Italian term. *Vincolo* is always rendered as "bond" and is the only term so rendered. Finally, in the prologue on Debord, the term *clandestino* is variously translated as "clandestine," "secret," or "stowaway."

I owe a debt of gratitude to many people for their help and support. Above all, I must thank Carlo Salzani for carefully comparing my entire manuscript to the original Italian text and offering invaluable corrections and clarifications. I would also like to extend my gratitude to Agatha Slupek, Philippe Theophanidis, and Mark Westmoreland for their bibliographical assistance, and to Emily-Jane Cohen, Tim Roberts, Friederike Sundaram, and the entire staff at Stanford University Press.

Prefatory Note

Those who have read and understood the preceding parts of this work know that they should not expect a new beginning, much less a conclusion. In fact, we must decisively call into question the commonplace according to which is it a good rule that an inquiry commence with a *pars destruens* and conclude with a *pars construens* and, moreover, that the two parts be substantially and formally distinct. In a philosophical inquiry, not only can the *pars destruens* not be separated from the *pars construens*, but the latter coincides, at every point and without remainder, with the former. A theory that, to the extent possible, has cleared the field of all errors has, with that, exhausted its raison d'être and cannot presume to subsist as separate from practice. The *archè* that archeology brings to light is not homogeneous to the presuppositions that it has neutralized; it is given entirely and only in their collapse. Its work is their inoperativity.

The reader will thus find here reflections on some concepts—use, demand, mode, form-of-life, inoperativity, destituent potential—that have from the very beginning oriented an investigation that, like every work of poetry and of thought, cannot be concluded but only abandoned (and perhaps continued by others).

Some of the texts published here were written at the beginning of the investigation, which is to say, almost twenty years ago; others—the greater part—were written in the course of the last five years. The reader will understand that, in a writing process so prolonged in time, it is difficult to avoid repetitions and, at times, discordances.

Prologue

1. It is curious how in Guy Debord a lucid awareness of the insufficiency of private life was accompanied by a more or less conscious conviction that there was, in his own existence or in that of his friends, something unique and exemplary, which demanded to be recorded and communicated. Already in *Critique de la séparation*, he thus evokes at a certain point as intransmissible "cette clandestinité de la vie privée sur laquelle on ne possède jamais que des documents dérisoires" ("that clandestinity of private life regarding which we possess nothing but pitiful documents"; Debord 1, p. 49/33); and nevertheless, in his first films and again in *Panégyrique*, he never stopped parading one after the other the faces of his friends, of Asger Jorn, of Maurice Wyckaert, of Ivan Chtcheglov, and his own face, alongside that of the women he loved. And not only that, but in *Panégyrique* there also appear the houses he inhabited, 28 via delle Caldaie in Florence, the country house at Champot, the square des Missions étrangères at Paris (actually 109 rue du Bac, his final Parisian address, in the drawing room of which a photograph from 1984 shows him seated on the English leather sofa that he seemed to like).

Here there is something like a central contradiction, which the Situationists never succeeded in working out, and at the same time something precious that demands to be taken up again and developed—perhaps the obscure, unavowed awareness that the genuinely political element consists precisely in this incommunicable, almost ridiculous clandestinity of private life. Since clearly it—the clandestine, our form-of-life—is so intimate and close at hand, if we attempt to grasp it, only impenetrable, tedious everydayness is left in our hands. And nonetheless, perhaps precisely this homonymous, promiscuous, shadowy presence preserves the stowaway of the political, the other face of the *arcanum imperii*, on which every biography and every revolution makes shipwreck. And Guy, who was so shrewd and cunning when he had to analyze and describe the alienated forms of existence in the society of the spectacle, is equally innocent and helpless when he tries to communicate the form of his life, to look in the face and dissolve the stowaway with which he had shared his journey up to the end.

2. *In girum imus nocte et consumimir igni* (1978) opens with a declaration of war against its time and continues with a relentless analysis of the conditions of life that the market society at the last stage of its development had established over all the earth. Unexpectedly, however, around the middle of the film, the detailed and merciless description stops and is replaced by the melancholic, almost mournful evocation of personal memories and events, which anticipate the declared autobiographical intention of *Panégyrique*. Guy recalls the Paris of his youth, which no longer exists, in whose streets and cafés he had set out with his friends on the stubborn investigation of that "Graal néfaste, dont personne n'avait voulu" ("sinister Grail, which no one else had ever sought"). Although the Grail in question, "glimpsed fleetingly" but not "encountered," must unquestionably have had a political meaning, since those who sought it "found themselves capable of understanding false life in light of true life" (Debord 1, p. 252/172), the tone of the commemoration, punctuated by citations from Ecclesiastes, Omar Khayyam, Shakespeare, and Bossuet, is at the same time indisputably nostalgic and gloomy: "À la moitié du chemin de la vraie vie, nous étions environnés d'une sombre mélancolie, qu'ont exprimée tant des mots railleurs et tristes, dans le café de la jeunesse perdue" ("Midway on the journey of real life we found ourselves surrounded by a somber melancholy, reflected by so much sad banter in the cafés of lost youth," Debord 1, p. 240/164). From this lost youth, Guy recalls the confusion, the friends and lovers ("comment ne me serais-je pas souvenu des charmants voyous et des filles orgueilleuses avec qui j'ai habité ces bas-fonds . . . [I couldn't help remembering the charming hooligans and proud young women I hung out with in those shady dives . . .]"; p. 237/162), while on the screen there appear the images of Gil J. Wolman, Ghislain de Marbaix, Pinot-Gallizio, Attila Kotanyi, and Donald Nicholson-Smith. But it is toward the end of the film that the autobiographical impulse reappears more forcefully and the vi-

sion of Florence *quand elle était libre* ("when it was free") is interwoven with images of the private life of Guy and of the women with whom he had lived in that city in the seventies. One then sees pass by rapidly the houses in which Guy lived, the impasse de Clairvaux, the rue St. Jacques, the rue St. Martin, a parish church in Chianti, Champot, and, once more, the faces of friends, while one hears the words from Gilles' song in *Les visiteurs du soir*: "Tristes enfants perdus, nous errions dans la nuit . . . ." And, a few sequences before the end, pictures of Guy at 19, 25, 27, 31, and 45 years of age. The sinister Grail, which the Situationists had set out to investigate, has to do not only with the political, but in some way also with the clandestinity of private life, of which the film does not hesitate to exhibit, apparently without shame, the "pitiful documents."

3. The autobiographical intention was, however, already present in the palindrome that gives the film its title. Immediately after having evoked his lost youth, Guy adds that nothing expresses its dissipation better than that "ancient phrase that turns completely back on itself, being constructed letter by letter like an inescapable labyrinth, thus perfectly uniting the form and content of loss: *In girum imus nocte et consumimur igni*. 'We turn in the night, consumed by fire'" (Debord 1, p. 242/165–166).

The phrase, at times defined as the "devil's verse," actually comes, according to a short article by Heckscher, from emblematic literature and refers to moths inexorably drawn by the flame of the candle that will consume them. An emblem consists of an *impresa*—which is to say, a phrase or motto—and an image; in the books that I have been able to consult, the image of moths devoured by flame appears often, yet it is never associated with the palindrome in question but rather with phrases that refer to amorous passion ("thus living pleasure leads to death," "thus to love well brings torment") or, in some rare cases, to imprudence in politics or war ("non temere est cuiquam temptanda potentia regis," "temere ac periculose"). In Otto van Veen's *Amorum emblemata* (1608) a winged love contemplates the moths who hurl themselves toward the flame of the candle, and the *impresa* reads: *brevis et damnosa voluptas*.

It is thus probable that Guy, in choosing the palindrome as a title, was comparing himself and his companions to moths who, amorously and rashly attracted by the light, are destined to lose themselves and be consumed in the flame. In *The German Ideology*—a work that Guy knew perfectly well—Marx evokes this image critically: "and it is thus that nocturnal moths, when the sun of the universal has set, seek the light of the lamp of the particular." It is thus all the more striking that, despite this warning, Guy had continued to pursue this light, to stubbornly peer into the flame of singular and private existence.

4. Toward the end of the nineties, on the shelves of a Parisian bookstore, the second volume of *Panégyrique*, containing iconography—by chance or out of an ironic intention of the bookseller—was next to the autobiography of Paul Ricoeur. Nothing is more instructive than to compare the use of images in the two cases. While the photographs in Ricoeur's book depicted the philosopher solely in the course of academic conferences, almost as though he had had no life outside them, the images of *Panégyrique* aspired to a state of biographical truth that concerned the existence of the author in all his aspects. "L'illustration authentique," the brief preamble informs us, "éclaire le discours vrai . . . on saura donc enfin quelle était mon apparence à différentes âges; et quel genre de visages m'a toujours entouré; et quels lieux j'ai habités . . . ." ("An authentic illustration sheds light on a true discourse. . . . People will at last be able to see what I looked like at various stages of my life, the kinds of faces that have always surrounded me, and what kind of places I have lived in . . . ."; Debord 2, p. 1691/73–74). Once again, notwithstanding the obvious insufficiency and banality of its documents, life—the clandestine—is in the foreground.

5. One evening in Paris, when I told her that many young people in Italy continued to be interested in Guy's writings and were hoping for a word from him, Alice responded: "on existe, cela devrait leur suffire" ("we exist, this should be sufficient for them"). What did she mean by: *on existe*? Certainly, in those years, they were living in seclusion and without a telephone between Paris and Champot, in a certain sense with eyes turned to the past, and their "existence" was, so to speak, entirely hidden in the "clandestinity of private life."

And again, shortly before his suicide in November 1994, the title of the last film prepared for Canal Plus: *Guy Debord, son art, son temps* does not seem—despite the truly unexpected phrase *son art*—completely ironic in its biographical intention, and before concentrating with an extraordinary vehemence on the horrors of "his time," this (sort of) spiritual last will and testament reiterates, with the same candor and the same old photographs, the nostalgic evocation of his past life.

What does it mean, then: *on existe*? Existence—that concept that is in every sense fundamental for the first philosophy of the West—perhaps has to do constitutively with life. "To be," writes Aristotle, "for the living means to live." And centuries later, Nietzsche specifies: "To be: we have no other representation than to live." To bring to light—beyond every vitalism—the intimate interweaving of being and living: this is today certainly the task of thought (and of politics).

6. *The Society of the Spectacle* opens with the word "life" ("Toute la vie des sociétés dans lesquelles règnent les conditions moderns de production s'annonce comme une immense accumulation de spectacles"; "In societies where modern conditions of production prevail, all of life presents itself as an immense accumulation of spectacles"; Debord 3, §1), and up to the end the book's analysis never stops making reference to life. The spectacle, in which "everything that was directly lived has moved away into a representation" (§1), is defined as a "concrete inversion of life" (§2). "The more his life is now his product, the more he is separated from his life" (§33). Life under spectacular conditions is a "counterfeit life" (§48) or a "survival" (§154) or a "pseudo-use of life" (§49). Against this alienated and separated life, what is asserted is something that Guy calls "historical life" (§139), which appears already in the Renaissance as a "joyous rupture with eternity": "in the exuberant life of Italian cities . . . life is experienced as enjoyment of the passage of time." Already years previously, in *Sur le passage de quelques personnes* and *Critique de la séparation*, Guy says of himself and his companions that "they wanted to reinvent everything every day, to become masters and possessors of their own life" (Debord 1, p. 22/14), that their meetings were like "signals emanating from a more intense life, a life that has not truly been found" (p. 47/32).

What this "more intense" life was, what was inverted and falsified in the spectacle, or even what one should understand by "life of society" is nowhere clarified; and yet it would be too easy to reproach the author for incoherence or terminological imprecision. Guy is doing nothing here but repeating a constant attitude in our culture, in which life is never defined as such but is time after time articulated and divided into *bios* and *zoè*, politically qualified life and bare life, public life and private life, vegetative life and a life of relation, so that each of the partitions is determinable only in its relation to the others. And perhaps it is in the last analysis precisely the undecidability of life that makes it so that it must each time be decided politically and singularly. And Guy's indecision between the secrecy of his private life—which, with the passing of time, had to appear to him as ever more fleeting and undocumentable—and historical life, between his individual biography and the obscure and unrenounceable epoch in which it was inscribed, betrays a difficulty that, at least under present conditions, no one can be under the illusion of having resolved once and for all. In any case, the stubbornly sought-after Grail, the life that is uselessly consumed in the flame, was not reducible to either of the opposed terms, neither to the idiocy of private life nor to the uncertain prestige of public life, and it indeed calls into question the very possibility of distinguishing them.

7. Ivan Illich has observed that the conventional notion of life (not "a life," but "life" in general) is perceived as a "scientific fact," which has no relationship with the experience of the singular living person. It is something anonymous and generic, which can designate at times a spermatozoon, a person, a bee, a cell, a bear, an embryo. It is this "scientific fact," so generic that science has given up on defining it, that the Church has made the ultimate receptacle of the sacred and bioethics the key term of its impotent foolishness. In any case, "life" today has more to do with survival than with the vitality or form of life of the individual.

Insofar as a sacral remainder has crept into it in this way, the secret that Guy pursued has become even more elusive. The Situationist attempt to bring life back to the political runs up against a further difficulty, but it is not for this reason less urgent.

8. What does it mean that private life accompanies us as a secret or a stowaway? First of all, that it is separated from us as clandestine and is, at the same time, inseparable from us to the extent that, as a stowaway, it furtively shares existence with us. This split and this inseparability constantly define the status of life in our culture. It is something that can be divided—and yet always articulated and held together in a machine, whether it be medical or philosophico-theological or biopolitical. Thus, not only is private life to accompany us as a stowaway in our long or short voyage, but corporeal life itself and all that is traditionally inscribed in the sphere of so-called intimacy: nutrition, digestion, urination, defecation, sleep, sexuality. . . . And the weight of this faceless companion is so strong that each seeks to share it with someone else—and nevertheless, alienation and secrecy never completely disappear and remain irresolv-

able even in the most loving life together. Here life is truly like the stolen fox that the boy hid under his clothes and that he cannot confess to even though it is savagely tearing at his flesh.

It is as if each of us obscurely felt that precisely the opacity of our clandestine life held within it a genuinely political element, as such shareable par excellence—and yet, if one attempts to share it, it stubbornly eludes capture and leaves behind it only a ridiculous and incommunicable remainder. The castle of Silling, in which political power has no object other than the vegetative life of bodies, is in this sense the cipher of the truth and, at the same time, of the failure of modern politics—which is, in reality, a biopolitics. We must change our life, carry the political into the everyday—and nevertheless, in the everyday, the political can only make shipwreck.

And when, as it today happens, the eclipse of the political and of the public sphere allows only private and bare life to subsist, the clandestine, left as sole master of the field, must, insofar as it is private, publicize itself and attempt to communicate its own no longer risible documents (though they remain such), which at this point correspond immediately with it, with its identical days recorded live and transmitted on screens to others, one after another.

And yet, only if thought is able to find the political element that has been hidden in the secrecy of singular existence, only if, beyond the split between public and private, political and biographical, *zoè* and *bios*, it is possible to delineate the contours of a form-of-life and of a common use of bodies, will politics be able to escape from its muteness and individual biography from its idiocy.

PART I

The Use of Bodies

§ 1 The Human Being without Work

1.1. The expression "the use of the body" (*he tou somatos chresis*) is found at the beginning of Aristotle's *Politics* (1254b 18), at the point where it is a question of defining the nature of the slave. Aristotle has just affirmed that the city is composed of families or households (*oikiai*) and that the family, in its perfect form, is composed of slaves and free people (*ek doulon kai eleutheron*—the slaves are mentioned before the free; 1253b 3–5). Three types of relations define the family: the despotic (*despotikè*) relation between the master (*despotes*) and the slaves, the matrimonial (*gamikè*) relation between the husband and wife, and the parental (*technopoietikè*) relation between the father and the children (7–11). That the master/slave relation is in some way, if not the most important, at least the most evident is suggested—aside from its being named first—by the fact that Aristotle specifies that the latter two relations are "nameless," lacking a proper name (which seems to imply that the adjectives *gamikè* and *technopoietikè* are only improper denominations devised by Aristotle, while everyone knows what a "despotic" relation is).

In any case, the analysis of the first relation, which immediately follows, in some way constitutes the introductory threshold of the treatise, almost as if only a correct preliminary understanding of the despotic relation would allow access to the properly political dimension. Aristotle begins by defining the slave as a being that, "while being human, is by its nature of another and not of itself," asking himself immediately after "if a similar being exists by nature or if, by contrast, slavery is always contrary to nature" (1254a 15–18).

The answer proceeds by means of a justification of the command ("to command and be commanded are not only necessary parts of things but also expedient"; 21–22), which in living beings are distinguished into des-

3

potic commands (*archè despotikè*) and political commands (*archè politikè*), exemplified respectively in the command of the soul over the body and that of the intelligence over the appetite. And just as in the preceding paragraph he had affirmed in general the necessity and natural (*physei*) character of command not only among animate beings but also in inanimate things (in Greek, the musical mode is the *archè* of the harmony), now he seeks to justify the command of some men over others:

> The soul commands the body with a despotic command, whereas the intellect commands the appetites with a political and royal command. And it is clear that the command of the soul over the body, and of the mind and the rational element over the passionate, is natural and expedient; whereas the equality of the two or the command of the inferior is always hurtful. . . . The same must therefore also happen among human beings. . . . (1254b 5–16)

‎‫א‬‎.   The idea that the soul makes use of the body as an instrument and at the same time commands it was formulated by Plato in a passage of the *Alcibiades* (130a 1) that Aristotle very likely must have in mind when he is seeking to found the dominion of the master over the slave through that of the soul over the body.

What is decisive, however, is the genuinely Aristotelian specification, according to which the command that the soul exercises over the body is not of a political nature (the "despotic" relation between master and slave is after all, as we have seen, one of the three relations that, according to Aristotle, define the *oikia*, the household). This means—according to the clear distinction that separates the household (*oikia*) from the city (*polis*) in Aristotle's thought—that the relationship soul/body (like master/slave) is an economic-domestic relationship and not a political one, as is, by contrast, that between intellect and appetite. But this also means that the relation between master and slave and that between soul and body are defined by one another and even that we must attend to the first if we want to understand the second. The soul is to the body as the master is to the slave. The caesura that divides the household from the city persists in the same threshold that separates and at the same time unites body and soul, master and slave. And it is only by interrogating this threshold that the relationship between economy and politics among the Greeks can become truly intelligible.

1.2. It is at this point that there appears, almost in the form of a parenthesis, the definition of the slave as "the being whose work is the use of the body":

> These human beings differ among themselves like the soul from the body or the human from the animal—as in the case of those whose work is the use of the

body [*oson esti ergon he tou somatos chresis*], and this is the best [that can come] from them [*ap'auton beltiston*]—the lower sort are by nature slaves, for whom it is better to be commanded with this command, as said above. (1254b 17–20)

The problem of what is the *ergon*, the work and proper function of the human being, had been posed by Aristotle in the *Nicomachean Ethics*. To the question of whether there was something like a work of the human being as such (and not simply of the carpenter, the tanner, or the shoemaker), or whether the human being was not instead born without work (*argos*), Aristotle had there responded by affirming that "the work of the human being is the being-at-work of the soul according to the *logos*" (*ergon anthropou psyches energeia kata logon*; 1098a 7). All the more striking, then, is the definition of the slave as the human being whose work consists only in the use of the body. That the slave is and remains a human being is, for Aristotle, beyond question (*anthropos on*, "while being a human being"; 1254a 16). This means, however, that there are some human beings whose *ergon* is not properly human or is different from that of other human beings.

Already Plato had written that the work of each being (whether it is a matter of a human being, a horse, of or whatever other living thing) is "what it alone does or what it does better than anything else" (*monon ti e kallista ton allon apergazetai*; *Republic*, 353a 10). Slaves represent the emergence of a dimension of human beings in which the best work ("the best for them"—the *beltiston* of the *Politics* probably refers to the *kallista* of the *Republic*) is not the being-at-work (*energeia*) of the soul according to the *logos* but something for which Aristotle can find no other denomination than "the use of the body."

In the two symmetrical formulas—

ergon anthropou psyches energeia kata logon
ergon (doulou) he tou somatos chresis

  the work of the human being is the being-in-action of the soul
    according to the *logos*
  the work of the slave is the use of the body

—*energeia* and *chresis*, being-at-work and use, seem to be juxtaposed precisely as are *psychè* and *soma*, soul and body.

1.3. The correspondence is all the more significant since we know that in Aristotle's thought there is a strict and complex relation between the two terms *energeia* and *chresis*. In an important study, Strycker (pp. 159–160) has shown that the classical Aristotelian opposition of potential (*dynamis*) and act (*energeia*, literally "being-at-work") originally had the form of an opposition between *dynamis* and *chresis* (being in potential and being in use). The paradigm of the opposition is found in Plato's *Euthydemus* (280d), which distinguishes between possession (*ktesis*) of a technique and the appropriate instruments without making use of them and their active employment (*chresis*). According to Strycker, Aristotle had begun, based on his master's example, by distinguishing (for example, in *Topics*, 130a 19–24) between possessing a science (*epistemen echein*) and using it (*epistemei chresthai*) and had later technicalized the opposition by substituting for the common *chresis* a word of his own invention, unknown to Plato: *energeia*, being-at-work.

In effect, in his early works, Aristotle made use of *chresis* and *chresthai* in a sense similar to that of the later *energeia*. Thus, in the *Protrepticus*, where philosophy is defined as *ktesis kai chresis sophias*, "possession and use of wisdom" (Düring, fragment B8), Aristotle carefully distinguishes between those who possess vision while keeping their eyes closed and those who effectively use it and, in the same way, between those who make use of science and whose who simply possess it (ibid., fragment B79). That use here has an ethical connotation and not only an ontological one in a technical sense is obvious in the passage in which the philosopher seeks to specify the meaning of the verb *chresthai*:

> To use [*chresthai*] anything, then, is this: if the capacity [*dynamis*] is for a single thing, then it is doing just that thing; if it is for several things, then it is doing whichever is best of these, as happens in the use of flutes, when someone uses the flute in the only and best way. . . . One must say, therefore, that the one who uses uses correctly, since for the one who uses correctly uses for the natural end and in the natural way. (fragment B84)

In the later works, Aristotle continues to make use of the term *chresis* in a sense similar to that of *energeia*, and yet the two terms are not simply synonymous but are often placed side by side as if to include and complete one another. Thus, in the *Magna Moralia*, after having affirmed that "use is more desirable than habit" (*hexis*, which indicates the possession of a *dynamis* or of a *techne*) and that "no one would care to have sight, if he were destined never to see but always to have his eyes shut," Aristotle writes that "happiness consists in a certain use and in *energeia*" (*en chresei tini kai energeiai*; 1184b 13–32). The formula, which is also found in the *Politics* (*estin eudaimonia aretes energeia kai chresis tis teleios*, "happiness is a being-at-work and a certain perfect use of virtue"; 1328a 38), shows that for Aristotle, the two terms are at once similar and distinct. In the definition of happiness, being-at-work and being-in-use, an ontological perspective and an ethical perspective, include and condition one another.

Since Aristotle does not define the term *energeia* except in a negative way with respect to potential (*esti d' he energeia to hyparchein to pragma me outos hosper legomen dynamei*, "*energeia* is the existing of a thing, but not in the sense in which we say that it is in potential"; *Metaphysics*, 1048a 31), it is all the more urgent to try to understand the meaning of the term *chresis* (and of the corresponding verb *chresthai*) in this context. It is certain, in any case, that Aristotle's abandonment of the term *chresis* in favor of *energeia* as key term of ontology has determined to some extent the way in which Western philosophy has thought being as actuality.

‏ℵ.‏ Like keeping one's eyes closed, so also is sleep the paradigm par excellence of potential and *hexis* for Aristotle, and in this sense, it is counterposed and subordinated to use, which by contrast is assimilated to wakefulness: "for both sleeping and waking presuppose the existence of the soul, but waking corresponds to knowing in act, sleeping to a having without exercising" (*echein kai me energein*; *On the Soul*, 412a 25). The inferiority of sleep, as figure of potential, with respect to *energeia* is affirmed even more decisively in the ethical works: "That happiness is an *energeia* can be seen also from the following consideration. For supposing someone to be asleep all his life, we should hardly consent to call such a person happy. Life indeed he has, but life according to virtue he has not" (*Magna Moralia*, 1185a 9–14).

1.4. In modern studies of slavery in the ancient world, the problem—with a striking anachronism, seeing that the ancients lacked even the corresponding term—is considered solely from the point of view of "labor" and production. That the Greeks and Romans saw in it a phenomenon of another order, which called for a conceptualization completely different from ours, seems irrelevant. It thus appears all the more scandalous to moderns that ancient philosophers not only did not problematize slavery but seemed to accept it as obvious and natural. Hence it is unsurprising to read, in the preamble of a recent exposition of Aristotle's theory of slavery, that this presents frankly "despicable" aspects, while the most elementary methodological caution would have suggested, in place of outrage, a preliminary analysis of the problematic context in which the philosopher inscribes the question and the conceptuality through which he seeks to define its nature.

There fortunately exists an exemplary reading of Aristotle's theory of slavery, which focuses on the entirely special character of the treatment that the philosopher makes of the problem. In a 1973 study, Victor Gold-schmidt shows that Aristotle here reverses his habitual methodology, according to which, when confronted with a phenomenon, it is first necessary to ask oneself if it exists and only subsequently to attempt to define its essence. With respect to slavery, he does exactly the opposite: first he defines—in truth, much too hastily—its essence (the slave is a human being who is not of himself but of another) in order to then pass over into interrogating its existence, but also does this latter in a completely peculiar way. The question does not in fact concern the existence and legitimacy of slavery as such but the "physical problem" of slavery (Gold-schmidt, p. 75): that is to say, it is a matter of establishing *whether there exists in nature a body corresponding to the definition of the slave.* Thus, the inquiry is not dialectical but physical, in the sense in which Aristotle distinguishes in *On the Soul* (403a 29) the method of the dialectic, which defines, for example, anger as a desire for vengeance, from that of physics, which will see in it only a boiling of blood in the heart.

Taking up and developing Goldschmidt's suggestion, we can thus affirm that the novelty and specificity of Aristotle's thesis is that the foundation of slavery is of a strictly "physical" and non-dialectical order, that is to say, that it can consist only in a bodily difference with respect to the body of the free person. The question becomes at this point: "does there exist something like a body (of the) slave?" The response is affirmative, but with such restriction that it has legitimately been asked whether the doctrine of Aristotle, which the moderns have always understood as a jus-tification of slavery, would not have had to appear to his contemporaries as an attack (Barker, p. 369). "Nature," writes Aristotle,

would like [*bouletai*] to distinguish between the bodies of freemen and slaves, making the one strong for the necessary use [*pros ten anankaian chresin*], the other upright, and though useless for such services, useful for political life. . . . But the opposite often happens—that some have the souls and oth-ers the bodies of freemen. And doubtless if human beings differed from one another in the mere forms of their bodies as much as the statues of the gods do from human beings, all would acknowledge that the inferior class should be slaves of the superior. And if this is true of the body, how much more just that a similar distinction should exist in the soul? But the beauty of the soul is not as easy to see as that of the body. (*Politics*, 1254b 28ff.)

The conclusion that Aristotle immediately draws from it is therefore uncertain and partial: "It is clear, then [*phaneron*, which here in no way indicates a logical conclusion, but means rather: 'it is a fact'], that there are some [*tines*] who are free by nature and others who are slaves, and for these latter to serve is both expedient and just [*sympherei to douleuein kai dikaion estin*]" (1255a 1–2). As he repeats a few lines later: "nature wants [*bouletai*] to do this [*scil*. that from a noble and good father comes a son similar to him], but it often cannot [*dynatai*]" (1255b 4).

Far from securing a certain foundation for it, the "physical" treatment of slavery leaves unanswered the only question that could have founded it: "does a bodily difference between the slave and the master exist or not?" This question implies at least in principle the idea that another body is possible for the human being, that the human body is constitutively divided. Seeking to understand what "use of the body" means will also mean thinking this other possible body of the human being.

‫‬ℵ. The idea of a "physical" foundation of slavery is taken up unreservedly many centuries later by Sade, who puts in the mouth of the libertine Saint-Fond this peremptory argumentation:

Glance at the works of nature and judge for yourself whether she has not, in forming the two classes of men [masters and slaves], made them vastly unalike; I ask you to put aside partiality, and to decide: have they the same voice, the same skin, the same limbs, the same gait, the same tastes, have they—I venture to inquire—the same needs? It will be to no purpose if someone attempts to persuade me that circumstances or education have made for these differences and that the slave and the master, in a state of nature, as infants, will be indistinguishable. I deny the fact; and it is after having pondered the matter and sifted much personal observation, after having examined the findings of clever anatomists, that I affirm there is no similarity between the conformations of these several infants. . . . Therefore, Juliette, cease to doubt these inequalities; and admitting their existence, let's not hesitate to take full advantage of them, and to persuade ourselves that if it so suited nature to have us born into the upper of these two classes, we have but to extract profit and pleasure from our situation by worsening that or our inferiors, and despotically to press them into the service of all our passions and our every need. (Sade, pp. 322–323)

Aristotle's reserve has disappeared here, and nature unfailingly accomplishes what it wants: the bodily difference between masters and slaves.

1.5. It is thus all the more surprising that Goldschmidt, after having noted with such precision the "physical" character of Aristotle's argumentation, does not in any way put it in relation with the definition of the slave in terms of the "use of the body" that immediately precedes it, nor does he draw from this latter any consequence as to the very conception of slavery. It is possible, rather, that comprehension of the strategy that drives Aristotle to conceive the slave in a purely "physical" way will be revealed only if one seeks in a preliminary way to understand the meaning of the formula "the human being whose work is the use of the body." If Aristotle reduces the problem of the existence of the slave to that of the existence of his body, this is perhaps because slavery defines a quite singular dimension of the human being (that the slave is a human being is, for him, beyond any doubt), which the syntagma "use of the body" seeks to name.

To understand what Aristotle means by this expression, it will be necessary to read the passage, a little earlier, in which the definition of slavery intersects with the question of its being just or violent, according to nature (*physei*) or convention (*nomoi*) and with the problem of the administration of the household (1253b 20–1254a 1). After having recalled that according to some, the power of the head of the family over slaves (*to despozein*) is contrary to nature and thus unjust and violent (*biaion*), Aristotle introduces a comparison between the slave and *ktemata*, household equipment (tools, in the broad sense that this term originally had) and the instruments (*organa*) that are parts of the administration of a household:

> Household equipment [*ktesis*] is part of the household, and the art of using household equipment [*ktetikè*] is part of the economy (for no one can live well, or indeed live at all, without necessary things). And as in the arts that have a definite sphere the workers must have their own proper instruments [*oikeiai organa*], so it is for those who manage the household [*oikonomikoi*]. Now instruments are of various sorts; some are living, others lifeless (for the one who commands a ship, the rudder is inanimate, the lookout person, a living instrument; for in the arts the servant [*hyperetes*] exists in the form of an instrument). Thus, too, equipment [*ktema*] is an instrument for life [*pros zoen*], and the ensemble of household equipment [*ktesis*] is a multitude of instruments, and the slave is in a certain sense animate equipment [*ktema ti empsychon*]; and the servant is like an instrument for instruments [*organon pro organon*, or an instrument that comes before the other instruments]. For

if every instrument could accomplish its own work, obeying or anticipating the will of others, like the statues of Daedalus or the tripods of Hephaestus, which, says the poet, "of their own accord [*automatous*] entered the assembly of the gods," if, in like manner, the shuttle would weave and the plectrum touch the lyre, then architects would not want servants, nor masters slaves.

The slave is here compared to equipment or to an animate instrument, which, like the legendary automatons constructed by Daedalus and Hephaestus, can move itself on command. We will be returning to this definition of the slave as "automaton" or animate instrument; for now, let us note that for a Greek, the slave plays, in modern terms, more the part of the machinery or fixed capital than of the worker. But as we will see, it is a matter of a special machine, which is not directed to production but only to use.

ℵ.   The term *ktema*, which we have rendered as "equipment," is often translated as "object of property." This translation is misleading, because it suggests a characterization in juridical terms that is lacking in the Greek term. Perhaps the most exact definition of the term is that of Xenophon, who explains *ktema* as "what is advantageous for the life of all," specifying that what is advantageous is "everything of which one can make use" (*Oeconomicus*, 6.4). The word, as is in any case obvious in the subsequent passages of Aristotle's text, refers to the sphere of use and not to that of ownership. In his treatment of the problem of slavery, that is to say, Aristotle seems to intentionally avoid the definition of slavery in the juridical terms that we would expect as the most obvious in order to displace his argumentation onto the level of the "use of the body." The fact that even in the definition of the slave as "the human being who is not of himself but of another," the opposition *autou/allou* is not necessarily understood in terms of ownership is also proven—beyond the fact that "being owner of oneself" would be meaningless—by the analogous formula that Aristotle uses in the *Metaphysics*, where it refers to the sphere of autonomy and not to that of ownership: "Just as we call free the person who exists for himself and not another [*ho autou heneka kai me allou on*], in the same way we say that wisdom is the only free science" (982b 25).

1.6. Immediately after, Aristotle, in a decisive development, links the theme of the instrument to that of use:

The instruments just mentioned [shuttles and plectra] are productive organs [*poietika organa*], while equipment is by contrast a practical [*praktikon*] instrument. From a shuttle, we get something else besides the use of it [*heteron ti genetai para ten chresin autes*], whereas of a garment or of a bed there is only the use [*he chresis monon*]. Further, as production [*poiesis*] and praxis [*praxis*] are different in kind, and both require instruments, the instruments that they employ must likewise differ in kind. The mode of life [*bios*] is a praxis and not a production, and therefore the slave is an assistant for things of praxis. Now "equipment" has the same meaning as "part" [*morion*, "piece," what belongs to an ensemble]; for the part is not only a part of something else [*allou*] but totally belongs to it [*holos*—some manuscripts have *haplos*, "absolutely," or with a still stronger expression, *haplos holos*, "absolutely and totally"]. This same can be said for equipment. The master is only the master of the slave and is not [part] of him; the slave is not only slave of the master but is totally [part] of him.

Hence we see what is the nature [*physis*] and the potential [*dynamis*] of the slave: the one who, while being human [*anthropos on*], is by nature of another, is a slave by nature; and the one who is of another who, while being human, is equipment, that is, a practical and separate instrument [*organon praktikon kai choriston*]. (1254a 1–17)

The assimilation of the slave to equipment or to an instrument is here developed by first of all distinguishing instruments into productive instruments and instruments of use (which produce nothing, except their use). In the expression "use of the body," use must therefore be understood not in a productive sense but in a practical one: *the use of the slave's body is similar to that of a bed or clothing, and not to that of a spool or plectrum.*

We are so accustomed to thinking of use and instrumentality as a function of an external goal that it is not easy for us to understand a dimension of use entirely independent of an end, such as that suggested by Aristotle: for us the bed serves for rest and clothing to protect us from the cold. In the same way, we are accustomed to consider the labor of the slave to be just like the eminently productive labor of the modern worker. A first, necessary precaution is therefore that of abstracting the slave's "use of the body" from the sphere of *poiesis* and production, in order to restore it to the sphere—according to Aristotle by definition unproductive—of praxis and mode of life.

ℵ. The distinction between the operation that produces something external and that from which there results only a use was to be so important for Aristotle that he develops it from a properly ontological perspective in book Theta of the *Metaphysics*, dedicated to the problem of potential and act. "The work [*ergon*]," he writes, is the end, and the being-at-work [*energeia*] is the work. Therefore even the term "being-at-work" derives from "work," which means also possessing-oneself-in-the-end [*entelecheia*]. And while in some cases the use [*chresis*] is the ultimate thing (e.g., in sight [*opseos*] the ultimate thing is seeing [*horasis*], and no other product besides this results from sight), but from some things a product follows (e.g., from the art of building there results a house as well as the act of building [*oikodomesin*]). . . . Where, then, the result is something apart from the use, the being-at-work is in the thing produced, e.g., the act of building is in the thing that is being built and the act of weaving in the thing woven . . . ; but when there is no product apart from the being-at-work, the being-at-work resides in them, in the sense that the act of seeing is in the one seeing and contemplation [*theoria*] in the one who contemplates and life in the soul. (*Metaphysics*, 1050a 21–1050b 1)

Aristotle seems here to theorize an excess of *energeia* over the *ergon*, of being-at-work over the work, which in some way implies a primacy of operations in which nothing is produced other than use over poietic operations, whose *energeia* resides in an external work and which the Greeks tended to hold in low regard. It is certain, in any case, that the slave, whose *ergon* consists only in the "use of the body," is to be inscribed, from this point of view, in the same class in which vision, contemplation, and life figure.

1.7. For Aristotle, the assimilation of the slave to a *ktema* implies that he is a part (*morion*) of the master, and part in an integral and constitutive sense. The term *ktema*, which, as we have seen, is not a technical term of law but of *oikonomia*, does not mean "property" in a juridical sense, and in this context, it designates things insofar as they are part of a functional whole and not insofar as they belong to an individual in ownership (for this latter sense, a Greek would say not *ta ktemata* but *ta idia*). For this reason, as we have seen, Aristotle can consider *ktema* as synonymous with *morion* and takes care to specify that the slave "is not only slave of the master but is totally part of him" (1254a 13). In the same sense, it is necessary to restore to the Greek term *organon* its ambiguity: it indicates both the instrument and the organ as a part of the body (in writing that the slave is an *organon praktikon kai choriston*, Aristotle is obviously playing on the double sense of the term).

The slave is a part (of the body) of the master, in the "organic" and not simply instrumental sense of the term, to such an extent that Aristotle can speak of a "community of life" between slave and master (*koinonos zoes*; 1260a 40). But then how are we to understand the "use of the body" that defines the work and condition of the slave? And how are we to think the "community of life" that unites him to the master?

In the syntagma *tou somatos chresis*, the genitive "of the body" is not to be understood only in an objective sense but also (analogously to the expression *ergon anthropou psyches energeia* in the *Nicomachean Ethics*) in a subjective sense: in the enslaved human being, the body is in use just as, in the free human being, the soul is at work in accordance with reason.

The strategy that leads Aristotle to define the slave as an integral part of the master shows its subtlety at this point. By putting in use his own body, the slave is, for that very reason, used by the master, and in using the body of the slave, the master is in reality using his own body. The syntagma "use of the body" represents a point of indifference not only between subjective genitive and objective genitive but also between one's own body and that of another.

‫‪ℵ.‬‬   It is helpful to read the theory of slavery that we have delineated up to this point in light of Sohn-Rethel's idea according to which in the exploitation of one human being on the part of another there occurs a rupture and a transformation in the immediate relationship of organic exchange between the living being and nature. For the relationship of the human body with nature, there is substituted a relation of human beings among themselves. The exploiters live, that is to say, from the products of the exploited's labor, and the productive relationship between human beings and nature becomes the object of a relationship between human beings, in which the relation itself is reified and appropriated. "The productive relationship humans-nature becomes the object of a human-human relationship, is subjected to its order and to its laws and therefore 'denatured' with respect to the 'natural' state, by being subsequently realized solely according to the laws of the forms of mediation that represent its affirmative negation" (Adorno and Sohn-Rethel, p. 32).

In Sohn-Rethel's terms, one could say that what happens in slavery is that the relationship of the master with nature, as Hegel had intuited in his dialectic of self-recognition, is now mediated by the relationship of the slave with nature. The slave's body in its relationship of organic exchange with nature is thus used as a medium of the relationship of the master's body with nature. One can ask, however, whether mediating one's own relation with nature through the relation with another human being is not from the very beginning what is properly human and whether slavery does not contain a memory of this original anthropogenetic operation. The perversion begins only when the reciprocal relation of use is appropriated and reified in juridical terms through the constitution of slavery as a social institution.

Benjamin once defined the just relation with nature not as "dominion of the human being over nature" but as "dominion of the relationship between the human being and nature." One can say, from this perspective, that while the attempt to master the dominion of humanity over nature gives rise to contradictions that ecology does not manage to work out, a dominion of the relation between the human being and nature is rendered possible precisely by the fact that the relation of the human being with nature is not immediate but mediated by his or her relation with other human beings. I can constitute myself as ethical subject of my relationship with nature solely because this relationship is mediated by the relationship with other human beings. However, if I seek, through what Sohn-Rethel calls "functional socialization," to appropriate mediation for myself by means of the other, then the relation of use decays into exploitation, and, as the history of capitalism sufficiently shows, exploitation is defined by the impossibility of being mastered (for this reason, the idea of a sustainable development in a "humanized" capitalism is contradictory).

1.8. Let us reflect on the singular condition of the human being whose *ergon* is the use of the body and, at the same time, on the peculiar nature of this "use." Unlike the cobbler, the carpenter, the flute player, or the sculptor, the slave, even if he carries out these activities—and Aristotle knows perfectly well that this can happen in the *oikonomia* of the household—is and remains essentially without work, in the sense that, in contrast to what happens with an artisan, his praxis is not defined by the work that he produces but only by the use of the body.

This is all the more surprising in that—as Jean-Paul Vernant has shown in an exemplary study (Vernant and Vidal-Naquet, pp. 28–33)— the classical world never considered human activity and its products from the point of view of the labor process that they entailed but solely from that of their result. Yan Thomas has thus observed that work contracts never determine the value of the commissioned object according to the amount of labor that it requires but solely according to the characteristics proper to the object produced. Historians of law and economy are, for this reason, accustomed to affirming that the classical world does not know the concept of labor. (It would be more exact to say that they do not distinguish it from the work it produces.) The first time—this is Yan Thomas's discovery—that, in Roman law, something like labor appears as an autonomous juridical reality is in contracts for the *locatio operarum* of the slave by someone who had ownership or—in the case that is exemplary according to Thomas—the usufruct of that slave.

It is significant that the isolation of something like a "labor" of the slave could happen only by conceptually separating the use (*usus*)—

which could not be alienated by the *usuarius* and coincided with the personal use of the slave's body—from the *fructus*, which the *fructuarius* could alienate on the market:

> The labor to which the *usuarius* has a right is mixed together with the personal or domestic use that he has of the slave—a use that excludes mercantile profit. The labor to which the *fructuarius* has a right can, on the contrary, be alienated on the market in exchange for a price: it can be rented out. In both cases, that is to say, whether it is a matter of use or usufruct of the slave, the slave concretely labors. But his activity, which common language would call his labor, does not have the same value for the law. In one case, the slave remains at the disposal of the usuary in person: it is a matter, then, of a service so to speak in nature, which we could call a labor of use, in the sense in which one speaks of use value. In the other case, his *operae*, separated from him, represent a "thing" alienable to third parties, in the juridical form of a contract. For the usufructary, it will then only be a matter of a monetary income. To the labor of use there is added in this way a labor that can be defined as merchandise, in the sense in which one speaks of market value. (Thomas 1, p. 222; cf. Thomas 2, p. 227)

The use of the slave, even when the owner has ceded it to others, always remains inseparable from the use of his body. "If anyone," writes Ulpian, "has received in inheritance the use of service personnel, he can use them for himself or for his children or for his relatives . . . but he cannot lease the work of the slave of whom he has use, nor concede the use of him to others" (Thomas 1, pp. 217–218). This is even more clear in the case of slaves from whom there was no possible work, like infants, the use of whom coincided with the delight (*delicia, voluptas*) that is derived from them. When we read in the *Digest* "if only the use of an infant slave should be bequeathed . . ." (*Digest*, 7, 1, *de usuf.*, 55), it is clear that here the juridical term *usus* is confounded with the use of the body without remainder.

It is necessary to reflect on this inseparable and personal character of the use of the slave. As we have seen, even when Roman jurists, using the notion of *fructus*, distinguished the labor (*operae* does not indicate the product but the activity in itself) of the slave from use in the strict sense, the latter is and remains personal and inseparable from the body itself. The separation of something like a labor activity is here possible only by separating the body as object of use from its activity as alienable and remunerable: "the worker is divided between two zones of law that correspond respectively to what he is as body and what he is as merchandise, as incorporeal good" (Thomas 2, p. 233). At this point, the slave enters into the centuries-long process that will be able to transform him into a worker.

From the perspective that interests us here, we can hypothesize that the late appearance of the dimension of labor happened in the case of the slave before that of the artisan precisely because the activity of the slave is by definition deprived of a proper work and therefore cannot be valued on the basis of his *ergon*, as would happen for the artisan. Precisely because his *ergon* is the use of the body, the slave is essentially *argos*, deprived of work (at least in the poietic sense of the term).

1.9. The peculiar nature of the use of the slave's body appears clearly in a sphere that has curiously escaped the attention of historians. Already in 1980, in his study on *Ancient Slavery and Modern Ideology*, Moses Finley, taking up an observation of Joseph Vogt, lamented the lack of any study on the relation between slavery and sexual relationships. Unfortunately, Kyle Harper's recent study (*Slavery in the Late Roman World*, 2011), which dedicates a lengthy chapter to this problem, concerns only late Roman antiquity and must therefore make use of Christian sources that are not always objective. His study, however, shows beyond any doubt that sexual relationships between the master and his slaves were considered totally normal. The sources examined by Harper suggest, in fact, that they functioned in some way as a counterpart to the institution of marriage and that it was even thanks to them that this latter institution was able to maintain its strength in Roman society (Harper, pp. 290–291).

What interests us here, rather, is that the sexual relationship made up an integral part of the use of the slave's body and was not in any way perceived as an abuse. Nothing is more significant, from this perspective, than the fact that the testimony of Artemidorus's *Interpretation of Dreams* lists sexual relationships with slaves among those that are "natural, legal, and customary" (*kata physin kai nomon kai ethos*; Artemidorus, 1.78). In perfect coherence with the Aristotelian doctrine of the slave as equipment, sexual use of the slave in dreams is here the symbol of the best possible relationship with one's own objects of use: "to dream of having sex with one's slave, whether male or female, is good; for slaves are equipment [*ktemata*] of the dreamer, so that uniting oneself with them will mean, quite naturally, that the dreamer will derive pleasure from his equipment, which will grow greater and more valuable." As proof of its completely normal character, the sexual relationship with the slave can also appear as a key for the interpretation of a dream: "If one dreams of masturbating with one's hands, it means that one will have sexual relations with a male or female slave, insofar as the hands that approach the genitals are serviceable [*hyperetikas*]." Naturally, a slave can also be the one to dream: "I know of a slave who dreamt that he masturbated his master, and he became the companion and attendant of his children, for in his hands he held his master's penis, which is the symbol of his children"; the prediction can, however, also be unfavorable: "I know another who, by contrast, dreamed of being masturbated by his master; he was tied to a pillar and received many lashes" (Artemidorus, 1.78).

What Artemidorus's oneirocritical acumen seems to suggest here is that not only does the use of the slave's body include the use of his sexual parts, but also that, in the indetermination of the two bodies, the "serviceable" hand of the master is equivalent to the service of the slave. Hence the striking promiscuity that always defines relationships with servants, whom masters (or mistresses) have bathe them, clothe them, and comb their hair without this corresponding to any real necessity.

However, precisely for this reason and in confirmation of the personal and non-mercantile character of the use of the slave's body, the master who prostitutes a slave dishonors himself and his household.

1.10. The slave's activity has often been identified with that which moderns have called "labor." As is well known, this is the more or less explicit thesis of Arendt: the victory of *homo laborans* in modernity and the primacy of labor over all other forms of human activity (producing, *Herstellen*, which corresponds to the Aristotelian *poiesis* and acting, *Handeln*, which corresponds to *praxis*) in actuality implies that the condition of the slave, that is to say, of the one who is entirely occupied with the reproduction of bodily life, has, with the end of the ancien régime, been extended to all human beings. That the modern worker is more comparable to the slave than to the creator of objects (with whom modernity tends, according to Arendt, to confound the worker) or the political man is unquestionable, and already Cicero affirmed that for those who sell their labor, the compensation is "a pledge of their slavery" (*auctoramentum servitutis*; Cicero I, 1, 42, 150). However, one must not forget that the Greeks were ignorant of the concept of labor and, as we have seen, conceived the activity of the slave not as an *ergon* but as a "use of the body."

If in Greece there can be no general notion of labor comparable to our own, this is because, as Vernant has shown, productive activities are not conceived in relation to the unitary referent that the market is for us, but with respect to the use value of the object produced.

> By means of the market, all labors effectuated in a society in their totality are put in relation with one another, compared among themselves, and equalized. . . . This universal equalization of the products of labor on the market, in the same instant that it transforms diverse labors, completely diverse from the point of view of their use, into merchandise comparable from the point of view of their value, also transmutes all human labors, entirely diverse and particular, into one same general and abstract labor activity. By contrast, in the sphere of ancient technique and economy, labor appears only in its concrete aspect. Every task is defined as a function of the product that it proposes to fabricate: the cobbler with respect to the shoe, the potter with respect to the pot. Labor is not considered in the perspective of the producer, as an expression of one same human effort that creates a social value. For this reason, in classical Greece there does not exist a single great human function, called labor, which includes all trades, but rather a plurality of diverse trades, each of which defines a particular type of activity that produces its own work. (Vernant and Vidal-Naquet, p. 28)

It is in this context that one must situate Aristotle's reflection on *poiesis* in the above-cited passage from the *Metaphysics* (1050a 21–1050b 1): while the one who acts or uses without producing possesses *energeia* in his very action, the artisan who produces an object does not possess in himself the *energeia* of his activity, which instead resides outside him in the work. For this reason his activity, constitutively submitted to an external end, is presented as inferior to praxis. Vernant can thus rightly affirm that

> in a similar social and mental system, the human being "acts" when he uses things and not when he makes them. The ideal of the free and active human being is to be always and universally a "user" and never a producer. The true problem of action, at least insofar as it concerns the relationship of the human being with nature, is that of the "good use" of things and not of their transformation through labor. (Vernant and Vidal-Naquet, p. 33)

In this perspective, the interpretation of the slave's activity in terms of labor appears, even aside from the anachronism, extremely problematic.

Insofar as it seems to dissolve into an unproductive use of the body, it seems almost to constitute the other face of the good use of things on the part of the free person. That is to say, it is possible that the "use of the body" and the absence of work of the slave are something more or, at any rate, different from a labor activity and that they instead preserve the memory or evoke the paradigm of a human activity that is reducible neither to labor, nor to production, nor to praxis.

1.11. Hannah Arendt has recalled the difference that separates the ancient concept of slavery from that of the moderns: while for the latter the slave is a means of procuring labor-power at a good price with the goal of profits, for the ancient it was a matter of eliminating labor from the properly human life, which was incompatible with it and which slaves, by taking it upon themselves, rendered possible. "Since human beings are subjected to the necessities of life, they can be free only if they subject others, forcefully constraining them to endure those necessities for them" (Arendt, p. 78).

It is necessary to add, however, that the special status of slaves—at once excluded from and included in humanity, as those not properly human beings who make it possible for others to be human—has as its consequence a cancellation and confounding of the limits that separate *physis* from *nomos*. Both artificial instrument and human being, the slave properly belongs neither to the sphere of nature nor to that of convention, neither to the sphere of justice nor to that of violence. Hence the apparent ambiguity of Aristotle's theory of slavery, which, like ancient philosophy in general, seems constrained to justify what it can only condemn and to condemn that of which it cannot deny the necessity. The fact is that the slave, although excluded from political life, has an entirely special relation with it. The slave in fact represents a not properly human life that renders possible for others the *bios politikos*, that is to say, the truly human life. And if the human being is defined for the Greeks through a dialectic between *physis* and *nomos*, *zoè* and *bios*, then the slave, like bare life, stands at the threshold that separates and joins them.

ℵ.   The anthropology that we have inherited from classical philosophy is modeled on the free man. Aristotle developed his idea of the human being starting from the paradigm of the free man, even if this latter implies the slave as his condition of possibility. One can imagine that he could have developed an entirely other anthropology if he had taken account of the slave (whose "humanity" he never intended to negate). This means that, in Western culture, the slave is something like the repressed. The reemergence of the figure of the slave in the modern worker thus appears, according to the Freudian scheme, as a return of the repressed in a pathological form.

1.12. How are we to understand the peculiar sphere of human acting that Aristotle calls "use of the body"? What does "using" mean here? Is it really a matter, as Aristotle seems to suggest, possibly through distinguishing it from production, of a sort of praxis (the slave is a "practical instrument")?

In the *Nicomachean Ethics*, Aristotle had distinguished *poiesis* and *praxis* on the basis of the presence or absence of an external end (*poiesis* is defined by an external *telos* that is the object produced, while in praxis "acting well [*eupraxia*] is in itself the end"; 1140b 6). Aristotle unreservedly affirms many times that the use of the body does not belong to the productive sphere of *poiesis*; nor does it seem possible to simply inscribe it in the ambit of praxis. The slave is indeed assimilated to an instrument and defined as an "instrument for life [*zoè*]" and "assistant for praxis": but precisely for this reason, it is impossible to say of his actions that, as happens in praxis, acting well is in itself the end.

This is so true that Aristotle explicitly limits the possibility of applying to the action of the slave the concept of virtue (*aretè*) that defines the acting of the free man: insofar as the slave is useful for the necessities of life, "it is clear that he needs some small virtue, such as will prevent him from abandoning his work through cowardice or lack of self-control" (*Politics* 1260a 35–36). There is not an *aretè* of the slave's use of the body, just as (according to the *Magna Moralia*, 1185a 26–35) there cannot be an *aretè* of nutritive life, which is for this reason excluded from happiness.

And just as it seems to escape the opposition between *physis* and *nomos*, *oikos* and *polis*, neither is the activity of the slave classifiable according to the dichotomies *poiesis/praxis*, acting well/acting badly that would seem, according to Aristotle, to define human operations.

ℵ.   In the above-cited passage from the *Magna Moralia* (1185a 26–35), Aristotle asks if a virtue of nutritive life is possible (that is to say, that part of human life that human beings have in common with plants and that, beginning with late-ancient commentators, will be defined as "vegetative"): "What happens if we ask if there is a virtue for that part of the soul? For if it does, it is clear that there will be here also a being-at-work [*energeia*] and happiness is the being-at-work of a perfect virtue. Now whether there is or is not a virtue of this part is another question; but, if there is, it has no being-at-work."

It is interesting to reflect on the analogy between a human activity deprived of *ergon* and virtue, which that of the slave is, and vegetative life, as human life excluded from virtue. And just as Aristotle seems to suggest for this latter the possibility of a virtue without being-at-work ("if it even exists, there is no being-at-work of it"), in the same way one could think for the body of the slave an *aretè* that knows neither *ergon* nor *energeia* and nevertheless is always in use. Perhaps one of the limits of Western ethics has been precisely the incapacity to think an *aretè* of life in all its aspects.

The reason why Aristotle cannot admit an *energeia* and a virtue in an act of vegetative life is that it is, according to him, deprived of *hormè*, of impulse or *conatus*. "For those things that have no *hormè*," continues the cited passage, "will not have any *energeia* either; and there does not seem to be any impulse in this part, but it seems to be on par with fire. For that also will consume whatever you throw in it, but if you do not throw anything in, it has no impulse to get it. So it is also with this part of the soul, for if you give it food, it nourishes, but if you fail to throw in food, it has no impulse to nourish. There is no being-at-work of that which has no impulse. So that this part in no way contributes to happiness."

By all indications, it is the will to exclude nutritive life from ethics (to say that something does not contribute to happiness means, for a Greek, to exclude it from ethics) that leads Aristotle to deny to it anything like a *conatus*. An ethics that does not want to exclude a part of life will have to be in a position not only to define a *conatus* and an *aretè* of life as such but also to rethink from the very beginning the very concepts of "impulse" and "virtue."

1.13. Let us attempt to fix in a series of theses the characteristics of the activity that Aristotle defines as "use of the body."

1. It is a matter of an unproductive activity (*argos*, "inoperative," "without work" in the terminology of the *Nicomachean Ethics*), comparable to the use of a bed or a garment.

2. The use of the body defines a zone of indifference between one's own body and the body of another. The master, in using the body of the slave, uses his own body, and the slave, in using his own body, is used by the master.

3. The body of the slave is situated in a zone of indifference between the artificial instrument and the living body (it is an *empsychon organon*, an animate organ) and, therefore, between *physis* and *nomos*.

4. The use of the body is, in Aristotelian terms, neither *poiesis* nor *praxis*, neither a production nor a praxis, but neither is it assimilable to the labor of moderns.

5. The slave, who is defined by means of this "use of the body," is the human being without work who renders possible the realization of the work of the human being, that living being who, though being human, is excluded—and through this exclusion, included—in humanity, so that human beings can have a human life, which is to say a political life.

Yet precisely insofar as the use of the body is situated at the undecidable threshold between *zoè* and *bios*, between the household and the city, between *physis* and *nomos*, it is possible that the slave represents the capture within law of a figure of human acting that still remains for us to recognize.

ℵ.   From Aristotle on, the tradition of Western philosophy has always put at the foundation of the political the concept of action. Still in Hannah Arendt, the public sphere coincides with that of acting, and the decadence of the political is shown by the progressive substitution, in the course of the modern era, of making for acting, of *homo faber* and, later, of *homo laborans* for the political actor.

The term *actio*, however, from which the word "action" derives and which, beginning with the Stoics, translates the Greek *praxis*, originally belongs to the juridical and religious sphere and not to the political. *Actio* designates in Rome first of all a trial. The Justinian *Institutes* thus begin by dividing the sphere of law into three great categories: the *personae* (personal laws), the *res* (property law), and the *actiones* (trial law). *Actionem constituere* therefore means "to start proceedings," just as *agere litem* or *causam* means "to conduct a trial." On the other hand, the verb *ago* originally means "to celebrate a sacrifice," and, according to some, it is for this reason that in the most ancient sacramentaries the mass is defined as *actio* and the Eucharist as *actio sacrificii* (Casel, p. 39; Baumstark, pp. 38–39).

It is a term that comes from the juridico-religious sphere that has furnished to the political its fundamental concept. One of the hypotheses of the current study is, by calling into question the centrality of action and making for the political, that of attempting to think use as a fundamental political category.

§ 2 Chresis

2.1. In March 1950, Georges Redard discussed before the *École pratique de hautes études* a *mémoire* on the meaning of the Greek words *chre*, *chresthai*. The committee was presided over by Émile Benveniste, who was also the supervisor for this research. The *mémoire*, which the subtitle defines as "a study of semantics," was conceived as a chapter of a fuller study on mantic terminology (the words in question, which we normally refer to the sphere of use, belong originally in Greek, according to Redard, to the family of "oracular words").

What is most surprising when one first examines the ample lexical material collected by Redard is that the verb *chresthai* does not seem to have a proper meaning but acquires ever different meanings according to the context. Redard thus lists twenty-three meanings of the term, from "to consult an oracle" to "have sexual relations," from "to speak" to "be unhappy," from "to punch someone" to "feel nostalgia." The common strategy in our dictionaries, which consists in distinguishing the "different" meanings of a term, in order then to defer to the etymology the attempt to lead them back to a unity, here shows its insufficiency. The fact is that the verb in question seems to draw its meaning from that of the term that accompanies it, which is not normally, as we moderns would expect, in the accusative but in the dative or, at times, the genitive. Let us consider the following list, gathered in large part from examples mentioned by Redard:

> *chresthai theoi*, lit. "to make use of the god" = to consult an oracle
>
> *chresthai nostou*, lit. "to use return" = to feel nostalgia

chresthai logoi, lit. "to use language" = to speak

chresthai symphorai, lit. "to use misfortune" = to be unhappy

chresthai gynaikì, lit. "to use a woman" = to have sexual relations with a woman

chresthai te polei, lit. "to make use of the city" = to participate in political life

chresthai keiri, lit. "to use one's hands" = to punch someone

chresthai niphetoi, lit. "to use snow" = to be caught in a snowstorm

chresthai alethei logoi, lit. "to use a true discourse" = to tell the truth

chresthai lotoi, lit. "to use the lotus" = to eat lotus

chresthai orgei, lit. "to use anger" = to be angry

chresthai eugeneiai, lit. "to use good birth" = to be of noble stock

chresthai Platoni, lit. "to use Plato" = to be friends with Plato

The situation is completely analogous for the corresponding Latin verb *uti*:

uti honore, lit. "to use an office" = to hold a position

uti lingua, lit. "to use the tongue" = to speak

uti stultitia, lit. "to use foolishness" = to be foolish (or give proof of foolishness)

uti arrogantia, lit. "to use arrogance" = to be arrogant (or give proof of arrogance)

uti misericordia, lit. "to use mercy" = to be merciful (or give proof of mercy)

uti aura, lit. "to use the breeze" = to have a favorable wind

uti aliquo, lit. "to make use of someone" = to be on familiar terms with someone

uti patre diligente, lit. "to use a hardworking father" = to have a hardworking father

2.2. What these examples render immediately evident is that the verb in question cannot mean, according to the modern meaning of the verb *to use*, "to make use of, to utilize something." Each time it is a matter of a relationship with something, but the nature of this relationship is, at least in appearance, so indeterminate that it seems impossible to define a unitary sense of the term. This is so much the case that Redard, in his attempt to identify this meaning, must content himself with a generic and, in the last analysis, tautological definition, because it is limited to displacing the problem onto the French term *utilisation*: *chresthai* would mean *rechercher l'utilisation de quelque chose* (even if one cannot see how "to be caught in a snowstorm" could mean "to seek the utilization of snow" or in what way "to be unhappy" could be equivalent to "to seek the utilization of misfortune").

It is likely that a more or less conscious projection of the modern meaning of the verb *to use* onto that of *chresthai* has kept the scholar from grasping the meaning of the Greek term. This is evident in the way in which he characterizes the relation between the subject and object of the process expressed by the verb.

> If we now seek to define the process expressed by the verb, we can state that it is carried out within the sphere of the subject. . . . The construction of *chresthai* is intransitive: the object is in the dative or the genitive. . . . Whether we are dealing with a person or a thing, the object each time affirms its independence with respect to the subject. . . . The god who is consulted, the jewel with which one adorns oneself, the lotus that one eats, the javelin that one utilizes, the name of which one makes use, the language that one speaks, the clothes that one wears, the eulogy to which one makes recourse, the activity that one carries out, the opinion that one follows, the customs that one observes, the cold of which one is a victim, the chance to which one is submitted, the anger that seizes one, the author with whom one associates, the return to which one aspires, the nobility from which one descends, all these notions are realities independent of the one who makes recourse to them: the object exists outside the subject and never modifies it. (Redard, p. 42)

It is truly striking that Redard can speak of "exteriority," of intransitivity and absence of modification between subject and object, precisely when he has just evoked the "return to which one aspires," the "anger that seizes one," the "cold of which one is a victim," and the "nobility from which one descends," examples among many others of a relation so close between subject and object that not only is the subject intimately modified, but the boundaries between the two terms of the relationship even seem to be indeterminated.

It is perhaps because of his awareness of this intimacy between subject and object of use that Redard seems at a certain point to nuance his definition of the meaning of the verb *chresthai*, adding that it expresses an attempt at accommodation and appropriation on the part of the subject:

The appropriation can be actualized as in *arpagei iemasi chresthai* (to be greedy) or virtual, as in the case of *nostou chresthai*. . . . In any case, the appropriation is always occasional, and this is its specificity. Whether one consults an oracle, whether one feels a need, rents out a plow, or catches rabies, it is always as a function of an event. An expression like *symphorai chresthai* (to be unhappy) is not an exception to the rule: "to be unhappy" means more precisely "to attract misfortune upon oneself." . . . The subject-object relationship is defined as a relationship of occasional appropriation, of the lightning-lightning rod type, to take up Mr. Benveniste's lovely image. (Ibid., p. 44)

Once again, the examples belie the thesis point by point: "to be unhappy" cannot mean to occasionally appropriate misfortune to oneself, nor "to feel nostalgic" to appropriate return to oneself.

2.3. It is probable that precisely the subject/object relationship—so marked in the modern conception of the utilization of something on the part of someone—emerges as inadequate to grasp the meaning of the Greek verb. And yet an indication of this inadequacy is present precisely in the very form of the verb, which is neither active nor passive but in the diathesis that ancient grammarians called "middle" (*mesotes*). Redard, noting this fact, refers to an article of Benveniste's that appeared the same year in which his *mémoire* was discussed ("Actif et moyen dans le verbe," 1950). Benveniste's thesis is clear: whereas in the active, verbs denote a process that is realized starting from the subject and beyond him, "in the middle . . . the verb indicates a process that takes place in the subject: the subject is internal to the process" (Benveniste, p. 172/148). The examples of verbs that have a middle diathesis (*media tantum*) illustrate well this peculiar situation of the subject inside the process of which he is an agent: *gignomai*, Latin *nascor*, "to be born"; *morior*, "to die"; *penomai*, Latin *patior*, "to suffer"; *keimai*, "to lie"; *phato*, Latin *loquor*, "to speak"; *fungor*, *fruor*, "to enjoy," etc. In all these cases, "here the subject is the seat of the process, even if this process, as is the case for the Latin *fruor* or Sanskrit *manyate*, demands an object; the subject is the center as well as the agent of the process; he achieves something that is being achieved in him" (p. 172/149).

The opposition with the active is obvious in those middle-voice verbs that also allow an active diathesis: *koimatai*, "he sleeps," in which the subject is internal to the process, thus becomes *koima*, "he causes to sleep, puts to sleep," in which the process, no longer having its place in the subject, is transitively transferred into another term that becomes its object. Here the subject, "placed outside the process, governs it thenceforth as an agent," and the action must consequently take as its end an external object. Almost immediately after, Benveniste further specifies with respect to the active the peculiar relation that the middle voice presupposes between the subject and the process of which he is both the agent and the place: "they always finally come down to situating positions of the subject with respect to the process, according to whether it is exterior or interior to it, and to qualifying it as an agent, depending on whether it effects, in the active, or whether it effects while being affected [*il effectue en s'affectant*], in the middle" (ibid., p. 173/149–50).

2.4. Let us reflect on the striking formula by which Benveniste seeks to express the meaning of the middle diathesis: *il effectue en s'affectant*. On the one hand, the subject who achieves the action, by the very fact of achieving it, does not act transitively on an object but first of all implies and affects himself in the process; on the other hand, precisely for this reason, the process presupposes a singular topology, in which the subject does not stand over the action but is himself the place of its occurring. As is implicit in the name *mesotes*, the middle voice is situated in a zone of indetermination between subject and object (the agent is in some way also object and place of action) and between active and passive (the agent receives an affection from his own action). One can understand, then, why Redard, in insisting on the subject/object relation and on the modern meaning of "utilization," does not manage to lead the unaccountable polysemy of the verb *chresthai* back to a unity. Thus, it is all the more urgent to investigate, in the case that interests us here, the singular threshold that the middle voice establishes between subject and object and between agent and patient.

It also becomes clear, from this "middle-voice" perspective, why the object of the verb *chresthai* cannot be in the accusative but is always in the dative or genitive. The process does not pass from an active subject toward the object separated from his action but involves in itself the subject, to the same degree that this latter is implied in the object and "gives himself" to it.

We can therefore attempt to define the meaning of *chresthai*: *it expresses the relation that one has with oneself, the affection that one receives insofar as one is in relation with a determinate being.* The one who *synphorai chretai* has an experience of himself as unhappy, constitutes and shows himself as unhappy; the one who *utitur honore* puts himself to the test and defines himself insofar as he holds an office; the one who *nosthoi chretai* has an experience of himself insofar as he is affected by the desire for a return. *Somatos chresthai*, "to use the body," will then mean *the affection that one receives insofar as one is in relation with one or more bodies.* Ethical—and political—is the subject who is constituted in this use, the subject who testifies of the affection that he receives insofar as he is in relation with a body.

2.5. Perhaps nowhere has this singular status of the agent been described with greater precision than in Spinoza. In the twentieth chapter of the *Compendium grammatices linguae hebraeae*, he introduced an ontological meditation in the form of an analysis of the meaning of a Hebrew verbal form, the reflexive active verb, which is formed by adding a prefix to the intensive form. This verbal form expresses an action in which agent and patient, active and passive are identified. To clarify its meaning, the first Latin equivalent that comes to his mind is *se visitare*, "to visit-oneself," but this seems to him so insufficient that he later specifies it in the form: *se visitantem constituere*, "to constitute-oneself as visiting." A second example, *se ambulationi dare*, "to give oneself over to a walk," also inadequate, is clarified with an equivalent drawn from the mother tongue of his people. "To walk" is said in Ladino (that is, in the Spanish that the Sephardic Jews spoke at the time of their expulsion from Spain) as *pasearse*, to "walk-oneself." As an expression of an action of the self on the self, in which agent and patient enter into a threshold of absolute indistinction, the Ladino term is particularly appropriate.

A few pages earlier, in speaking of the corresponding form of the infinitive noun, Spinoza defines its semantic sphere by means of the idea of an immanent cause: "It was therefore necessary to invent another kind of infinitive, which expressed an action referred to the agent as immanent cause . . . , which means to visit-oneself, or to constitute-oneself as visiting or, finally, to manifest-oneself as visiting" (Spinoza 1, p. 342). Here the sphere of the action of the self on the self corresponds to the ontology of immanence, to the movement of autoconstitution and of autopresentation of being, in which not only is it not possible to distinguish between agent and patient but also subject and object, constituent and constituted are indeterminated.

It is according to this paradigm that one must understand the singular
nature of the process that we call "use." Just as, in the experience of making a visit expressed by the Hebrew verb, the subject constitutes himself
as visiting and, in the experience of walking, the subject first of all walks
himself, has an experience of himself as walking, in the same way every
use is first of all use of self: to enter into a relation of use with something,
I must be affected by it, constitute myself as one who makes use of it.
Human being and world are, in use, in a relationship of absolute and
reciprocal immanence; in the using of something, it is the very being of
the one using that is first of all at stake.

It may be helpful to reflect on the peculiar conception of the subject
and of action implicit in use. While in the act of visiting what is essential, according to the meaning of the active diathesis, is the action of the
agent outside himself, in use (in constituting-oneself as visiting) what is
in the foreground is not the *energeia* of the visitor but the affection that
the agent-user (who thus becomes patient) receives from it. The same can
be said of the term that, in the passive diathesis, is object of the action:
in use, it constitutes-itself as visited, is active in its being passive. To the
affection that the agent receives from his action there corresponds the
affection that the patient receives from his passion. Subject and object
are thus deactivated and rendered inoperative, and, in their place, there
follows use as a new figure of human praxis.

ℵ.   It is from this perspective that one can understand the striking proximity
between use and love that Dante institutes in the *Convivio* (Dante 1, IV, 22). After having affirmed that the natural appetite (which he also calls, using a Greek
word, *hormen*) first of all loves itself and, through this love of self, also other
things ("and thus, loving itself primarily and other things for its own sake, and
loving the better part of itself better, it is clear that it loves the mind better than
the body or aught else"), he writes: "wherefore if the mind always delights in the
use of the thing it loves (which is the fruition of love), use in that thing which it
loves most is the most delightful." Love is here, in some way, the affection that
is received by use (which is always also use of self) and remains in some way
indiscernible from it. In the syntagma "use of the loved thing," the genitive is at
once subjective and objective. The subject-object of use is love.

§ 3   Use and Care

3.1. In the course on *L'herméneutique du sujet*, Foucault had come up against the problem of the meaning of the verb *chresthai* while interpreting the passage from Plato's *Alcibiades* in which Socrates, in order to identify the "self" of which one must take care, seeks to demonstrate that "the one who uses" (*ho chromenos*) and "that which one uses" (*hoi chretai*) are not the same thing. To this end, he has recourse to the example of the cobbler and the lyre player, who make use of a cobbler's knife and a plectrum as well as their hands and eyes as instruments to cut leather or to play the cithara. If the one who uses and that of which one makes use are not the same thing, this then means that the human being (who "uses his whole body," *panti toi somati chretai anthropos*; 129e) does not coincide with his body and therefore, in taking care of it, he is taking care of "a thing that is his own" (*ta heautou*) but "not of himself" (*ouk hauton*). What uses the body and that of which one must take care, Socrates concludes at this point, is the soul (*psychè*).

It is in the course of commenting on this passage from Plato that Foucault seeks to define the meaning of *chresthai*, with considerations not very different from what we have already seen in connection with Redard's *mémoire*.

Of course, *chraomai* means: I use, I utilize (an instrument, a tool). But equally *chraomai* may designate my behavior or my attitude. For example, in the expression *ubrikhos chresthai*, the meaning is: behaving violently (as when we say, "using violence," when "using" does not mean utilizing, but rather behaving violently). So *chraomai* is also a certain attitude. *Chresthai* also designates a certain type of relationship with other people. When one says, for example, *theois chresthai* (using the gods), this does not mean that one utilizes the gods for any end whatever. It means having appropriate and legitimate relationships with the gods. . . . *Chraomai, chresthai* also designate a certain attitude towards oneself. In the expression *epithumiais chresthai*, the meaning is not "to use one's passions for something" but quite simply "to give way to one's passions." (Foucault 1, pp. 55–56/56)

The insistence on the specification of the semantic sphere of *chresthai* is not by chance. According to Foucault, in fact, this verb develops a strategic function in Plato's argumentation, insofar as Socrates makes use of it to respond to the question of what this "oneself" is that is the object of care-of-oneself ("in what way will it be possible to find the self itself"— *auto tauto*, a technical formula for the expression of the idea: the "itself in itself"; 129b). By concentrating his examples on the verb *chresthai*, that is to say, Plato intends to suggest that taking care of the self means, in reality, to concern oneself with the subject of a series of "uses." And here the attempt to define the meaning of *chresthai* shows its full pertinence. When Plato—Foucault suggests—makes use of the notion of *chresthai/ chresis* to identify the *heauton* in the expression "to take care of oneself," in reality he intends to designate "not an instrumental relationship of the soul to the rest of the world or to the body, but rather the subject's singular, transcendent position, as it were, with regard to what surrounds him, to the objects available to him, but also to other people with whom he has a relationship, to his body itself, and finally to himself" (Foucault 1, p. 56/56–57). What Plato discovers in this way is not, that is to say, "the soul-substance" but "the soul-subject":

> Taking care of oneself will be to take care of the self insofar as it is the "subject of" a certain number of things: the subject of instrumental action, of relationships with other people, of behavior and attitudes in general, and the subject also of relationships to oneself. It is insofar as one is this subject who uses, who has certain attitudes, and who has certain relationships, etc., that one must take care of oneself. It is a question of taking care of oneself as subject of *chresis* (with all that word's polysemy: subject of actions, behavior, relationships, attitudes). (Ibid., p. 56/57)

3.2. Anyone who has any familiarity with the investigations of the late Foucault will have recognized in this passage one of the essential characteristics of the ethical subjectivity that they seek to define. If Foucault returns so insistently in his courses to Plato's *Alcibiades*, it is not only because one of the central themes of the dialogue is care-of-oneself, with which he was very concerned in those years. In the Foucauldian laboratory, the *Alcibiades* above all furnishes the occasion to articulate in all its complexity and in all its aporias that notion of the subject with which, according to his testimony, he had never ceased to concern himself.

Just as the subject is not a substance for Foucault but a process, so also does the ethical dimension—care-of-oneself—not have an autonomous substance: it has no other place and no other consistency than the relation of use between the human being and the world. Care-of-oneself presupposes *chresis*, and the self that names the ethical subject is not something other with respect to the subject of use but remains immanent to it. For this reason Foucault, in his reading of the *Alcibiades*, insists on the distinction between soul-substance and soul-subject, and for this reason he can write, in the notes published by Frédéric Gros at the end of the course, that "the self with which one has the relationship is nothing other than the relationship itself . . . it is in short the immanence, or better, the ontology adequation of the self to the relationship" (ibid., p. 514/533).

The difficulty with which these feverish remarks seek to settle accounts is decisive: if that of which one takes care is the very subject of relations of use with others, the risk here is that the active subject of care will be configured in its turn in a transcendent position as subject with respect to an object or that, in any case, ethical subjectivity will be drawn into a *regressio ad infinitum* (the one that takes care of the subject of use will demand in its turn another subject that takes care of it, etc.).

The question is all the more urgent and delicate insofar as it is precisely here that we see the reappearance of that problem of governmentality that constitutes the privileged object of Foucault's courses beginning from the mid-1970s. The theme of care-of-oneself in this way risks resolving itself entirely into that of the governance of the self and of others, just as, in the passage from the *Alcibiades*, the theme of the use of the body on the part of the soul is resolved at a certain point into that of the command (*archè*) of the soul over the body (130a).

What is crucial here is the way in which one thinks the relationship between care and use, between care-of-oneself and use-of-oneself. As we have seen, in connection with use, Foucault evokes the relationship with oneself, but while the concept of care-of-oneself remains at the center of his analyses, that of "use-of-oneself" is almost never thematized as such. The relation of use, which constitutes precisely the primary dimension in which subjectivity is constituted, thus remains in the shadows and gives way to a primacy of care over use that seems to repeat the Platonic gesture in which *chresis* was resolved into care (*epimeleia*) and command (*archè*). This is all the more fraught with consequences insofar as the separation between care-of-oneself and use-of-oneself is at the root of that between ethics and politics, which is as alien to classical thought at least up to Aristotle as it is to the preoccupations of the late Foucault.

3.3. The relation between care and use seems to entail something like a circle. The formula "to concern oneself with oneself as subject of *chresis*" suggests, in fact, a genetico-chronological primacy of the relations of use over care-of-oneself. It is only insofar as a human being is introduced as subject into a series of relations of use that a care-of-oneself may perhaps become possible. On the other hand, if "the self with which one has a relationship is nothing other than the relationship itself," the subject of *chresis* and that of care are the same subject. It is this coincidence that the enigmatic expression "the immanence or ontological adequation of the self to the relationship" seems to want to express (Foucault 1, p. 514/533). The subject of use must take care of itself insofar as it is in a relationship of use with things or persons: that is to say, it must put itself into relationship with the self insofar as it is in a relationship of use with another. But a relationship with the self—or an affection of the self—is already implicit, as we have seen, in the middle-voice meaning of the verb *chresthai,* and this seems to call into question the very possibility of distinguishing between care-of-oneself and use. If "to use" means "to enter into a relationship with the self insofar as one is in relationship with another," in what way could something like a care-of-oneself legitimately claim to define a dimension other than use? That is to say, how would ethics distinguish itself from use and obtain a primacy over it? And why and how has use been transformed into care? This is all the more the case given that, as Foucault suggests many times, the subject of *chresis* can enter into a relationship of use also with itself, can constitute a "use-of-oneself."

It is perhaps out of awareness of these aporias that, alongside the theme of care-of-oneself, we see the appearance in the late Foucault of the at least apparently contrary motif that he designates with the formula: *se déprendre de soi-même.* Care-of-oneself here gives place to a dispossession and abandonment of the self, where it again becomes mixed up with use.

3.4. It is from this perspective that Foucault's interest in sadomasochistic practices can be properly situated. It is not only a matter of the fact that here, as Foucault emphasizes many times, the slave can in the end find himself in the position of the master, and vice versa: rather, what defines sadomasochism is the very structure of subjectivation, its *ethos*, insofar as the one whose body is (or seems to be) used is actually constituted to the same extent as subject of its being used, assumes it and experiences pleasure in it (even here what is in question, in the terms of the course on *L'herméneutique du sujet*, is the relationship that one has with the self as subject of one's own sexual relations). Vice versa, the one who seems to use the body of the other can in some way be used by the other for his own pleasure. Master and slave, sadist and masochist here are not two incommunicable substances, but in being taken up into the reciprocal use of their bodies, they pass into one another and are incessantly indeterminated. As the language expresses so well, the masochist "causes to be done to him" what he suffers, is active in his very passivity. That is to say, *sadomasochism exhibits the truth of use, which does not know subject and object, agent and patient.* And in being taken up in this indetermination, pleasure is also made non-despotic and common.

It is striking that the analyses of sadomasochism from the Freudian perspective, despite noting the inversion of roles between the two subjects, do not mention the master/slave relation. Thus, in the by-now classic monograph that he dedicated to masochism, Theodor Reik notes many times the reciprocal transformation of the active element into the passive element and the reversal toward the ego of what is originally a sadistic tendency; but the terms "master" and "slave" never appear. By contrast, Foucault not only makes use of these terms but seems to suggest that it is precisely the assumption of these two roles that allows for a new and more enjoyable relation to the body. "I think it's a kind of creation," he writes in connection with his experience in California bathhouses, "a creative enterprise, which has as one of its main features what I call the desexualization of pleasure . . . ." (Foucault 2, p. 738/Rabinow, p. 165); ". . . wouldn't it be marvelous . . . to encounter bodies that are both present and fleeting? Places where you desubjectivize and desexualize yourself . . . ?" (Foucault and Le Bitoux, p. 399).

It is possible, then, that what is in question in sadomasochism is a ritualized re-creation of the master/slave relation, insofar as this relation paradoxically seems to allow access to a freer and fuller use of bodies.

By means of this, the subject pursues the traces of a "use of the body" beyond the subject/object and active/passive scissions: in the words of Foucault, he has an experience of his own desubjectivation.

And if it is true, as Deleuze observed, that masochism always entails a neutralization of the juridical order by means of its parodic exaggeration, then one can form the hypothesis that the master/slave relation as we know it represents the capture in the juridical order of the use of bodies as an originary prejuridical relation, on whose exclusive inclusion the juridical order finds its proper foundation. In use, the subjects whom we call master and slave are in such a "community of life" that the juridical definition of their relationship in terms of property is rendered necessary, almost as if otherwise they would slide into a confusion and a *kononia tes zoes* that the juridical order cannot admit except in the striking and despotic intimacy between master and slave. And what seems so scandalous to us moderns—namely, property rights over persons—could in fact be the originary form of property, the capture (the *ex-ceptio*) of the use of bodies in the juridical order.

ℵ.   The ancient world knew of festivals in which the originary indetermination that defines the use of bodies reemerged into the light by means of the role reversal between master and slave. Thus, during the Saturnalia, which was celebrated on December 17, not only did masters serve the slaves, but the entire order of social life was transformed and subverted. It is possible to see in these anomic festivals not only a state of suspension of the law that characterizes certain archaic juridical institutions but also, by means of this suspension, the reemergence of a sphere of human action in which not only master and slave but also subject and object, agent and patient are indeterminated.

3.5. One can therefore understand why in the *Phenomenology of Spirit*, the dialectic between master and slave and the recognition that is in question in it has a constitutive anthropological function. What is decisive here is not only, as Hegel never stops reminding us, that the recognition of self-consciousness can happen only by means of another self-consciousness but also that, in the relationship between master and slave, what is at stake is what Hegel unreservedly calls enjoyment (*der Genuss*):

The master relates himself mediately to the thing through the slave; the slave, *qua* self-consciousness in general, also relates himself negatively to the thing and abolishes it [*hebt es auf*]; but at the same time the thing is independent vis-à-vis the slave, whose negating of it, therefore, cannot go to the length of being altogether done with it to the point of annihilation; in other words, he only works on it. For the master, on the other hand, the immediate relation becomes through this mediation the sheer negation of the thing, or the enjoyment of it. What desire failed to achieve, he succeeds in doing, viz., to have done with the thing altogether, and to achieve satisfaction in the enjoyment of it. Desire failed to do this because of the thing's independence; but the master, who has interposed the slave between it and himself, takes to himself only the dependent aspect of the thing and has the pure enjoyment of it . . . .

In both of these moments [*scil.* the slave's labor and the enjoyment that it renders possible] the master achieves his recognition through another consciousness. . . . (Hegel, pp. 115–116)

Hegel sees the intimate relation between master and slave that we have sought to define as use of the body; however, while in the *koinonia tes zoes* that is here in question, the body of the master and that of the slave, distinct in the juridical order, tend to become undecidable. Hegel dwells upon precisely what makes it possible to separate and recognize the two positions: the distinction between the labor of the slave and the enjoyment of the master. Naturally, as in sadomasochism according to Foucault, the two roles tend to be reversed, and, in the end, since "the truth of the master's consciousness is servile consciousness" (Hegel, p. 117), the labor of the servant, as "desire held in check and fleetingness staved off" (p. 118), acquires its independence with respect to the fleeting enjoyment of the master.

Even in this dialectical reversal, what is nonetheless lost is the possibility of another figure of human praxis, in which enjoyment and labor (which is restrained desire) are in the last analysis unassignable. From this perspective, sadomasochism appears as an insufficient attempt to render inoperative the dialectic between master and slave by parodically finding in it the traces of that use of bodies to which modernity seems to have lost all access.

§ 4   The Use of the World

4.1. Despite his *boutade* on not reading *Being and Time*, it is difficult to imagine that Foucault was not familiar with the chapter that bears the significant title "Dasein's Being as Care [*die Sorge*]," which concludes and almost summarizes the first division of the work and where what is in question is an analogous—and equally aporetic—primacy of care over use. Here care is not understood simply as preoccupation (*Besorgnis*, as opposed to carelessness, *Sorglosigkeit*; Heidegger 1, p. 192/237) but in an ontological sense as the fundamental structure of Dasein, as "the originary totality of Dasein's structural whole" (*die ursprüngliche Ganzheit des Strukturganzen des Daseins*; ibid., p. 180/225). The "primacy" (*Vorrang*) that belongs to care as "originary totality" implies that it comes before "every factical 'attitude' [*Verhaltung*] and 'situation' [*Lage*] of Dasein" (p. 193/238) and that it is "ontologically 'earlier' [*früher*]" than phenomena like "willing and wishing or urge and addiction" (p. 194/238).

However, if we seek to understand how this ontological priority of care is articulated, we realize that it is neither chronological nor genetic but on the contrary has the striking form of a finding oneself always already in something else. The phrase that we just cited in an incomplete form reads in its entirety: "Care, as a primordial structural totality, lies 'before' every factical 'attitude' and 'situation' of Dasein, and it does so existentially *a priori* [*existential-apriorisch*]" (p. 193/238). The existential *a priori* of care, like every *a priori*, always already inheres in something other than care itself. This character of "being-in" is, however, implied in the definition of the structure of care that immediately precedes it: "the Being of Dasein means ahead-of-itself-Being-already-in-(the-world) as Being-alongside" (*Sich-vorweg-schon-Sein-in (der Welt) als Sein-bei*; p. 192/236).

Dasein, which has the structure of care, finds itself always already factically thrown into the world and inserted into that series of references and relations that according to Heidegger define the "worldhood of the world." And immediately afterward, he specifies what the "where" of this being-alongside is: "Ahead-of-itself-Being-already-in-a-world essentially includes one's falling and one's *Being-alongside* those things ready-to-hand within-the-world with which one concerns oneself" (*besorgten innerweltlichen Zuhanden*; p. 192/237).

Heidegger dedicates paragraphs 15 and 22 of *Being and Time* in particular to the definition of "handiness," being-ready-to-hand (*Zuhandenheit*); but the entire analysis of being-in, starting from paragraph 12 up to the end of the third chapter of the book, attempts to define the "familiarity that uses and handles" (*der gebrauchende-hantierende Umgang*) that constitutes the originary relation of Dasein to its world.

4.2. In his book entitled *Umgang mit Göttlichem*, Kerényi dwelled on the untranslatability of the German term *Umgang*, with which he expresses the originary relationship of the human being with the divine. The English word "intercourse" seems to him to be insufficient, because "it is limited to the total exchangeability of subject and object, to a running back and forth of the event" between the two terms of the relationship; in French and Italian one would have to choose between *commerce* and *commercio,* on the one hand, and *familiarité* and *dimestichezza,* on the other, while the German term unites both meanings in itself. The peculiarity of the term *Umgang* is that it entails both exchangeability between subject and object ("the object of familiarity must be able to change itself at any moment into the subject of that same familiarity; and we, who cultivate familiarity with it, must be able to become its object"; Kerényi, p. 5) and immediacy ("the relationship between subject and object that stands at the basis of familiarity excludes every mediation on the part of a third"; p. 8).

It is in this semantic perspective that one must situate the "familiarity that uses and handles" in *Being and Time*. Like Kerényi's *Umgang*, it is immediate, because nothing separates it from the world, and at the same time it is a place of indetermination between subject and object, because Dasein, which is always ahead of itself, finds itself always already in the power of the things of which it takes care. Analogous considerations could be made for the other two terms by means of which Heidegger characterizes the immediate and originary relation of being-in between Dasein and the world: "handiness" and relevance (*das Bewandtnis*, the being satisfactory or sufficient of something with respect to something else). In every case, it is a matter of something so immediate and constitutive for Dasein that this latter cannot at all be conceived as a subject "which sometimes has the inclination to take up a 'relation' with the world" (Heidegger 1, p. 57/84); familiarity, handiness, and relevance name the very structure of Dasein in its originary relation to the world.

4.3. That this relation has to do with the sphere of use, that what is in question in it is something like a "use of the world" is implied in the fact that the paradigm of handiness is equipment (*das Zeug*, something like Aristotle's *organon* or *ktema*), exemplified par excellence in the hammer:

> Straightforward familiarity with equipment can genuinely show itself only in dealings cut to its own measure (hammering with a hammer, for example); but in such dealings an entity of this kind is not *grasped* thematically as an occurring thing, nor is the equipment-structure known as such even in the using [*das Gebrauchen*]. The hammering does not simply have knowledge about the hammer's character as equipment, but it has appropriated this equipment in a way that could not possibly be more suitable. In this familiarity that makes use [*gebrauchenden Umgang*], our concern [*das Besorgen*] subordinates itself to the end-oriented characteristic [*Um-zu*, "in-order-to"] which is constitutive for the equipment we are employing at the time; the less we just stare at the hammer-thing, and the more we seize hold of it and use it [*gebraucht*], the more originary does our relationship to it become, and the more unveiledly is it encountered as that which it is—as equipment. The hammering itself uncovers the specific "manipulability" [*Handlichkeit*] of the hammer. The mode of Being which equipment possesses—in which it manifests itself in its own right—we call "handiness" [*Zuhandenheit*]. (Heidegger 1, p. 69/98)

This originary and immediate relation with the world—which Heidegger, to emphasize its inescapable character, also calls "facticity" (*Faktizität*)—is so involved and absolute that, to express it, it is necessary to make recourse to the same term that, in juridical language, designates the state of arrest: "the concept of 'facticity' implies that an entity 'within-the-world' has Being-in-the-world in such a way that it can understand itself as captured [*verhaftet*] in its 'destiny' with the Being of those entities which it encounters within its own world" (p. 56/82). And it is due to this unheard-of involvement of Dasein that Heidegger can speak of an originary "intimacy" (*Vertrautheit*, "confident familiarity") between Dasein and the world: "Any concern [*das Besorgen*] is always already as it is, because of some intimacy with the world. In this intimacy Dasein can lose itself in what it encounters in the world and be fascinated [*benommen*] by it" (p. 76/107).

In familiarity with the world we again find the plurality of senses and forms, of "ways of being-in" (*Weisen des In-Seins*), that we had seen to define the polysemy of the Greek *chresis*: "having to do with something [*zutunhaben mit etwas*], producing [*herstellen*] something, attending to something and looking after it, making use of [*verwenden*] something, giving something up and letting it go, undertaking, accomplishing, evincing, interrogating, considering, discussing, determining . . ." (p. 56/83). And all these modalities of being-in are included in that "familiarity with the world and with entities within-the-world" that Heidegger expressly defines as "those entities which we encounter first of all" (*nächstebegegnenden Seienden*; p. 66/95). These first and immediate entities are pre-thematic, because they "are not objects for knowing the world theoretically, they are rather what gets used [*das Gebrauchte*], what gets produced, and so forth. As entities so encountered, they become the preliminary theme for the purview of a 'knowing' which, as phenomenological, looks primarily toward Being, and which, in thus taking Being as its theme, takes these entities as its accompanying theme" (p. 67/95). And Dasein has no need to transpose itself (*sich versetzen*) into this familiarity: it "*is* always already in this mode of Being: when I open the door, for instance, I use the latch" (p. 67/96). The use of the world is, once again, the first and immediate relationship (*die nächste Art des Umganges*; ibid.) of Dasein.

ℵ. The relation between use and care can be compared with that between use value and exchange value, which Marx deduces from the economists. The privilege that Marx seems to grant to use value is founded on the fact that, for him, the process of production is in itself oriented to use value and not to exchange value, and only the surplus of use values over demand allows them to be transformed into means of exchange and commodities. However, Marx did not clearly show what one is to understand by a surplus of use values and seems, on the other hand, to conceive use value only as utilizability of an object. Now it is obvious that at the moment when an object is brought to market to sell it one cannot use it, which implies that use value in some way constitutively exceeds effective utilization. Exchange value is founded on a possibility or surplus contained in use value itself, which can be suspended and maintained in the potential state, just as, according to Heidegger, the suspension of handiness allows care to appear. From the perspective that interests us, it will be a question of thinking a surplus—or an alterity—of use with respect to utilizability that is intrinsic to use itself, independently of its surplus with respect to demand.

4.4. It is over this "familiarity that uses and handles" that care must affirm its primacy. It is a matter, on the one hand, even before confronting it thematically in the analysis of paragraphs 39–43, of presupposing and inscribing care into the very structure of being-in that defines the originary relation of Dasein with its world. In paragraph 12, at a point where he is characterizing the essential spatiality of Dasein and the ways of its being-in-the-world, Heidegger anticipates with these words the theme of care:

> All these ways of Being-in have concern [*Besorgen*] as their mode of Being— a mode of Being which we have yet to characterize in detail. . . . This term has been chosen not because Dasein happens to be proximally and to a large extent "practical" and economic, but because the Being of Dasein itself must [*soll*] be made visible as *care*. This term must be understood [*istzu fassen*] as an ontological structural concept. (p. 57/83–84)

Even though neither handiness nor relevance nor any of the other characteristics that define familiarity with the world seem to imply anything like a "taking care" (indeed, in their immediacy and their "nearness" they would seem to presuppose the contrary; cf. §22), here care is inserted as a necessity that does not need to be argued for and whose explanation is postponed to a later time.

It is another apparatus, however, that proves to be decisive in the strategy directed toward establishing the primacy of care. I am speaking of anxiety. Already in paragraph 16, familiarity had displayed points of fracture: a tool can be damaged and unusable and, precisely for this reason, can surprise us; it can be missing and, precisely for this reason, become intrusive; finally, it can be out of place or in the way, almost as though it was rebelling against every possibility of use. In all these cases, familiarity gives way to a simple availability (*Vorhandenheit*) but does not for this reason disappear. Since it appears to be a matter of accessory or subsequent phenomena, which do not call into question the primary characteristic of handiness, Heidegger can write that "handiness does not vanish simply, but takes its farewell, as it were, in the conspicuousness of the unusable. Handiness still shows itself, and it is precisely here that the worldly character of the handy shows itself too" (p. 74/104).

In anxiety, by contrast, the first and immediate relationship with the world proper to familiarity is called radically into question. "Here the total-ity of relevance of the handy and the available discovered within-the-world, is, as such, of no consequence; it collapses into itself; the world has the character of completely lacking significance" (p. 186/231). It is not simply a matter, as in the preceding cases, of an occasional unutilizability. The spe-cific power of anxiety is rather that of annihilating handiness, of producing a "nothing of handiness" (*Nichts von Zuhandenheit*; p. 187/232). In annihi-lating handiness, anxiety does not withdraw from the world but unveils a relation with the world more originary than any familiarity:

> That in the face of which anxiety is anxious is nothing handy within-the-world. . . . The "nothing" of handiness is grounded in the most primordial "something"—in the *world*. . . . *Being-in-the-world itself is that in the face of which anxiety is anxious.* Being-anxious discloses, originarily and directly, the world as world. (p. 187/231–232)

It is with this neutralization of handiness that, with a radical subver-sion of the rank (up until then primary) of the "familiarity that uses and handles," he can propose the striking thesis according to which intimacy with the world "is a mode of Dasein's uncanniness [*Unheimlichkeit*], not the reverse. *From an existential-ontological point of view, the 'not-at-home' [das Un-zu-hause] must be conceived as the more primordial phenomenon*" (p. 189/234).

And it is only after the apparent primacy of familiarity has been swept aside thanks to anxiety that care can appear, in the paragraph immedi-ately following, as the original structure of Dasein. That is to say, the primacy of care has been rendered possible only by means of an operation of annulling and neutralizing familiarity. The originary place of care is situated in the non-place of handiness, its primacy in making the pri-macy of use disappear.

א. To the primacy of care over use there corresponds, in the second division of the book, the primacy of temporality over spatiality. In paragraphs 22–24 of *Being and Time*, the sphere of the "familiarity that uses and handles" defined the "spatiality" of Dasein, its constitutive character as "being-in." The concepts Heidegger uses here are all of a spatial order: "de-removal" (*die Ent-fernung*), "proximity" (*dis Nähe*), "region" (*die Gegend*), "making room" (*Einräumen*). And spatiality is not something in which Dasein finds itself or that at a certain point happens to it: "Dasein is originarily spatial," and "in every encounter with the handy" of which it takes care "the encounter with space as region" is already inherent (p. 111/145).

Starting from paragraph 65, by contrast, not only is it temporality and not spatiality that constitutes the ontological meaning of care, but the very structure of this latter (being-already-ahead-of-oneself in a world as being-alongside the beings that one encounters in the world) acquires its proper sense from the three "ecstasies" of temporality: future, past, and present. It is not an accident that while "being-already" and "being-ahead-of-oneself" refer immediately to the past and the future, Heidegger observes that "we lack such an indication" (p. 328/376) proper to that third constitutive moment of care—the being-alongside that defines the sphere of handiness. The attempt to return being-alongside as well to temporality in the form of a "making-present" (*Gegenwärtigen*, p. 328/376) appears necessarily forced since in paragraphs 22–23, being-alongside defines Dasein's spatiality, a spatial nearness (*Nähe*) and not a temporal present. It is for this reason that in paragraphs 69 and 70, Heidegger persistently seeks to lead spatiality back to temporality ("Only on the basis of its ecstatico-horizonal temporality is it possible for Dasein to break into space "; p. 369/421). But it is significant that many years later, in the seminar on *Time and Being*, we read the laconic admission that "the attempt in *Being and Time*, §70, to derive human spatiality from temporality is untenable" (Heidegger 2, p. 24/23).

4.5. The primacy of care over use can be inscribed without difficulty in the peculiar dialectic that defines the analytic of Dasein: that between the improper (*Uneigentlich*) and the proper (*Eigentlich*). What appears as primary, the dimension in which Dasein is "already and for the most part," can only "fall" always already into impropriety and inauthenticity; but precisely for this reason, the proper does not have another place and substance with respect to the improper: it is "existentially only a modified way in which the latter is seized upon" (*nur ein modifiziertes Ergreifen dieser*; Heidegger 1, p. 179/224). This means that the primacy of the proper over the improper (like that of care over handiness, of temporality over spatiality) rests on a singular structure of being, in which something exists and is given reality solely by grasping a being that precedes and, nevertheless, disperses and removes itself. That something like a dialectical process is in question here is suggested by the analogy with the dialectic that opens the *Phenomenology of Spirit*, in which sense certainty, which "is primary and our immediate object," is later revealed to be the experience that is most abstract and lacking in truth, which may become true only through a process of mediation and negation, which nevertheless has need of it as the beginning that must be removed in order, only at the end, to be understood. Just as, for Hegel, perception (*Wahrnehmung*, taking as true) is possible only by grasping the untruth of sense certainty, so also in *Being and Time*, the proper is only a modified grasp of the improper, and care a grasping of the impropriety of use. But why, in our philosophical tradition, does not only consciousness but the very Dasein, the very being-there of the human being, need to presuppose a false beginning, which must be abandoned and removed to give place to the true and the most proper? Why can the human being find itself only by presupposing the not-truly-human; why can it only find free political action and the work of the human being by excluding—and at the same time including—the use of the body and the inoperativity of the slave? And what does it mean that the most proper possibility can be seized upon only by recovering itself from lostness and the fall into the improper?

‫‬‫א.‬   Heidegger cautions many times against the temptation to interpret the "falling" (*das Verfallen*) of Dasein into the improper in theological terms, as if it referred to the doctrine of the *status corruptionis* of human nature ("Ontically, we have not decided whether man is 'drunk with sin' and in the *status corruptionis*, whether he walks in the *status integritatis*, or whether he finds himself in an intermediate stage, the *status gratiae*"; ibid., p. 180/224). It is difficult to believe, however, that he was not aware (as Hegel, on the other hand, had been in his own way with respect to the doctrine of redemption) of having secularized in the analytic of Dasein the theological doctrine of the fall and original sin. But once again, it would probably have been a matter—for him as for Hegel—of "properly" grasping on the ontological plane what had been "improperly" theorized on the ontic level. The shift in level worked out by secularization often coincides not with a weakening but with an absolutization of the secularized paradigm.

4.6. In his 1946 essay *Der Spruch des Anaximander*, Heidegger seems to want to restore to use the centrality that, in *Being and Time*, he had taken away from it in the name of care. The occasion is provided by the translation of a Greek term closely related to *chre* and *chresthai*: *to chreon*, often translated as "necessity," but which Heidegger unreservedly renders with *der Brauch*, "use." First of all, by adopting the etymology proposed by Bréal and rejected by the majority of linguists, Heidegger inscribes this term into the semantic context of the hand and of handling (and, in this way, puts it implicitly into relation with the dimension of *Zuhandenheit* in *Being and Time*):

> *Chreon* is derived from *chrao, chraomai*. This suggests *he cheir*, the hand. *Chrao* means: *ich be-handle etwas*, I handle something, reach for it, extend my hand to it [*gehe es an und gehe ihm an die Hand*]. Thus, at the same time, *chrao* means: to place in someone's hands, to hand over and deliver [*in die Hand geben, einhändigen*], to let something belong to someone. Such a giving into the hand [*Aushändigen*, "delivery"] is, however, of a kind which keeps the transfer in hand [*in der Hand behält*], and with it what is transferred. (Heidegger 3, p. 337/276)

What is decisive here, however, is that a fundamental ontological function belongs to use, thus carried into the sphere of the hand, because it names the very difference between being and beings, between presence (*Answesen*) and the present (*Anwesendes*) of which Heidegger never stops reminding us:

> The term [*to chreon*] can only name the essentification in the presence *of* the present [*das Wesende im Anwesen des Anweseden*], together with the relation which is announced—obscurely enough—in the genitive. *To chreon* is thus the handing over [*das Einhändigen*] of presencing, a handing over which hands out [*aushändigt*] presencing to what is present, and therefore keeps in hand, in other words, preserves in presencing, what is present as such. (Ibid.)

By translating *chreon* with *Brauch*, Heidegger situates use in an ontological dimension. The relation of use now runs between being and beings, between presence and what comes to presence. This implies, naturally, that "use" and "to use," *Brauch* and *brauchen*, are abstracted from the sphere of meaning of utilization and, as we have seen for *chresis* and *chresthai*, restored to their originary semantic complexity:

> Generally, we understand "to use" to mean to utilize and need within the area of that to the use of which we enjoy rights. That of which one has need in the act of a utilization then becomes the usual [*üblich*]. The used is in use [*das Gebrauchte ist im Brauch*]. As the translation of *to chreon*, "use" is not to be understood in these customary but secondary meanings. Rather, we attend to the root meaning: *brauchen*, to use, is *bruchen*, to brook, in Latin *frui*, in German *fruchten, Frucht* [to bear fruit, fruit]. We translate this freely

as "to enjoy [*geniessen*]," which in its original form [*niessen*] means to take joy in something and so to have it in use. Only in its secondary meaning does "to enjoy" come to mean to consume and gobble up. We encounter what we have called the root meaning of "to use" as *frui* when Augustine says, "*Quid enim est aliud quod dicimus frui, nisi praesto habere, quod diligis?*" ("For what else do we mean when we say *frui* if not to have at hand something especially prized?"). *Frui* contains: *praesto habere. Praesto, praesitum* means in Greek *hypokeimenon*, that which already lies before us in unconcealment, the *ousia*, that which presences awhile. Accordingly, "to use" says: to let something that is present come to presence as such. *Frui, bruchen* [to brook], *brauchen* [to use], *Brauch* [use], means: to hand something over to its own essence and, as so present, to keep it in the protecting hand. In the translation of *to chreon*, use is thought of as the essentification in being itself. *Bruchen* [to brook], *frui*, is now no longer predicated of enjoyment as human behavior; nor is it said in relation to any entity whatever, even the highest (*fruitio dei* as *beatitudo hominis*). Rather, "use" now designates the way in which being itself presences as the relationship to what is present which is concerned and handles it as what is present: *to chreon*. (Ibid., pp. 338–339/277)

4.7. What relation is there between this "use" understood as a fundamental ontological dimension in which being maintains beings in presence and the "familiarity that uses and handles" that in *Being and Time* named the mode of being of the beings that Dasein first encounters in the world?

There is certainly more than an analogy between the affirmation "to use means: to let something present be present as such" and the one in paragraph 18 of *Being and Time*, according to which "'letting something be relevant' signifies ontically: letting something handy be so-and-so *as* it is already and *in order that* it be such" (and the text immediately specifies that "the way we take this ontical sense of 'letting be' is in a fundamentally ontological way"; Heidegger 1, pp. 84–85/117). However, with respect to the "familiarity that uses and handles," the shift of use from the level of the analytic of Dasein to that of the ontological difference seems to deprive it of any concreteness and distinctness. What does it in fact mean that being uses beings, that the originary ontological relation has the form of a use?

At a certain point, Heidegger assimilates use to *energeia*. The present being, he writes, is brought into presence and into unlatency "insofar as, surging into presence, it is brought into being by itself," and, at the same time, "it is brought into being, insofar as it is pro-duced by the human being." From this perspective, what comes into presence has the character of an *ergon*, that is, "thought in a Greek way, of a pro-duct, something brought forth" (*Hervor-gebrachtes*); for this reason, the presence of what is present, the being of beings is called in Greek: *energeia* (Heidegger 3, p. 342/279). In accordance with the proximity between *chresis* and *energeia* that we have already encountered in Aristotle, use (*chreon*) and being-at-work (*energeia*) "name the same thing" (ibid., p. 342/280).

The specificity of the term *chreon*, understood as "use" (*Brauch*) here seems to fade away. But what if use instead implied, with respect to potential, a relationship other than *energeia*? What if we had to think a use of potential that did not simply mean its being put-into-work, its passage to the act? *What if use in fact implied an ontology irreducible to the Aristotelian duality of potential and act that, through its historical translations, still governs Western culture?*

§ 5 Use-of-Oneself

5.1. In Stoic thought, the terms "use" and "to use" develop a function so central that it has been affirmed that in the last analysis Stoicism comes down to a doctrine of the use of life. In his study dedicated to this argument, Thomas Bénatouïl (pp. 21–22) has shown that the theme of use—in particular of the use of its own body parts by the animal—intersects with that of *oikeiosis*, of the appropriation or familiarization of the self to the self, whose fundamental importance in Stoic ethics has long been known to scholars (it is "the beginning and the foundation of Stoic ethics"; Pohlenz, p. 11).

The hypothesis that we intend to suggest is that, well beyond a simple intersection, the doctrine of *oikeiosis* becomes intelligible only if one understands it as a doctrine of use-of-oneself.

This is the passage in which Diogenes Laertius (VII, 85 = SVF, III, 178) has transmitted to us the essentials of what we know about the doctrine of *oikeiosis*:

> A living thing's first impulse [*hormè*] is to self-preservation, because nature from the outset has rendered it familiar [*oikeios* comes from *oikos*, the household or family] to itself [*oiekiouses autoi tes physeos ap'arches*], as Chrysippus affirms in the first book of his work *On Ends*, affirming that for every living thing the first familiar thing [*proton oikeion*] is its own constitution [*systasin*] and the awareness [*syneidesin*, but in the text of Chrysippus it should probably be read as *synaisthesin*, "con-sensation" or "con-sentiment"; cf. Pohlenz, p. 7] of itself. For it was not likely that nature should estrange the living thing from itself [*allotriosai*] or that the nature which has generated it could render it extraneous and not familiar to itself. We are forced then to conclude that

nature in constituting the living thing has rendered it familiar to itself [*oikeio-sai pros heauto*]; for so it comes to repel all that is injurious and to give free access to all that is familiar [*ta oikeia*].

According to this passage, the *proton oikeion*, that which is from the very beginning familiar to each living thing, is its own constitution and the sensation it has of it. In the same sense, Hierocles expresses it in his *Foundations of Ethics*: "From birth the living thing has sensation of itself and familiarity with itself and with its constitution" (*aisthanesthai te hautou kai oikeiousthai heautoi kai tei heautou systasei*; 7, 48; qtd. in Pohlenz, p. 1). *Oikeiosis*, familiarity with the self, is thinkable, in this sense, only on the basis of a *synaisthesis*, a con-sentiment of the self and of one's own constitution. And it is on this last notion, therefore, that the attention of the Stoics is concentrated, in order to seek to secure its reality at any cost.

It is at this point that the concept of use appears with a decisive function. The proof that animals possess sensation of their own body parts is, Hierocles suggests, the fact that they are familiar with their function, know what their function is, and make use of them: thus, "the winged animals perceived that their wings are adapted in advance to flight and for each of the parts of their bodies they perceive that they have them and, at the same time, what their use is" (*chreia*, proper functionality; Bénatouïl, p. 28). That we in some way perceive our eyes, our ears, and the other parts of our body is proven, Hierocles continues, by the fact that "if we want to look at something, we direct our eyes and not our ears at it, and when we want to listen, we incline our ears and not our eyes, and if we want to walk, we do not use [*chrometha*] our hands for this but our feet and legs" (ibid., p. 29). And in a subsequent passage, a further proof of self-perception is the fact that animals that are endowed with hooves, teeth, tusks, or venom do not hesitate "to make use of them to defend themselves in combat with other animals" (p. 34).

A passage from Galen's treatise traditionally entitled *De usu partium* insists on the decisive character of use for understanding the function of each part of the body: "When I first saw this," he writes concerning the elephant's proboscis,

I thought it superfluous and useless, but when I saw the animal using it like a hand, it no longer seemed so. . . . If the animal did not make use of this part, it would be superfluous and nature, who formed it, would not be perfectly skillful, but now, since the animal performs most useful actions with it, the part itself is shown to be useful and nature to be skillful. . . . When I also learned that in crossing a river or lake so deep that its entire body is submerged, the animal raises its proboscis high and breathes through it, I perceived that nature is provident not only because she constructed excellently all parts of the body but also because she taught the animal to use them. (Galen 1, pp. 438–439/725)

In all these texts—whether it is a matter, as for the physician Galen, of affirming the providential character of nature or, as for the philosopher Hierocles, of proving the familiarity of each animal with itself—the decisive element every time is in fact use. Only because the animal makes use of its body parts can something like a self-awareness and therefore a familiarity with itself be attributed to it. The familiarity, the *oikeiosis* of the living being with itself is dissolved without remainder into its self-perception, and this latter coincides in turn with the capacity of the living being to make use of its own body parts and its own constitution. It is this constitutive connection between *oikeiosis* and use-of-oneself that it will therefore be necessary to clarify.

‫א‬.   It is in Lucretius, much more radically than in the Stoics, that use seems to be completely emancipated from every relation to a predetermined end, in order to affirm itself as the simple relation of the living thing with its own body, beyond every teleology. Pushing to the extreme the Epicurean critique of every teleologism, Lucretius thus affirms that no organ was created in view of an end, neither the eyes for vision, nor the ears for hearing, nor the tongue for speech: "Whatever thing is born generates its own use [*quod natum est id procreat usum*]. There was no seeing before eyes were born, no verbal pleading before the tongue was created. The origin of the tongue was far anterior to speech. The ears were created long before a sound was heard. All the limbs, I am well assured, existed before their use" (IV, 835–841).

The reversal of the relation between organ and function amounts to liberating use from every established teleology. The meaning of the verb *chresthai* here shows its pertinence: the living being does not make use of its body parts (Lucretius does not speak of organs) for some one predetermined function, but by entering into relation with them, it so to speak gropingly finds and invents their use. The body parts precede their use, and use precedes and creates their function.

It is what is produced in the very act of exercise as a delight internal to the act, as if by gesticulating again and again the hand found in the end its pleasure and its "use," the eyes by looking again and again fell in love with vision, the legs and thighs by bending rhythmically invented walking.

‫א‬.   The testimony of Cicero agrees with that of Diogenes Laertius: "[The Stoics] maintain that immediately upon birth (for that is the proper point to start from) a living creature is rendered familiar and given in care to itself [*sibi concili-ari et commendari*, with which Cicero renders *oikeiousthai*] in order to preserve itself and to feel affection for its own constitution [*status*, which translates *systa-sis*] and for those things which tend to preserve that constitution and is rendered foreign [*alienari*, corresponding to *allotriosai*] to its own death and that which appears to threaten it" (Cicero 2, III, 16). The theme of self-consciousness ap-pears immediately afterward: "it would not be possible that they should feel de-sire at all unless they possessed self-sensation and loved themselves" (*nisi sensum haberent sui eoque se diligerent*).

5.2. We possess a brief treatise whose theme is precisely the relation between familiarity, sensation, and use of self: Seneca's Letter 121 to Lu-cilius. The question to which the letter intends to respond is "whether all living beings have sensation of their constitution" (*an esset omnibus animalibus constitutionis suae sensus*). Seneca's response refers to the innate capacity that each living being has of "use-of-oneself":

> That this is the case is proved particularly by their moving their members with fitness and nimbleness, as though they were trained for the purpose. There is none that does not show agility with respect to his own members. The skilled workman handles his tools with an ease born of experience; the pilot knows how to steer his ship skillfully; the painter can quickly lay on the colors which he has prepared in great variety for the purpose of rendering the likeness, and passes with ready eye and hand from palette to canvas. In the same way the animal is agile in all that pertains to the use of its body [*sic animale in omnem usum sui mobilest*]. We are apt to wonder at skilled dancers because their gestures are perfectly adapted to the meaning of the piece and its accompanying emotions, and their movements match the speed of the dialogue. But that which art gives to the craftsman, is given to the animal by nature. No animal handles its members with difficulty, no animal is at a loss how to use itself [*in usu sui haesitat*]. (Seneca, vol. 3, pp. 399–401)

To the objection that what drives the animal to move is fear of pain, Sen-eca responds that animals incline toward their natural movement despite the impediment of pain:

> Thus the child who is trying to stand and is becoming used to carrying his own weight, on beginning to test his strength, falls and rises again and again with tears until through painful effort he has trained himself to the demands of nature. . . . The tortoise on his back feels no suffering; but he is restless because he misses his natural condition [*naturalis status*], and does not cease

to shake himself about until he stands once more upon his feet. So all living things have a sensation of their own constitution [*constitutionis suae sensus*], and for that reason can manage their limbs as readily as they do [*membrorum tam expedita tractatio*]; nor have we any better proof that they come into being equipped with this knowledge [*notitia*] than the fact that no animal is clumsy in use-of-itself [*nullum animal ad usum sui rude est*]. (Ibid., p. 401)

After having thus confirmed the constitutive connection between use of self and self-consciousness, *usus sui* and *constitutionis suae sensus*, Seneca tackles the closely intertwined theme of *oikeiosis* (which, following Cicero's example, he renders with *conciliatio* and *conciliari*):

"You maintain, do you," says the objector, "that every living thing is at the start familiarized with its constitution [*constitutioni suae conciliari*], and that the human constitution is a reasoning one, and hence the human being is familiarized with itself not as animal, but as rational. For the human being loves himself in respect of that wherein he is human. How, then, can a child, not yet having reason, be familiarized with its rational constitution?" But each age has its own constitution, different in the case of the child, the body, and the old man. The child is toothless, and he is familiarized with this constitution. Then his teeth grow, and he is familiarized with that constitution. Vegetation also, which will develop into grain and fruits, has a special constitution when young and scarcely peeping over the tops of the furrows, another when it is strengthened and stands upon a stalk which is soft but strong enough to bear its weight, and still another when the color changes to yellow, prophesies threshing time, and hardens in the ear—no matter what may be the constitution into which the plant comes, it keeps it, and conforms to it. The periods of infancy, boyhood, youth, and old age, are different; but I, who have been infant, boy, and youth, am still the same. Thus, although each has at different times a different constitution, the familiarization with its own constitution is always the same [*conciliatio constitutioni suae eadem est*]. For nature does not render dear to me [*commendat*, the other verb with which Cicero translated *oikeiosai*] boyhood or youth or old age, but myself. Therefore, the child is familiarized with its present constitution, not with that which will be his in youth. For even if there is in store for him any higher phase into which he must be changed, the state in which he is born is also according to nature. It is with itself that the animal is first of all familiarized [*primum sibi ipsum conciliatur animal*], for there must be a pattern to which all other things may be referred. I seek pleasure: for whom? For myself. I am therefore taking care of myself [*mei curam ago*]. I shrink from pain; on behalf of whom? Myself. Therefore, I am taking care of myself. Since I do everything for care of myself, therefore care of myself is anterior to all [*ante omnia est mei cura*]. This quality inheres in all living beings and is not added to them at a second time, but is innate. (Ibid., pp. 405–407)

Let us reflect on the extraordinary intertwining of familiarity and self-hood, of consciousness and use-of-oneself that Seneca, though of course not without some contradictions, develops in these very dense pages. *Oikeiosis* or *conciliatio* does not have as its ultimate object the constitution of the individual, which can change over time, but, by means of it, its very self (*non enim puerum mihi aut iuvenem aut senem, sed me natura commendat*). This self—despite the fact that the Stoics seem at times to preconstitute it in a nature or an innate knowledge—is therefore not something substantial or a preestablished end but coincides entirely with the use that the living being makes of it (*usus sui*—which Seneca also declines as care-of-oneself, *cura mei*).

If one accepts this relational and non-substantial interpretation of the Stoic self, then—whether it is a matter of self-sensation, of *sibi conciliatio*, or of use-of-oneself—the self coincides each time with the relation itself and not with a predetermined telos. And if use, in the sense that we have seen, means being affected, constituting-oneself insofar as one is in relation with something, then use-of-oneself coincides with *oikeiosis*, insofar as this term names the very mode of being of the living being. The living being uses-itself, in the sense that in its life and in its entering into relationship with what is other than the self, it has to do each time with its very self, feels the self and familiarizes itself with itself. *The self is nothing other than use-of-oneself.*

ℵ.   In the *De anima libri mantissa*, Alexander of Aphrodisias refers to the Stoic doctrine of *oikeiosis* in these terms: "The Stoics . . . affirm that the animal is for itself the first familiar thing [*to proton oikeion einai to zoon hautoi*] and that each animal—and also the human being—upon being born is familiarized with itself [*pros hauto oikeiousthai*]" (Alexander, p. 150/151); a similar doctrine is attributed in almost the same terms to Aristotle ("Some say that, according to Aristotle, we ourselves are the first thing familiar to ourselves"—*einai proton oikeion emin emas autous*; p. 150/152).

It is significant that Alexander resolutely identifies familiarity and seity. Familiarity and relation with oneself are the same thing.

ℵ.   The familiarity and self-sensation of which the Stoics speak do not entail a rational consciousness but seem to be obscurely immanent to the very use-of-oneself. The living being, Seneca writes in the above-cited letter, "does not know

what a constitution is, but knows its own constitution, does not know what a
living creature is, but feels that it is a living being. . . . Everyone of us understands that there is something that stirs his impulses, but he does not know what
it is and where it comes from" (*quid sit constitutio non novit, constitutionem suam
novit . . . quid sit animal nescit, animal esse se sentitconatum sibi esse scit, quid sit
aut unde sit nescit*; Seneca, vol. 3, p. 403). The self becomes aware of itself by
means of the articulation of a zone of non-awareness.

5.3. It is perhaps in a passage from the *Enneads* (VI, 8, 10) that the
specificity of use-of-oneself finds, so to speak, its ontological formulation. Seeking a provisional expression for the mode of being of the One,
here Plotinus, after having denied that it could accidentally be what it is,
definitively opposes use to substance, *chresthai* to *ousia*:

> Well then, suppose he did not come to be, but is as he is and is not of his own
> substance. And if he is not master of his substance [*ouk on tes autou ousias
> kyrios*], but is who he is, not hypostatizing himself but using-himself as what
> he is [*ouk hypostesas heaouton, chromenos de heautoi hoios estin*], then he is what
> he is of necessity, and could not be otherwise.

What is decisive for us in this passage is not the strategy of Plotinus, who is
looking to exclude from the One both accidentality and necessity, so much
as the striking opposition that he establishes between use and hypostasis.
Dörrie has shown that beginning with Neoplatonism the term *hypostais* acquires the meaning of "realization": *hyphistamai* thus means "to be realized
in an existence" (Dörrie, p. 45). Using-oneself means not pre-supposing
oneself, not appropriating being to oneself in order to subjectivate oneself
in a separate substance. The self of which use makes use is expressed, for
this reason, only by the anaphora *hoios*, "some such," which always recov-
ers being from its hypostatization into a subject. And precisely because it
maintains itself in use-of-itself, the One is abstracted not only from the
categories of modality (it is neither contingent nor necessary: "Neither his
being such nor any way of being happen to him by accident: he is such
and not otherwise. . . . Now he is not as he is because he cannot be otherwise, but because being what he is is best"; Plotinus, VI, 8, 9–10), but
also from those of being and its fundamental divisions ("beyond being
means . . . that he is not a slave to being or to himself"; VI, 8, 19).

Let us attempt to develop the idea of a non-hypostatic, non-substan-
tializing use-of-oneself, which Plotinus seems to let to the side immediately after having formulated it. Use-of-oneself, in this sense, precedes

being (or is beyond it and, therefore, also beyond the division between essence and existence), is—as Plotinus writes a little after of the One with a willfully paradoxical expression—"a primary *energeia* without being," in which the self itself takes the place of hypostasis ("it itself is, as it were, its hypostasis," *autò touto ton hoion hypostasin*; VI, 8, 20). Or—one can also say, reversing the argument—*being, in its originary form, is not substance* (ousia*), but use-of-oneself, is not realized in a hypostasis, but dwells in use.* And "to use" is, in this sense, the archimodal verb, which defines being before or, in any case, outside its articulation in the ontological difference existence/essence and in the modalities: possibility, impossibility, contingency, necessity. It is necessary that the self first be constituted in use outside any substantiality in order that something like a subject—a hypostasis—can say: I am, I can, I cannot, I must . . . .

5.4. It is from this perspective that we can read the messianic theory of use that Paul elaborates in the First Letter to the Corinthians. "Were you called in the condition of a slave?" he writes. "Do not be concerned about it. Even if you can gain your freedom, rather make use" (*mallon chresai*—that is, of your condition as a slave; 1 Corinthians 7:21). That is to say, the factical and juridico-political conditions in which each one finds himself must be neither hypostatized nor simply changed. The messianic call does not confer a new substantial identity but consists first of all in the capacity to "use" the factical condition in which each one finds himself. And the way this new capacity of use must be understood is stated a little further down: "I mean, brothers and sisters, time has grown short; what remains is so that those who have wives may be as not [*hos me*] having, and those who mourn as not mourning, and those who rejoice as not rejoicing, and those who buy as not possessing, and those who use the world as not abusing. For the present form of this world is passing away. I want you to be without care" (7:29–32). The Pauline "as not," by putting each factical condition in tension with itself, revokes and deactivates it without altering its form (weeping *as not* weeping, having a wife *as not* having a wife, slaves *as not* slaves). That is to say, the messianic calling consists in the deactivation and disappropriation of the factical condition, which is therefore opened to a new possible use. The "new creature" is only the capacity to render the old inoperative and use it in a new way: "if one is in the messiah, a new creature [*kaine ktisis*]: the old things have passed away, behold they have become new" (2 Corinthians 5:17).

From this perspective, we can better understand the sense of the antitheses of verses 30–31: "those who buy as not possessing, and those who use the world as not abusing." What is in question is an explicit reference to the definition of ownership according to Roman law as *ius utendi et abutendi*. That is to say, Paul counterposes *usus* to *dominium*: to dwell in the call in the form of the "as not" signifies never making of the world an object of ownership but only of use.

§ 6 Habitual Use

6.1. The tradition of Aristotelianism that culminates in Scholasticism understands use as synonymous with *energeia* and therefore seeks to keep it separate from potential and habit. "Use," Aquinas writes, "denotes the being-in-act of some habit or other [*usus significat actum cuiuslibet habitus*]. The act of any habit and the use of potential belong to the one (or the thing) to which the act belongs. Hence the term 'use' means the act and in no way the potential or the habit" (Aquinas 1, q. 17, a. 1). Against this tradition, it is necessary to think being-in-use as distinct from being-in-act and, at the same time, to restore it to the dimension of habit, but of a habit that, insofar as it happens as habitual use and is therefore always already in use, does not presuppose a potential that must at a certain point pass into the act or be put into work.

Galen had to think a dimension of this kind when, in his *De usu partium*, he decisively opposes use to *energeia*, just as a state or a habit is opposed to a movement and an operation: "Now the use of a part differs from its *energeia*, from its being-in-act, because *energeia* is an active motion (*kinesis drastike*), and use is what is commonly called *euchrestia*" (Galen 1, p. 437/724). *Euchrestia* means the adequacy of a part to develop a certain function, good functionality, which is to say, not an operation and passage from potential to act but something like a habitual condition. It is in this sense that we intend to think here a "habitual use," a *chresis-chreia*, a being-always-already-in-use of habit and potential: that is, a potential that is never separate from act, which never needs to be put to work, because it is always already in use, is always already *euchrestia*.

This means, however, entirely rethinking and correcting, starting from habit and use, the Aristotelian doctrine of *dynamis* and *energeia*, of potential and act. Aristotle—one could say—has divided what we are here seeking to think as use and has called *dynamis* and *energeia* that which results from the division. The concept of habit (*hexis*) was thought by Aristotle precisely to eliminate the aporias implicit in this doctrine and to assure to potential some reality. If being (use) is divided into potential and act, something that articulates and renders possible the passage from one to the other will indeed be necessary. If potential were always and only generic potential, such as the purely chimerical potential that belongs to a baby, of whom we say that he could become a writer or carpenter, an architect or a flute player, then the concept of potential would dissolve and its being put to work would be unthinkable. Habit is what renders possible the passage of potential from mere genericity to the effective potential of the one who writes or plays the flute, builds tables or houses. Habit is the form in which potential exists and is given reality as such.

The aporias of generic potential, which are neutralized in this way, are, however, immediately reproduced in the new reality that it has been given. In order that a distinction between habit and being-at-work be maintained, in order that *hexis* not always already blindly cross over into *energeia*, it is in fact necessary that the one who has the habit of a technique or of a knowledge be able not to exercise it, be able not to pass to the act. For this reason, in book nine of the *Metaphysics*, the decisive thesis on potential-habit reads: "every potential is impotential of the same and according to the same" (*tou autou kai kata to auto pasa dynamis adynamia*; *Metaphysics* 1046a 30). Impotential, *adynamia*, here means to be able not to pass to the act and, in accordance with the philosopher's intense antipathy for sleep that we have already noted, habit is in this sense compared to sleep and the act to wakefulness: "waking corresponds to knowing in act, sleeping to a having without exercising" (*echein kai me energein*; *On the Soul*, 412a 25). The ambiguity of the notion of "potential not to" here appears clearly: it is what permits habit to be given existence as such, and at the same time it is constitutively inferior to the act to which it is irrevocably destined. As Aristotle never stops repeating against the Megarians, the one who truly has a potential is the one who can both put it and not put it into action; but *energeia*, being-at-work, remains the end of potential. In this way, however, the aporia that was thought to be eliminated reappears in an even more acute form: if in every potential-habit there irreducibly inheres a potential not to pass to the act, how will it be possible to lead it to this passage; how will it be possible to stir it from its sleep?

By assimilating use to *energeia* and being-at-work and by separating it from habit as wakefulness from sleep, Aristotle set thought durably off course. Only if we think habit not only in a negative mode, beginning from impotential and from the possibility of not passing into act, but rather as habitual use, is the aporia, against which Aristotelian thought on potentiality has made shipwreck, dissolved. Use is the form in which habit is given existence, beyond the simple opposition between potential and being-at-work. And if habit is, in this sense, always already use-of-oneself and if this latter, as we have seen, implies a neutralization of the subject/object opposition, then there is no place here for a proprietary subject of habit, which can decide to put it to work or not. The self, which is constituted in the relation of use, is not a subject, is nothing other than this relation.

6.2. In the concept of *hexis-habitus* (*hexis* is the nominalization of *echein*, "to have"), philosophy has thought the constitutive connection that unites being to having, which remains a still uninvestigated chapter in the history of ontology. In an exemplary study, Benveniste sought to define the linguistic function and relation of "being" and "having" in Indo-European languages. They are both verbs that indicate a state: "*To be* is the state of being, of that which is something; *to have* is the state of having, of that to which something is. The difference thus emerges. *To be* establishes an intrinsic relationship of equivalence between the two terms which it joins: it is the consubstantial state. In contrast, the two terms joined by *to have* remain distinct; the relationship between them is extrinsic and establishes a belonging" (Benveniste, p. 198/172). According to Benveniste, moreover, *to have* is nothing but an inverted "being to (or of)": *habeo aliquid*, "I have something," is only a secondary and derivative variant of *mihi est aliquid*, "something is to me, belongs to me."

One must pursue Benveniste's analysis beyond the limits of linguistics. In reality, the relation between "being" and "having" is more intimate and complex. *Hexis*, potential insofar as it is a habit, is according to Aristotle one of the ways in which being is said. Namely, it indicates the state of being, insofar as it is attributed to a subject. What is had in *hexis* is a certain mode of being, a *diathesis*, a being disposed in a certain way (being knowledgeable, being an architect, being a flute player . . .). Aristotle calls this being that one has *dynamis*, "potential," and the one who has this certain state and this certain being is *dynatos*, "potent." In any case, having (*echein*) is here always "having a being."

This means that the doctrine of *habitus* delimits the logical place in which a doctrine of subjectivity would have been possible. For this reason, in the philosophical dictionary in book Delta of the *Metaphysics* (1022b 4–6), Aristotle can write, in an apparent contradiction, that *hexis* means both "a certain being-at-work [*energeia*] of the one having and the thing had" and "the disposition [*diathesis*] according to which what is disposed is disposed well or badly": it is both a mode of being and the state or disposition of a subject. And for this reason, apropos of the rational potentials, which are capable of a thing as much as of its contrary, he can say that it is necessary that there be a sovereign (*kyrion*) element that is in a position to decide the potential in one direction or the other and that it must be "something else" (*heteron ti*) with respect to potential (*Metaphysics* 1048a 11). Habit is the point at which a subjectivity seeks to make itself master of being, the place in which, with a perfect circularity, having, which derives from being, appropriates the latter to itself. Having is nothing but the appropriation of a being.

6.3. There is a text of Aristotle in which a different conception of habit could perhaps have been founded. In the above-cited passage from book Delta of the *Metaphysics*, one reads that if habit is defined as the relation between the one who has and that which is had, then "it is impossible to have a habit, because if it were possible to have the habit that one has, there would be infinite regress" (1022b 7–10). It is in this elusive, fugitive place that modern thought will situate its subject, which is posited as master of what cannot be had.

In Aristotle's warning there comes to light the aporia inherent in the interweaving of being and having that has its place in habit. Against the scholastic doctrine according to which "the use of potential belongs to the one to whom habit belongs," it is necessary to affirm that use does not belong to any subject, that it is situated beyond both being and having. That is to say, use breaks the ambiguous implication of being and having that defines Aristotelian ontology. Glenn Gould, to whom we attribute the habit of playing the piano, does nothing but make use-of-himself insofar as he plays and knows habitually how to play the piano.

He is not the title holder and master of the potential to play, which he can put to work or not, but constitutes-himself as having use of the piano, independently of his playing it or not playing it in actuality. *Use, as habit, is a form-of-life and not the knowledge or faculty of a subject.*

This implies that we must completely redraw the map of the space in which modernity has situated the subject and its faculties.

A poet is not someone who has the potential or faculty to create that, one fine day, by an act of will (the will is, in Western culture, the apparatus that allows one to attribute the ownership of actions and techniques to a subject), he decides—who knows how and why—like the God of the theologians, to put to work. And just like the poet, so also are the carpenter, the cobbler, the flute player, and those who, with a term of theological origin, we call professionals—and, in the end, every human being—not transcendent title holders of a capacity to act or make: rather, they are living beings that, in the use and only in the use of their body parts as of the world that surrounds them, have self-experience and constitute-themselves as using (themselves and the world).

ℵ.   The thesis that potential is in some way always in use, even if it does not pass over into action, is affirmed by Pelagius in his impassioned defense of the human possibility not to sin, which Augustine vainly seeks to refute in his anti-Pelagian writings (in particular, in *De natura et gratia*). Potential, writes Pelagius, "inheres in me even if I do not will it and it never contains in itself any idleness" (qtd. in Augustine 1, 57, 49). Nevertheless, insofar as it is given to us by God, to whom it essentially belongs, it is not in our power (*in nostra potestate*).

6.4. But what is habitual use, and how is a habit used without causing it to pass over into action, without putting it to work? It is clear that this does not mean inertia or simple absence of works but a totally other relation to them. The work is not the result or achievement of a potential, which is realized and consumed in it: the work is that in which potential and habit are still present, still in use; it is the dwelling of habit, which does not stop appearing and, as it were, dancing in it, ceaselessly reopening it to a new, possible use.

In book IV of the *Ethics*, Spinoza has provided the key to understanding the special relation with potential that is in question here and that he calls *acquiescentia in se ipso*. "Acquiescence in oneself," he writes, "is the pleasure arising from a person's contemplation of himself and his potential for acting" (Spinoza 2, p. 183). What does it mean for a human being to contemplate himself and his potential for acting? Acquiescence is certainly a figure of inoperativity—but what is an inoperativity that consists in contemplating the very potential to act?

Contemplation is the paradigm of use. Like use, contemplation does not have a subject, because in it the contemplator is completely lost and dissolved; like use, contemplation does not have an object, because in the work it contemplates only its (own) potential. Life, which contemplates in the work its (own) potential of acting or making, is rendered inoperative in all its works and lives only in use-of-itself, lives only (its) livability. We write "own" and "its" in parentheses because only through the contemplation of potential, which renders inoperative every *energeia* and every work, does something like the experience of an "own" and a "self" become possible. The self—whose place the modern subject will usurp— is what is opened up as a central inoperativity in every operation, as the "livability" and "usability" in every work. And if the architect and the carpenter remain such even when they are not building, that is not because they are title-holders of a potential of building, which they can also not put to work, but because they habitually live in use-of-themselves as architect or carpenter: habitual use is a contemplation and contemplation is a form of life.

6.5. At the end of *What Is Philosophy?* Deleuze defines life in its immediacy as "contemplation without consciousness" (Deleuze and Guattari, p. 213). Of this "passive creation" that "is but does not act," he furnishes the examples of sensation and habitual praxis (p. 212). In the same sense, in his *Mémoire sur la décomposition de la pensée*, Maine de Biran indefatigably seeks to grasp, beyond the ego and the will, a "mode of existence that is so to speak impersonal," which he calls "affectability" and defines as the simple organic capacity to be affected without consciousness or personality, which, like Condillac's statue, becomes all its modifications and all its sensations and yet constitutes "a positive and complete manner of existing in its kind" (Maine de Biran, p. 370).

What is decisive here is the separation between contemplation and consciousness and between affectability and personality. Contrary to the prestige of consciousness in our culture, it is always necessary to recall anew that sensation and habitual praxis, as use-of-oneself, articulate a zone of non-consciousness, which is not something like a mystical fog in which the subject loses itself but the habitual dwelling in which the living being, before every subjectivation, is perfectly at ease. If the gestures and acts of the animal are agile and graceful ("no animal is at a loss in use-of-itself"), this is because for it no act, no gesture constitutes a "work" of which it is posited as responsible author and conscious creator.

It is in this way that we must think contemplation as use-of-oneself. Every use is the articulation of a zone of non-consciousness. And this is not the fruit of a removal, like the unconscious of psychoanalysis, nor is it deprived of relation to the living thing that dwells in it: on the contrary, using-oneself means maintaining oneself in relation with a zone of non-consciousness, keeping it intimate and close just as habit is intimate to use. This relation is not inert but is preserved and constituted through a patient, tenacious deactivation of the *energeiai* and the works that cease-lessly surface in it, by means of the quiet cancellation of every attribution and every property: *vivere sine proprio*. And it is not important that cancellation and disappropriation are continually lost in the tradition, that contemplation and use-of-oneself never cease to make shipwreck in the history of works and subjects. Contemplation, the zone of non-consciousness, is the nucleus—unforgettable and at the same time immemorial—inscribed in every tradition and in every memory, which signs it with a mark of infamy or glory. The user, always unauthorized, is only the *auctor*—in the Latin sense of witness—who bears testimony of the work in the very gesture in which, in contemplation, he revokes it and constantly puts it back into use.

6.6. The most proper characteristic of habit as *ethos* and use-of-oneself was covered and rendered inaccessible by the medieval theory of virtue. According to this doctrine, which takes up and develops the Aristotelian definition of *aretè* as habit (*hexis*), virtue is an "operative habit," which causes potential or habit to pass into act in the best way. Human potential—thus the scholastics argue, who formulated and transmitted to Western ethics the doctrine of virtue—in contrast to natural potentials is constitutively undecided, insofar as it can indifferently want this or that object, the good as well as the bad. For this reason, it is necessary that there be produced in potential a habit that is essentially ordained to good action: this habit is virtue as *habitus operativus*. The Aristotelian primacy of *energeia* over habit is here confirmed: virtue is that by means of which habit, which in Aristotle is a category of ontology, is transformed into acting and crosses over into ethics (Aristotle had divided being into potential and act in order to insert movement and action into it). And yet precisely this indetermination of being and praxis, habit and *energeia*, marks the status of virtue with its ambiguity: it is the mode of being of a subject (the virtuous human being) and at the same time a quality of his action. The human being acts well insofar as he is virtuous, but he is virtuous insofar as he acts well.

In breaking the vicious circle of virtue, it is necessary to think the virtuous (or the virtual) as use, that is, as something that stands beyond the dichotomy of being and praxis, of substance and action. The virtuous (or the virtual) is not opposed to the real: on the contrary, it exists and is in use in the mode of habituality; however, it is not immaterial, but, insofar as it never ceases to cancel and deactivate being-at-work, it continually restores *energeia* to potential and to materiality. Use, insofar as it neutralizes the opposition of potential and act, being and acting, material and form, being-at-work and habit, wakefulness and sleep, is always virtuous and does not need anything to be added to it in order to render it operative. Virtue does not suddenly develop into habit: it is the being always in use of habit; it is habit as form of life. Like purity, virtue is not a characteristic that belongs to someone or something on its own. For this reason, virtuous actions do not exist, just as a virtuous being does not exist: what is virtuous is only use, beyond—which is to say, in the middle of—being and acting.

§ 7   The Animate Instrument and Technology

7.1. In *Being and Time*, familiarity and handiness define the place of the originary and immediate relation of Dasein with the world. This relation, however, is intrinsically determined by an irreducible instrumental character, which constitutes it as a relation of use: "when I open the door, I make use [*mache ich Gebrauch*] of the latch" (Heidegger 1, p. 67/96). What the human being primarily encounters in the world is, as we have seen, "equipment" (*Zeug*), but in the proper sense equipment "is" not but exists solely in the form of an "in-order-to" (*um-zu*), is always inserted into a multiplicity of instrumental relations (*Zeugganzes*; ibid., p. 68/97). The first of these relations is utility (*Dienlichkeit*, a term in which one must perceive proximity to service—*Dienst*—and servant—*Diener*). In this sense, familiarity with the world always necessarily has to do with a "serviceability," must "subordinate itself to the 'serves-for' [*um-zu*] which is always constitutive for the instrumentality of the equipment" (p. 69/98).

Years later, in the essay on *The Origin of the Work of Art*, Heidegger returns to the theme of equipment. And he does so by means of the analysis of the most common and ordinary equipment possible: a pair of peasant shoes (*ein paar Bauernschuhe*—evidently something of the kind still existed, even if he must exemplify it with a Van Gogh painting). The equipment chosen belongs to the class that Aristotle defined as *ktema praktikon*, "practical equipment," from which one obtains nothing other than its use. But even more than to the handle, the hammer, and the other equipment mentioned in *Being and Time*, to the peasant shoes there belongs the magical power, for the person—or to the woman, since it is a question of a peasant woman—who uses them, of disclosing

66

her world, conferring meaning and security on it. Certainly, "the being equipment of the equipment consists in its utility" (*Dienlichkeit*, "service-ability"), but this is not exhausted in simple instrumentality:

> The equipment vibrates with the silent call of the earth, its silent gift of the ripening grain, its unexplained self-refusal in the wintry field. This equipment is pervaded by uncomplaining worry as to the certainty of bread, wordless joy at having once more withstood want, trembling before the impending birth, and shivering at the surrounding menace of death. (Heidegger 3, p. 23/14)

That is to say, the essence of equipment, its "fullness," rests in something more than instrumentality, which Heidegger calls "reliability" (*Verlässlichkeit*).

> Thanks to this, the peasant woman is admitted into the silent call of the earth; in virtue of the reliability of the equipment she is certain of her world. World and earth exist for her and those who share her mode of being only here—in the equipment. We say "only" but this is a mistake; for it is the reliability of the equipment which first gives the simple world its security and assures the earth the freedom of its steady pressure. The equipmental being of the equipment, its reliability, keeps all things gathered within itself. . . . (Ibid., p. 23/14–15)

Here Heidegger refers to the conceptuality that he had developed in the 1929–30 winter semester course on *The Fundamental Concepts of Metaphysics*, in which the stone, the animal, and the human being were defined according to their having or not having a world. It is in virtue of equipment that the peasant woman, in contrast with the plant and the animal who remain imprisoned in their environment, has a world, "stays in the openness of being" (p. 34/23). Equipment, in its reliability, gives to the world its necessity and its proximity and to things their time and their proper measure. And yet it still remains in some way imprisoned in the sphere of utility. This essential limit of equipment appears clearly if one compares it to the work of art. While the work of art exposes beings in their truth (for example, the Van Gogh painting, which shows what the peasant shoes really are), the being equipment of the equipment always already dissipates into its "serviceability."

> The individual piece of equipment becomes worn out and used up. But also, use itself falls into disuse, becomes ground down and merely habitual. In this way equipmental being withers away, sinks to the level of mere equipment. Such dwindling of equipmental being is the disappear-

ance of its reliability. . . . Now nothing but sheer serviceability remains
visible. (p. 24/15)

Equipment, which opens to the human being its world, nevertheless always risks falling back into instrumentality and service. And yet this decadence of equipment, "to which the objects of use owe their boringly oppressive usualness," is still "a testament to their originary essence" (ibid.).

7.2. The human beings whom Heidegger describes are at the mercy of
equipment, they rely on its "serviceability," and only by means of it do
they enter into their world. In this sense, the relation with equipment
defines the human dimension. And yet one could say that Heidegger
seeks in every way to liberate the human being from the narrow limits
of this sphere, which coincides with that of use. And he does it in *Being
and Time* by substituting care for use and in the essay on *The Origin of
the Work of Art*, first by means of reliability and then by subordinating
equipment to the work of art, which puts to work that truth of being,
which equipment always ends up losing in serviceability.

It should not be surprising, then, that instrumentality appears once
again in the 1950 essay on *The Question Concerning Technology*, that is,
precisely in the context of the central problem of the late Heidegger's
thought. Against Spengler, who in his 1931 book on *Man and Technology*
had affirmed that technology cannot be understood starting from the instrument, the essay opens by affirming an essential connection between
technology and instrumentality. Technology is in fact nothing other than
a human action directed at a goal.

> For to posit ends [*Zwecke*] and procure and utilize the means [*Mittel*] to them
> is a human activity. The manufacture and utilization of equipment, tools, and
> machines, the manufactured and used things themselves, and the needs and
> ends that they serve, all belong to what technology is. The whole complex of
> these apparatuses [*Einrichtungen*] is technology. Technology is itself an appa-
> ratus—in Latin, an *instrumentum*. . . . This instrumental definition of tech-
> nology is indeed so uncannily correct that it even holds for modern technol-
> ogy, of which, in other respects, we maintain with some justification that it is,
> in contrast to the older handicraft technology, something completely different
> and therefore new. Even the power plant with its turbines and generators is a
> man-made means to an end established by man. Even the jet aircraft and the
> high-frequency apparatus are means to ends. (Heidegger 4, p. 10/312)

In the rest of the essay, however, this instrumental determination of technology is left aside as insufficient. Instrumentality is in fact only a form of causality, and only a correct understanding of this latter can allow access to the true nature of technology. But to cause means to carry something from non-being to being, which is to say, it is a form of what the Greeks called *poiesis*. This is explained in turn as a pro-ducing, a leading-forth from latency to illatency, from untruth to truth, in the Greek sense of *a-letheia*, "unveiledness, unconcealment." Technology is therefore an eminent mode of this unveiledness and, as such, belongs to the historical destiny of the West, from time immemorial held in the dialectic of latency and illatency, truth and untruth. For this reason, as long as we limit ourselves to viewing technology from the perspective of instrumentality, we will not understand its true nature and will remain held in the illusion of mastering it. Only if we instead understand the instrument as a mode of causality will technology then be revealed for what it is, which is to say, as a "destining of revealing" (ibid., p. 36/337).

Only at this point, when instrumentality has once again set aside and technology has been restored to its epochal rank in the historical destiny of Being, can Heidegger reconcile himself with it and perceive in it, according to one of his preferred citations from Hölderlin, both danger and salvation:

> If the essence of technology, the apparatus [*das Ge-stell*], is the extreme danger, if there is truth in Hölderlin's words, then the rule of technology cannot exhaust itself solely in blocking all lighting-up of every revealing, all splendor of truth. Rather, precisely the essence of technology must harbor in itself the growth of the saving power. (p. 32/333–334)

7.3. Let us attempt to go against the Heideggerian current and interrogate anew the idea of instrumentality as an essential characteristic of technology. As he is tracing instrumentality back to causality (and thus to ontology), Heidegger evokes Aristotle's doctrine of the four causes:

> the *causa materialis*, the material, the matter out of which, for example, a silver chalice is made; the *causa formalis*, the form, the shape into which the material enters; the *causa finalis*, the end, for example, the sacrificial rite in relation to which the required chalice is determined as to its form and matter; the *causa efficiens*, which brings about the effect that is the finished, actual chalice, in this instance, the silversmith. What technology is, when represented as a

means, discloses itself when we trace instrumentality back to fourfold causality. (pp. 11–12/313–314)

The project of bringing instrumentality into the sphere of Aristotle's doctrine of causality, however, is not easily realizable. In the *Metaphysics*, where the problem of the four causes is fully treated, Aristotle never mentions an instrument among the examples of causes. In the *Physics*, where the term "instrument" (*organa*) appears, it is referred not to the efficient cause (which Aristotle calls "principle of movement," *archè tes kyneseos*) but to the final cause; within this cause, instruments do not figure, as Heidegger seems to imply, as examples of causes but, obviously, as examples of what is caused: health is the final cause of walking, as much as it is of purification (*katharsis*), of medicine (*pharmaka*), and of instruments (*organa*, here understood, like the rest of the other terms, only in the originary medical sense of "surgical instruments"; 194b 36–195a 1). The classical world, which, as we have seen in Aristotle's conception of productive instruments like the spool and the plectrum, certainly did think the connection between the instrument and its product, seems to conceive this connection in such a narrow and immediate way that the instrument could not appear as an autonomous form of causality.

Heidegger could have recalled that, as he certainly knew, an attempt to insert the instrument within the category of causality had instead been achieved by medieval theologians. Beginning from the thirteenth century, alongside the efficient cause, they define a fifth cause, which they call *instrumentalis*. With a daring reversal, the instrument, which Aristotle could never have classified among the causes, is now considered as a special type of efficient cause. What defines the instrumental cause—for example, the axe in the hands of a carpenter who is making a bed—is the particularity of its action. On the one hand, it acts not in virtue of itself but in virtue of the principal agent (namely, the carpenter), but on the other hand, it works according to its own nature, which is that of cutting. That is to say, it serves the end of another, only to the degree that it realizes its own end. The concept of instrumental cause is thus born as a splitting of the efficient cause, which is divided into instrumental cause and principal cause, thus securing an autonomous status for instrumentality.

7.4. The place where Scholastic theology developed the theory of the instrumental cause is the doctrine of the sacraments. Thus, in the *Summa*

Theologica, it is treated in question 62 of the third part, the title of which reads: *De principali effectu sacramentorum, qui est gratia* ("On the principal effect of the sacraments, which is grace"). The function of the sacrament is to confer grace, and this can proceed only from God, who is its principal cause: what is proper to the sacrament, however, is that it produces its effect by means of an element that acts as instrumental cause (for example, water in baptism). More than the distinction between *agens* (or *causa*) *principalis* and *agens* (or *causa*) *instrumentalis*, Aquinas's specific achievement consists in the definition of the double action of the instrument: "An instrument," he writes,

> has a twofold action; one is instrumental, in respect of which it works not by its own power but by the power of the principal agent: the other is its proper action, which belongs to it in respect of its proper form: thus it belongs to an axe to cut asunder by reason of its sharpness, but to make a couch, insofar as it is the instrument of an art. But it does not accomplish the instrumental action save by exercising its proper action: for it is by cutting that it makes a couch. In like manner the corporeal sacraments by their operation, which they exercise on the body that they touch, accomplish through the Divine institution an instrumental operation on the soul; for example, the water of baptism, in respect of its proper power, cleanses the body, and thereby, inasmuch as it is the instrument of the Divine power, cleanses the soul: since from soul and body one thing is made. (Aquinas 2, III, q. 62, art. 1, sol. 2)

Let us reflect on the peculiar nature of this action, which, by acting according to its own law or form, seems to realize the operation of another and has been for this reason defined as "contradictory" and "difficult to understand" (Roguet, p. 330). In the first part of the *Summa*, Aquinas defines it, with a term that has often been misunderstood, as "dispositive operation": "The secondary instrumental cause," he writes, "does not participate in the action of the principal cause, except inasmuch as by something proper to itself [*per aliquid sibi proprium*] it acts dispositively [*dispositive operatur*, acts as an apparatus (It., *dispositivo*)] to the effect of the principal agent" (Aquinas 2, I, q. 45, art. 4). *Dispositio* is the Latin translation of the Greek term *oikonomia*, which indicates the way in which God, by means of his own trinitarian articulation, governs the world for the salvation of humanity. From this perspective, which implies an immediate theological meaning, a dispositive operation (or, we could say without forcing, an apparatus [It., *dispositivo*]) is an operation that, according to its own internal law, realizes a level that seems to transcend it but is in reality immanent to it, just as, in the economy of salvation, Christ works *dispositive*—that is, according to an "economy"— the redemption of humanity. As Aquinas specifies in no uncertain terms: "Christ's passion, which belongs to him in respect of his human nature, is the cause of justification, both meritoriously and efficiently, not as the principal cause thereof, or by his own authority, but as an instrument" (q. 64, art. 3). Insofar as he has been incarnated in a human body, Christ, who acts in the sacraments as a principal cause, is an instrumental and not principal cause of redemption. There exists a theological paradigm of instrumentality, and the trinitarian economy and the doctrine of the sacraments are its eminent *loci*.

ℵ.   The novelty and strategic importance of the concept of instrumental cause did not escape Dante, who made use of it in a decisive passage of the *Convivio* to found the legitimacy of imperial power. To those who split hairs and affirm that the authority of the Roman emperor was actually founded not on reason but on force, he responds that "force then was not the moving cause, as the caviler supposed, but was the instrumental cause, even as the blows of the hammer are the cause of the knife, whereas the mind of the smith is the efficient and moving cause. And thus not force but reason, and moreover divine reason, was the beginning of the Roman empire" (Dante 1, IV, 4).

7.5. Ivan Illich has drawn attention to the novelty implicit in the doctrine of the instrumental cause (Illich 1, pp. 72–73). By theorizing for the first time the sphere of the instrument as such and conferring on it a metaphysical standing, the theologians are responding in their way to the extraordinary technological change that characterizes the twelfth century, with the new horse harnesses that allow the full utilization of animal power and the multiplication of mechanisms that use water energy not only to cause mills to turn but to drive hammers that break rock and hooks that prepare wool for spinning. Listing in detail the instruments of the seven principal technologies of his time (the production of wool, the construction of weapons, mercantile navigation, agriculture, hunting, medicine, and—curiously— spectacles) in his *Didascalicon*, Hugh of St. Victor praises the human being who "by inventing these instruments, rather than possessing them as gifts of nature, has more brilliantly revealed his greatness" (I, 9).

Following up on the considerations of Illich, we can thus say that the discovery of the instrumental cause is the first attempt to give a conceptual figure to technology. While for antiquity the instrument is annulled in the *ergon* that it produces, just as labor disappears in its result, now the operation of equipment is divided into a proper end and an extrinsic finality, and in this way it allows the sphere of an instrumentality that can be directed toward any end whatsoever to emerge. The space of technology is opened at this point as the dimension of a mediality and of an availability that is properly unlimited, because while remaining in relationship with its own action, the instrument has here been rendered autonomous with respect to it and can be referred to any extrinsic finality whatsoever.

It is possible, in fact, that in the technical instrument, there is something other than simple "serviceability" but that this "other" does not coincide, as Heidegger maintained, with a new and decisive epochal unveiling-veiling of Being so much as with a transformation in the use of bodies and objects, of which originary paradigm is to be found in the "animate instrument" who is the slave, which is to say, the human being who in using his body is actually used by others.

7.6. In the *Questiones disputatae de veritate*, while treating the problem "whether the sacraments of the new law are the cause of grace," Aquinas insists on the division of the operation implicit in the idea of an instrumental cause: "Now although," he writes, "the saw has an action which attaches to it in accordance with its own form, that is, to divide, nevertheless it has an effect which does not attach to it except insofar as it is moved by a craftsman, namely, to make a straight cut agreeing with the pattern. Thus an instrument has two operations, one which belongs to it according to its own form, and another which belongs to it insofar as it is moved by the principal agent and which rises above the ability of its own form" (Aquinas 3, q. 27, art. 4).

It is significant that the principal operation is here defined by means of the concept of *ars*. In reality, the instrumental cause acquires its proper sense insofar as it is used in the context of a technology. What seems to define the instrumental cause is its indifference with respect to the end that the principal cause puts forward. If the end of the carpenter is to make a bed, the axe, which acts as instrumental cause, is used, on the one hand, simply according to its own function, which is that of cutting wood, but, on the other hand, according to the operation of the artisan. The axe knows nothing of the bed, and yet this latter cannot be made without it. *Technology is the dimension that is opened when the operation of the instrument has been rendered autonomous and at the same time is divided into two distinct and related operations.* This implies that not only the concept of instrument but also that of "art" now meet with a transformation with respect to their status in the ancient world.

The instrumental cause is not, therefore, only a specification of the efficient cause: it is also and to the same extent a transformation of the final cause and of the function proper to a certain being—the instrument—which are constitutively and necessarily subsumed by an external final cause, which in its turn depends just as much on them to be realized. The appearance of the apparatus [It., *dispositivo*] of the instrumental cause (which defines, as we have seen, the very nature of every "dispositive" action) coincides in this sense with a radical transformation in the mode of conceiving use. This is no longer a relation of twofold or reciprocal affection, in which subject and object are indeterminated, but a hierarchical relation between two causes, defined no longer by use but by instrumentality. The instrumental cause (in which the instrument—which in the ancient world seems to be no different from the hand that makes use of it—reaches its full autonomy) is the first appearance in the sphere of human action of those concepts of utility and instrumentality that determine the way in which modern human beings will understand their doing and making [It., *il suo fare*] in modernity.

7.7. In the sacraments, the character of an instrumental cause does not only belong to the material element (water, consecrated oil, etc.): it first of all concerns the celebrant himself. The minister is in fact fully an instrument ("the definition of the minister," one reads in Aquinas 2, III, q. 64, art. 1, "is identical to that of the instrument"); in contrast, however, to the material elements that, as inanimate instruments, are always and only moved by the principal agent, the minister is an "animate instrument" (*instrumentum animatum*), who "is not only moved, but in a sense moves itself, insofar as by his will he moves his bodily members to act" (q. 64, art. 8).

As we know, the term "animate instrument" comes from Aristotle's *Politics*, where it defined the nature of the slave. For that matter, the term *minister* originally means "servant." Aquinas is perfectly aware of this when he writes: "the minister comports himself in the mode of an instrument [*habet se ad modum strumenti*], as the Philosopher says in the first book of the *Politics*" (q. 63, art. 2). (In his *Commentary on Aristotle's* Politics, probably following the Latin translation that he had before him, he uses the expression *organum animatum*, "animate equipment," immediately specifying: "such as the assistants of a craftsman and slaves in a household"; Aquinas 4, p. 23).

The assimilation of the celebrant to a slave—who does not have legal personhood and whose acts are imputed to the "person" of his master—is therefore perfectly conscious, and it is in virtue of this awareness that Aquinas can write that "the minister of the sacrament acts *in persona* of the whole Church, whose minister he is" (Aquinas 2, q. 64, art. 8). This means that, by means of the paradigm of the "animate instrument," the sacramental priesthood is genealogically and not only terminologically connected to slavery.

The connection between the instrumental cause and the figure of the slave is, however, still more essential. It is implied in the very formula "the human being whose *ergon* is the use of the body" and in the definition (which we have seen to have an ontological and not a juridical character) of the slave as the one who, "while being human, is by nature of another and not of himself." The slave constitutes in this sense the first appearance of a pure instrumentality, which is to say, of a being that, while living according to its own end, is precisely for that reason and to the same extent used for another's end.

7.8. The peculiar "dispositive" efficacy that belongs to the sacraments thanks to the double nature of the instrumental cause is developed by theologians by means of a new scission, which in the sacrament divides the one working the work (*opus operans*, the action of the instrumental agent, in particular the celebrant) and the work worked (*opus operatum*, the sacramental effect in itself, which is unfailingly realized, whatever the condition of the celebrant may be). Insofar as the minister is the animate instrument of an operation whose principal agent is Christ, not only is it not necessary that he have faith and love, but even a perverse intention (baptizing a woman with the intention of abusing her) does not remove validity from the sacrament, because this latter acts *ex opere operato* and not *ex opere operante* (or *operantis*).

The distinction between the two works, which was devised in order to secure the validity of the sacrament, in fact transforms it into a perfect mechanism, a special apparatus, which unfailingly produces its effects.

The "instrumental" character of the sacraments, which they have in common with technologies and *artes*—Aquinas defines them as *instrumenta Dei* (Aquinas 5, IV, 56)—allows one to consider them as the paradigm of a superior technology, a *technologia sacra*, at whose center stands the most specialized action of the instrumental cause and the inexorable efficacy of the *opus operatum*.

They are in this sense a sort of prophecy of mechanization, which was only achieved five centuries later. Just as the machine, materializing the dream of the animate instrument, functions on its own and its maneuvers in reality do nothing but obey the possibilities of command prescribed by the machine itself, so also does the sacrament produce its effect *ex opere operato*, and the celebrant, of whom Aquinas says that "he is not merely a cause but also in a measure an effect insofar as it is moved by the principal agent" (Aquinas 2, III, q. 62, art. 1), does nothing but execute, more or less mechanically, the will of the principal agent. The analogy can be extended: if the advent of the machine, as Marx had already noted, had as a consequence the devaluation of the labor of the artisan, who in losing his traditional ability is transformed into an instrument of the machine, this corresponds point by point with the doctrine of the *opus operatum*, which by transforming the celebrant into an animate instrument in fact separates him from personal commitment and moral responsibility, which are no longer necessary to the efficacy of sacramental practices and remain confined to his interiority.

7.9. It is not surprising that a few centuries later, at the end of Scholasticism, the paradigm of the instrumental cause can be driven to the extreme, to the point of the rupture of the necessary connection between the instrument's own operation and that of the principal agent, and to the consequent affirmation of an unlimited "obediential" availability of the instrument to the intention of the principal agent. In his treatise on the sacraments, Suárez can thus write that

> in the divine instruments, the action connatural to the instrument precedent to the action and to the effect of the principal agent is not necessary. The reason is that . . . the divine instruments do not add a natural but an obediential [*obedientialem*] potential and moreover work beyond the limits of natural perfection, so that we do not expect a natural connection between their action and that of the principal agent. . . . Thus, while the diverse natural or artificial instruments are directed to diverse effects, because the condition of the in-

strument is adapted to this action and not to another, the divine instruments do not have this determination, because they are assumed only according to an obediential potential, which is indifferent to all that does not imply contradiction, because of the unlimitedness of the divine virtue. (Suárez 1, p. 149)

It is legitimate to suppose that the absolute instrumentality that is thought here constitutes in some way the paradigm of modern technologies, which tend to produce apparatuses that have incorporated in themselves the operation of the principal agent and can thus "obey" its commands (even if these are actually inscribed into the functioning of the apparatus, in such a way that the one using them, in pushing the "controls," obeys in turn a predetermined program). Modern technology does not derive only from the dream of the alchemists and magicians but also and more probably from that peculiar "magical" operation that is the absolute, perfect instrumental efficacy of the sacramental liturgy.

7.10. The constitutive connection that unites the slave and technology is implicit in Aristotle's ironic affirmation, according to which if instruments, like the legendary statues of Daedalus, could achieve their work by themselves, the architect would have no need of assistants nor the master of slaves.

The relation between technology and slavery has often been evoked by historians of the ancient world. According to the current opinion, in fact, the striking lack of technological development in the Greek world was due to the ease with which the Greeks, thanks to slavery, could procure manual labor. If Greek material civilization remained at the stage of the *organon*, that is, of the utilization of human or animal power by means of a variety of instruments and did not have access to machines, this happened, one reads in a classic work on this argument, "because there was no need to economize on manual labor, since one had access to living machines that were abundant and inexpensive, different from both human and animal: slaves" (Schuhl, pp. 13–14). It does not interest us here to verify the correctness of this explanation, whose limits have been demonstrated by Koyré (pp. 291ff.) and which, like every explanation of that kind, could be easily reversed (one could say just as reasonably, as Aristotle does in the end, that the lack of machines rendered slavery necessary).

What is decisive, rather, from the perspective of our study, is to ask ourselves if between modern technology and slavery there is not a connection more essential than the common productive end. Indeed, if it is clear that the machine is presented from its first appearance as the realization of the paradigm of the animate instrument of which the slave had furnished the originary model, it is all the more true that what both intend is not so much, or not only, an increase and simplification of productive labor but also, by liberating human beings from necessity, to secure them access to their most proper dimension—for the Greeks the political life, for the moderns the possibility of mastering the nature's forces and thus their own.

The symmetry between the slave and the machine thus goes beyond the analogy between two figures of the "living instrument": it concerns the ultimate achievement of anthropogenesis, the becoming fully human of the living human being. But this implies a further symmetry, this time with respect to the bare life that, being situated on the threshold between zoè and *bios*, between *physis* and *nomos*, enables, through its inclusive exclusion, political life. In this sense, slavery is to ancient humanity what technology is to modern humanity: both, as bare life, watch over the threshold that allows access to the truly human condition (and both have shown themselves to be inadequate to the task, the modern way revealing itself in the end to be no less dehumanizing than the ancient).

On the other hand, this study has shown that in Aristotle's definition of the slave, the dominant idea is that of a human life that unfolds entirely within the sphere of use (and not in that of production). What was in question in the animate instrument was, that is to say, not only liberation from labor but rather the paradigm of another human activity and another relation with the living body, for which we lack names and which for now we can only evoke by means of the syntagma "use of the body." Slavery (as a juridical institution) and the machine represent in a certain sense the capture and parodic realization within social institutions of this "use of the body," of which we have sought to delineate the essential characteristics. Every attempt to think use must necessarily engage with them, because perhaps only an archeology of slavery and, *at the same time*, of technology will be able to free the archaic nucleus that has remained imprisoned in them.

It is necessary, at this point, to restore to the slave the decisive meaning that belongs to him in the process of anthropogenesis. The slave is, on the one hand, a human animal (or an animal-human) and, on the other hand and to the same extent, a living instrument (or an instrument-human). That is to say, the slave constitutes in the history of anthropogenesis a double threshold, in which animal life crosses over to the human just as the living (the human) crosses over into the inorganic (into the instrument), and vice versa. The invention of slavery as a juridical institution allowed the capture of living beings and of the use of the body into productive systems, temporarily blocking the development of the technological instrument; its abolition in modernity freed up the possibility of technology, that is, of the living instrument. At the same time, insofar as their relationship with nature is no longer mediated by another human being but by an apparatus, human beings have estranged themselves from the animal and from the organic in order to draw near to the instrument and the inorganic to the point of almost identifying with it (the human-machine). For this reason—insofar as they have lost, together with the use of bodies, their immediate relation to their own animality—modern human beings have not truly been able to appropriate to themselves the liberation from labor that machines should have procured for them. And if the hypothesis of a constitutive connection between slavery and technology is correct, it is not surprising that the hypertrophy of technological apparatuses has ended up producing a new and unheard-of form of slavery.

§ 8   The Inappropriable

8.1. In *The Highest Poverty* (*Homo Sacer* IV.1), we have shown how the concept of use was at the center of the Franciscan strategy and how, precisely with respect to its definition and to the possibility of separating it from ownership, it had produced the decisive conflict between the order and the curia. Preoccupied solely with assuring the lawfulness of the refusal of every form of ownership, the Franciscan theorists therefore ended up enclosing themselves in a solely juridical polemic, without managing to furnish another definition of use that would not be put in purely negative terms with respect to the juridical order. Perhaps nowhere does the ambiguity of their argumentation appear more clearly than in the willfully paradoxical thesis of Hugh of Digne, according to whom the Franciscans "have only this right, not to have any rights" (*hoc ius nullum ius habere*; Hugh of Digne, p. 161).

The Franciscan vindication of poverty is thus founded on the possibility for a subject to renounce the right of ownership (*abdicatio iuris*). What they call "use" (and at times, as in Francis of Ascoli, "bodily use," *usus corporeus*) is the dimension that opens out from this renunciation. From the perspective that interests us here, the problem is not whether the Franciscan thesis, which ended up succumbing to the curia's attacks, could have been more or less rigorously argued: instead, what would have been decisive was a conception of use that was not founded on an act of renunciation—that is, in the last analysis, on the will of a subject—but, so to speak, on the very nature of things (as the frequent reference to the state of nature seems, after all, to imply).

8.2. In 1916, Benjamin jotted down in one of his *Notizblöcke* a brief text with the title "Notes toward a Work on the Category of Justice," which establishes a close connection between the concept of justice and that of inappropriability: "To every good," he writes,

> limited as it is by the spatio-temporal order, there accrues a possession-character. But the possession, as something caught in the same finitude, is always unjust. No order of possession, however articulated, can therefore lead to justice. Rather, this lies in the condition of a good that cannot be a possession [*das nicht Besitz sein kann*]. This alone is the good through which goods become possessionless [*besitzlos*]. (Benjamin 1, p. 41/257)

Justice, Benjamin continues, has nothing to do with the allotment of goods according to the needs of individuals, because the subject's claim to the good is not founded on needs but on justice, and as such it is directed not "toward the possession-right of the person but possibly toward the good-right of the good" (*ein Gutes-Recht des Gutes*; ibid.).

At this point, with a striking contraction of ethics and ontology, justice is presented not as a virtue but as a "state of the world," as the ethical category that corresponds not to having-to-be but to existence as such:

> Justice does not appear to refer to the good will of the subject, but, instead, constitutes a state of the world [*einen Zustand der Welt*]. Justice designates the ethical category of the existent, virtue the ethical category of the demanded. Virtue can be demanded; justice in the final analysis can only be as a state of the world or as a state of God.

And it is in this sense that it can be defined as "the striving to make the world into the highest good" (ibid.).

If we recall that justice, in the immediately preceding passage, coincided with the condition of a good that cannot be appropriated, to make of the world the supreme good can only mean: to experience it as absolutely inappropriable. In this fragment, which is radically Franciscan in a certain way, poverty is not found on a decision of the subject but corresponds to a "state of the world." And if, in the Franciscan theorists, use appeared as the dimension that is opened when one renounces ownership, here the perspective is necessarily reversed and use appears as *the relation to an inappropriable,* as the only possible relation to that supreme state of the world in which it, as just, can be in no way appropriated.

8.3. The testimony of experience, which daily offers us examples of inappropriable things with which we are nevertheless intimately in relation, testifies that a similar conception of use as relation to an inappropriable is not completely strange. Here I propose we examine three of these inappropriables: the body, language, and landscape.

A correct posing of the problem of the body was put durably off course by the phenomenological doctrine of the body proper. According to this doctrine—which finds its topical place in the polemic of Husserl and Edith Stein against Lipps's theory of empathy—the experience of the body would be, together with the I, what is most proper and originary. "The originary donation of the body," Husserl writes,

> can only be the donation of my body and no one else's [*meines und keines andern Leibes*]. The apperception "my body" is in any originally essential way [*urwesentlich*] the first and only one that can be fully originary. Only if I have constituted my body can I apperceive every other body as such, and this apperception principally has a mediated character. (Husserl 1, p. 7)

And yet precisely this apodictic pronouncement of the originary character as "mine" of the donation of a body never stops giving rise to aporias and difficulties.

The first is the perception of the body of the other. This latter is not actually perceived as an inert body (*Körper*) but as a living body (*Leib*), endowed like mine with sensibility and perception. In the notes and fragmentary drafts that make up volumes XIII and XIV of the *Husserliana*, pages and pages are dedicated to the problem of the perception of the hand of the other. How is it possible to perceive a hand as alive, that is, not simply as a thing, a marble, or painted hand but as a hand "of flesh and blood"—and yet not mine? If to the perception of the body there originarily belongs the character of being mine, what is the difference between the hand of another, which I see in this moment and which touches me, and mine? It cannot be a question of a logical inference or an analogy, because I "feel" the hand of the other, I identify with it, and its sensibility is given to me in a sort of immediate presentification (*Vergegenwärtigung*; Husserl 2, pp. 40–41). Then what keeps us from thinking that the hand of the other and mine are given co-originarily and that only in a second moment is the distinction produced?

The problem is particularly pressing because at the time when Husserl wrote his notes, the debate around the problem of empathy (*Einfüh-*

lung) was still very much alive. In a book published some years before (*Leitfaden der Psychologie*, 1903), Theodor Lipps had excluded the idea that empathetic experiences, in which the subject finds himself suddenly transferred into another's lived experience, could be explained by means of imitation, association, or analogy. When I observe with full participation the acrobats who are walking suspended in the void and cry out in terror when it looks like they will fall, I am in some way "with" them and feel their body as if it were my own and my own as if it were theirs. "It is therefore not the case," writes Husserl, "that I first solipsistically constitute my things and my world, and then empathetically grasp the other I, as solipsistically constituting his world for himself, and that only then is the one identified with the other; but rather my sensible unity, insofar as the external multiplicity is not separate from mine, is *eo ipso* empathetically perceived as the same as mine" (Husserl 1, p. 10). In this way, the axiom of the originarity of the body proper is seriously called into question. As Husserl could not fail to admit, empathetic experience introduces into the solipsistic constitution of the body proper a "transcendence," in which consciousness seems to go beyond itself and distinguishing one's own lived experience from another's becomes problematic (ibid., p. 8). This is especially the case since Max Scheler, who had sought to apply to ethics the methods of Husserlian phenomenology, had postulated unreservedly—with a thesis that Edith Stein had designated as "fascinating" even if erroneous—an originary, undifferentiated current of lived experience, in which the I and the body of the other are perceived in the same way as one's own.

None of the repeated attempts of Husserl and his student to restore the primacy and originarity of the body proper is finally convincing. As happens every time we persist in maintaining a certainty that experience has revealed to be fallacious, they come to a contradiction, which in this case takes the form of an oxymoron, of a "non-originary originarity." "Neither the external body nor external subjectivity," writes Husserl, "is given to me *originaliter*; and yet that human being is given to me originarily in my surrounding world" (Husserl 1, p. 234). And in an even more contradictory way, Edith Stein says:

> While I am living in the other's joy, I do not feel originary joy. It does not issue live from my "I." Neither does it have the character of having-once-been-lived like remembered joy. . . . This other subject is originary although I do not live it as originary; the joy that arises in him is originary even though I do

not live it as originary. In my non-originary lived experience I feel, as it were, accompanied by an originary lived experience not lived by me but still there, manifesting itself in my non-originary lived experience. (Stein, p. 11).

In this "non-originarily living an originarity," the originarity of the body proper is maintained so to speak in bad faith, only on condition of dividing empathetic experience into two contradictory moments. Immediate participation in external lived experience, which Lipps expressed as my being fully and distressingly transported "alongside" the acrobat who walks on the tightrope, is thus hastily set aside. In any case, what empathy—but, alongside it, it would be necessary to mention hypnosis, magnetism, and suggestion, which in those years seem to have obsessively captured the attention of psychologists and sociologists—shows is that however much one affirms the originary character of the "propriety" of the body and of lived experience, the intrusiveness of an "impropriety" shows itself to be all the more originary and strong in it, as if the body proper always cast a shadow, which can in no case be separated from it.

8.4. In the 1935 essay *De l'évasion* (*On Escape*), Emmanuel Levinas subjects to a merciless examination bodily experiences as familiar as they are disagreeable: shame, nausea, need. According to his characteristic gesture, Levinas exaggerates and drives to the extreme the analytic of Dasein of his teacher Heidegger so as to exhibit, so to speak, its dark side. If in *Being and Time* Dasein is irreparably thrown into a facticity that is improper to it and that it has not chosen, such that he always has to assume and grasp impropriety itself, this ontological structure now finds its parodic formulation in the analysis of bodily need, nausea, and shame. In fact, what defines the experiences is not a lack or defect of being, which we seek to fill up or from which we take our distance: on the contrary, they are founded on a double movement, in which the subject finds himself, on the one hand, irremissibly consigned to his body and, on the other, just as inexorably incapable of assuming it.

Let us imagine an exemplary case of shame: shame due to nudity. If in nudity we experience shame, it is because in it we find ourselves consigned to something that we cannot at any cost retract.

Shame arises each time we are unable to make others forget our basic nudity. It is related to everything we would like to hide and that we cannot bury or cover up. . . . What appears in shame is thus precisely the fact of being riveted to oneself, the radical impossibility of fleeing oneself to hide from oneself, the unalterably binding presence of the I to itself. Nakedness is shameful when it is the sheer visibility of our being, of its ultimate intimacy. . . . It is therefore our intimacy, that is, our presence to ourselves, that is shameful. (Levinas 1, pp. 86–87/64–67)

This means that, at the instant in which what is most intimate and proper to us—our body—is irreparably laid bare, it appears to us as the most foreign thing, which we cannot in any way assume and which we want, for that reason, to hide.

This double, paradoxical movement is even more evident in nausea and bodily need. Indeed, nausea is "the revolting presence of ourselves to ourselves" that, in the instant in which it is lived, "appears insurmountable" (ibid., p. 89/66). The more the nauseating state, with its vomiting, consigns me to my stomach, as to my sole and irrefutable reality, so much more does it seem to me to be foreign and inappropriable: I am nothing but nausea and vomiting, and yet I can neither accept it nor come out of it. "There is in nausea a refusal to remain there, an effort to get out. Yet this effort is always already characterized as desperate. . . . In nausea— which amounts to an impossibility of being what one is—we are at the same time riveted to ourselves, enclosed in a tight circle that smothers" (p. 90/66).

The contradictory nature of the relation to the body reaches its critical mass in need. At the moment that I experience an uncontestable urge to urinate, it is as if all my reality and all my presence are concentrated in the part of my body from which the need is coming. It is absolutely and implacably proper to me, and yet just for this reason, precisely because I am nailed down to it without escape, it becomes the most external and inappropriable thing. The instant of need, that is to say, lays bare the truth of the body proper: it is a field of polar tensions whose extremes are defined by a "being consigned to" and a "not being able to assume." My body is given to me originarily as the most proper thing, only to the extent to which it reveals itself to be absolutely inappropriable.

ℵ. The characteristics of inappropriability and externality that inhere ineliminably in the body proper emerge with particular obviousness in all those disturbances of gesturality and speech that, from the name of the French psychiatrist Gilles de la Tourette, are commonly defined with the term "Tourette's syndrome." The "tics," the compulsive utterances (generally of an obscene char-

acter), the impossibility of completing a movement, the tremors of the mus-
culature (*chorea*), and all the vast symptomatology that defines this syndrome
delimit a sphere of relationship to the body proper that eludes any possibility for
the patient to clearly distinguish between the voluntary and the involuntary, the
proper and the external, the conscious and the unconscious.

8.5. There exists, from this perspective, a structural analogy between
the body and language. Indeed, language also—in particular in the figure of the mother tongue—appears for each speaker as what is the most
intimate and proper; and yet, speaking of an "ownership" and of an "intimacy" of language is certainly misleading, since language happens to
the human being from the outside, through a process of transmission and
learning that can be arduous and painful and is imposed on the infant
rather than being willed by it. And while the body seems particular to
each individual, language is by definition shared by others and as such
an object of common use. Like the bodily constitution according to the
Stoics, that is to say, language is something with which the living being
must be familiarized in a more or less drawn-out *oikeiosis*, which seems
natural and almost inborn; and yet—as *lapsus*, stuttering, unexpected
forgetfulness, and aphasia testify—it has always remained to some degree
external to the speaker.

   This is all the more evident in those—the poets—whose trade is precisely that of mastering language and making it proper. They must for
this reason first of all abandon conventions and common use and, so to
speak, render foreign the language that they must dominate, inscribing
it in a system of rules as arbitrary as they are inexorable—foreign to such
a point that according to a firm tradition, it is not they who speak but
another, divine principle (the muse) who utters the poem for which the
poet is limited to providing the voice. The appropriation of language that
they pursue, that is to say, is to the same extent an expropriation, in such
a way that the poetic act appears as a bipolar gesture, which each time
renders external what it must unfailingly appropriate.

   We can call the ways in which this double gesture is signed in language style and manner. Here it is necessary to abandon the customary
hierarchical representations, for which manner would be a perversion and
a decline of style, which for them remains superior by definition. Style
and manner instead name the two irreducible poles of the poetic gesture:
if style marks its most proper trait, manner registers an inverse demand

for expropriation and non-belonging. Appropriation and disappropriation are to be taken literally here, as a process that invests and transforms language in all its aspects. And not only in literature, as in the last dialogues of Plato, in the late Goethe, and the final Caproni, but also in the arts (the exemplary case is Titian) one witnesses this tension of the field of language, which elaborates and transforms it to the point of rendering it new and almost unrecognizable.

8.6. If mannerism, in the history of art and in psychiatry, designates excessive adherence to a usage or a model (stereotype, repetition) and, at the same time, the impossibility of truly identifying oneself with it (extravagance and artifice), analogous considerations can be made for the relation of speakers to their inappropriable language: it defines a field of polar forces, held between idiosyncrasy and stereotype, the excessively proper and the most complete externality. And only in this context does the opposition between style and manner acquire its true sense. They are the two poles in the tension of which the gesture of the poet lives: style is disappropriating appropriation (a sublime negligence, a forgetting oneself in the proper), manner an appropriating disappropriation (a presenting oneself or remembering oneself in the improper).

We can therefore call "use" the field of tension whose poles are style and manner, appropriation and expropriation. And not only in the poet but in every speaking human being with respect to their language and in every living thing with respect to its body there is always, in use, a manner that takes its distance from style and a style that is disappropriated in manner. In this sense, every use is a polar gesture: on the one hand, appropriation and habit; on the other, loss and expropriation. To use— hence the semantic breadth of the term, which indicates both use in the strict sense and habitual praxis—means to oscillate unceasingly between a homeland and an exile: to inhabit.

ℵ.   Gregory the Great (*The Life of St. Benedict*, II, 3, 37) writes of St. Benedict that at a certain point in his life, "he returned to his beloved place of solitude and before the eyes of the supreme spectator alone *habitavit secum*, he inhabited with himself." What can it mean to "inhabit with oneself"? *Habitare* is an intensive form of *habere*. Use, as relation to an inappropriable, appears as a field of forces held between a propriety and an impropriety, a having and a not having. In this sense, if one recalls the proximity between use and habit and between use and use-of-oneself that we have evoked above, to inhabit means to be in a relation of use, thus understood, with something to the point of being able to lose and forget oneself in it, of constituting it as inappropriable.

To inhabit with oneself, to inhabit-oneself, therefore names the fundamental trait of human existence: the form of life of the human being is, in the words of Hölderlin, an "inhabiting life" (*Wenn in die Ferne geht der Menschen wohnend Leben . . .* ; Hölderlin, p. 314). But precisely for this reason, in the letter to Böhlendorff of December 4, 1801, in which Hölderlin formulated his supreme thought, use appears as always already divided into "proper" and "foreign," and the decisive thesis reads: "the free use of the proper [*der freie Gebrauch des Eignes*] is the most difficult thing."

8.7. A definition of the third example of the inappropriable, landscape, must begin from the exposition of its relationship with the environment and with the world. And this is not because the problem of landscape as it has been dealt with by art historians, anthropologists, and historians of culture is irrelevant. Rather, what is decisive is the observation of the aporias to which these disciplines remain prisoner whenever they seek to define landscape. Not only is it unclear whether it is a natural reality or a human phenomenon, a geographical place or a place in the soul; but in this second case, neither is it clear whether it should be considered as consubstantial to the human being or is instead a modern invention. It has often been repeated that the first appearance of a sensibility to landscape is the letter of Petrarch that describes the ascension of Mount Ventoux as motivated *sola videndi insignem loci altitudinem cupiditate ductus* ("by nothing but the desire to see its conspicuous height"; Petrarch, p. 36). In the same sense, it has been affirmed that landscape painting, unknown to antiquity, was the invention of the Dutch painters of the Quattrocento. Both affirmations are false. Not only are the place and the date of composition of the letter probably fictitious, but the citation of Augustine that Petrarch introduces there to stigmatize his *cupiditas vivdendi* implies that already in the fourth century human beings loved to contemplate landscape: *et eunt homines mirari alta montium et ingentes fluctus maris et latissimos lapsus fluminum*. Numerous passages testify, in fact, to a true and proper passion of the ancients for contemplation from the heights (*magnam capies voluptatem*, writes Pliny, *si hunc regionis situm ex monte prospexeris* ["You would be most agreeably entertained by taking a view of the face of this country from the mountains"]; Pliny 1,

V, vi, 13), which ethology has unexpectedly found in the animal kingdom, where one sees goats, vicuñas, felines, and primates climbing up
to an elevated place to then contemplate, for no apparent reason, the
surrounding landscape (Fehling, pp. 44–48). As for painting, not only
the Pompeian frescos but the sources as well show that the Greeks and
Romans were familiar with landscape painting, which they called *topio-
graphia* or "scenography" (*skenographia*), and they have preserved for us
the names of landscape painters like Ludius, *qui primus instituit amoenis-
simam parietum picturam* ("who first introduced the attractive fashion of
painting walls with pictures of country houses"; Pliny 2, XXXV, 116–17),
and Serapion, of whom we know that he could paint scenographies of
landscapes but not human figures (*hic scaenas optime pinxit, sed hominem
pingere non potuit*; ibid., XXXV, 113). And those who have observed the
petrified, dreamy landscapes painted on the walls of Campanian villas,
which Rostosvzev called idyllic-sacral (*sakral-idyllisch*), know that they
find themselves before something extremely difficult to understand but
that they recognize unequivocally as landscapes. The landscape is therefore a phenomenon that concerns the human being—and perhaps the
living being as such—in an essential way, and yet it seems to elude every
definition. Only to a philosophical consideration will it perhaps be able
to disclose its truth.

8.8. In the course of the winter semester of 1929–30 at Freiburg (published with the title *The Fundamental Concepts of Metaphysics: World,
Finitude, Solitude*), Heidegger seeks to define the fundamental structure of the human being as a passage from the "poverty in world" of
the animal to the being-in-the-world that defines Dasein. On the basis
of the work of Uexküll and other zoologists, extremely perceptive pages
are dedicated to the description and analysis of the relationship of the
animal with its environment (*Umwelt*). The animal is poor in world (*wel-
tarm*), because it remains a prisoner of the immediate relationship with a
series of elements (Heidegger calls "disinhibitors" what Uexküll defined
as "bearers of significance") that their receptive organs have selected in
the environment. The relationship with these disinhibitors is so strict and
totalizing that the animal is literally "stunned" and "captured" in them.
As a representative example of this stunning, Heidegger refers to the experiment in which a bee is placed in a laboratory in front of a glass full
of honey. If, after it has begun to suck, one removes the bee's abdomen,

it tranquilly continues to suck, while one sees honey flowing out where the abdomen has been cut off. The bee is so absorbed in its disinhibitor that it can never place itself before it to perceive it as something that exists objectively in and for itself. Certainly, with respect to the rock, which is absolutely deprived of world, the animal is in some way open to its disinhibitors and yet can never see them as such. "The animal," writes Heidegger, "can never apprehend something *as* something" (Heidegger 5, p. 360/248). For this reason the animal remains enclosed in the circle of its environment and can never open itself into a world.

The philosophical problem of the course is that of the boundary—that is to say, of the extreme separation and vertiginous proximity—between the animal and the human. In what way is something like a world opened for the human being? The passage from the environment to the world is not, in reality, simply the passage from a closure to an opening. The animal in fact not only does not see the open, beings in their unveiled being, but nor does it perceive its own non-openness, its own being captured and stunned in its own disinhibitors. The skylark that soars in the air "does not see the open," but neither is it in a position to relate to its own closure. "The animal," writes Heidegger, "is excluded from the essential domain of the conflict between unconcealedness and concealedness" (Heidegger 6, pp. 237–238/159–160). The openness of the world begins in the human being precisely from the perception of a non-openness.

This means, therefore, that the world does not open up onto a new or ulterior space, fuller and more luminous, conquered beyond the limits of the animal environment and without relation with it. On the contrary, it has been opened only through a suspension and deactivation of the animal relationship with the disinhibitor. The open, the free space of being do not name something radically other with respect to the non-open of the animal: they are only a grasping of a dis-unveiling, the suspension and the capture of the skylark-not-seeing-the-open. The openness that is in question in the world is essentially the openness to a closure, and the one who looks into the open sees only a closing up, sees only a non-seeing.

For this reason—that is to say, insofar as the world has been opened only through the interruption and nullification of the relationship of the living being with its disinhibitor—being is from the very beginning traversed by the nothing, and the world is constitutively marked by negativity and disorientation.

8.9. One can comprehend what landscape is only if one understands that it represents, with respect to the animal environment and the human world, an ulterior stage. When we look at a landscape, we certainly see the open and contemplate the world, with all the elements that make it up (the ancient sources list among these the woods, the hills, the lakes, the villas, the headlands, springs, streams, canals, flocks and shepherds, people on foot or in a boat, those hunting or harvesting . . .); but these things, which are already no longer parts of an animal environment, are now, so to speak, deactivated one by one on the level of being and perceived as a whole in a new dimension. We see them as perfectly and clearly as ever, and yet we already do not see them, lost—happily, immemorially lost—in the landscape. Being, *en état de paysage*, is suspended and rendered inoperative, and the world, having become perfectly inappropriable, goes, so to speak, beyond being and nothing. No longer animal nor human, to the one who contemplates the landscape is only landscape. That person no longer seeks to comprehend, only look. If the world is the inoperativity of the animal environment, landscape is, so to speak, inoperativity of inoperativity, deactivated being. And negativity, which inhered in the world in the form of the nothing and non-openness—because it comes from the animal closure, of which it was only a suspension—is now dismissed.

Insofar as it has in this sense gone beyond being, landscape is the outstanding form of use. In it, use-of-oneself and use of the world correspond without remainder. Justice, as a state of the world as inappropriable, is here the decisive experience. Landscape is a dwelling in the inappropriable as form-of-life, as justice. For this reason, if in the world the human being was necessarily thrown and disoriented, in landscape he is finally at home. *Pays! paese!* ("country," from *pagus*, "village") is according to the etymologists originally the greeting that is exchanged by those who recognize each other as being from the same village.

8.10. We can call "intimacy" use-of-oneself as relation with an inappropriable. Whether it is a matter of bodily life in all its aspects (understood as those elementary *ethe* that we have seen urinating, sleeping, defecating, sexual pleasure, nudity, etc., to be) or of the special presence-absence to ourselves that we live in moments of solitude, that of which we have an experience in intimacy is our being held in relation with an inappropriable zone of non-consciousness. Here familiarity with self reaches an intensity all the more extreme and jealous insofar as it is in no way translated into anything that we could master.

It is precisely this opaque sphere of non-awareness that in modernity becomes the most exclusive and precious content of "privacy" [*translator's note:* English in original here and throughout this passage]. The modern individual is defined first of all by means of his faculty (which can take the form of a true and proper right) to regulate access to his intimacy. According to the laconic definition of an English-speaking scholar, "privacy will be defined as: *selective control of access to the self.* . . . It is an interpersonal boundary process, whereby the openness-closedness from others shifts with the circumstances" (Altman, p. 8ff.). But what is at stake in this selective sharing of use-of-oneself is in reality the very constitution of the self. That is to say, intimacy is a circular apparatus, by means of which, by selectively regulating access to the self, the individual constitutes himself as the pre-supposition and proprietor of his own "privacy." As the same author suggests, albeit beyond his own intentions, what is vital for the definition of the self is not the inclusion or exclusion of others so much as the capacity to regulate contact when one desires to: "the privacy mechanisms serve to define the limits and boundaries of the self" (ibid., p. 26). The dominion of privacy therefore replaces, as a constitution of subjectivity, the use of bodies, in which subject and object were indeterminated.

One can therefore understand how, in a society formed from individuals, the transformation of use-of-oneself and of the relation to the inappropriable into a jealous possession in reality has a political significance that is all the more decisive insofar as it remains stubbornly hidden. It is in the work of Sade—that is to say, precisely at the moment when singular living beings as such became the bearers of the new national sovereignty—that this political meaning comes forcefully to light. In the manifesto "Français encore un effort si vous voulez être républicains" that the libertine Dolmancé reads in *Philosophie dans le boudoir*, the political locus par excellence becomes the *maisons* in which every citizen has a right to summon any other person to freely use his or her body. Intimacy becomes here what is at stake in politics; the *boudoir* is totally substituted for the *cité*. If the sovereign subject is first of all sovereign over his or her own body, if intimacy—which is to say, use-of-oneself as inappropriable—becomes something like the fundamental biopolitical substance, then one can understand that in Sade it can appear as the object of the first and unconfessed right of the citizen: each individual has the right to share his or her liking of the other's inappropriable. Common above all is the use of bodies.

What in Dolmancé's pamphlet was a juridical constitutional contract, founded on republican reciprocity, in the *120 Days of Sodom* instead appears as a pure object of dominion and of unconditioned violence (it is certainly not an accident that the loss of all control over one's own intimacy was, according to the testimonies of the deportees, an integral part of the atrocities of the *Lager*). The criminal pact that rules the castle of Silling, in which the four wicked potentates enclose themselves with their forty victims, establishes the absolute control on the part of the masters of the intimacy of their slaves—even their physiological functions are minutely regulated—the total and unlimited use of their bodies. The relation with the inappropriable, which constitutes the biopolitical substance of each individual, is thus violently appropriated by those who constitute themselves in this way as lords of intimacy, of that free use of the proper that, in the words of Hölderlin, appeared as "the most difficult thing."

Against this attempt to appropriate the inappropriable to oneself, by means of right or force, in order to constitute it as an *arcanum* of sovereignty, it is necessary to remember that intimacy can preserve its political meaning only on condition that it remains inappropriable. *What is common is never a property but only the inappropriable.* The sharing of this inappropriable is love, that "use of the loved object" of which the Sadean universe constitutes the most serious and instructive parody.

א.   In the course of this study of the use of bodies, a term has never stopped appearing: inoperativity. The elements of a theory of inoperativity had been elaborated in a previous volume (Agamben 2, passim and in particular §§8.22–8.24; but cf. also Agamben 3, §9); the concept of use that we have attempted to define can be correctly understood only if it is situated in the context of this theory. Use is constitutively an inoperative praxis, which can happen only on the basis of a deactivation of the Aristotelian apparatus potential/act, which assigns to *energeia*, to being-at-work, primacy over potential. Use is, in this sense, a principle internal to potential, which prevents it from being simply consumed in the act and drives it to turn once more to itself, to make itself a potential of potential, to be capable of its own potential (and therefore its own impotential).

The inoperative work, which results from this suspension of potential, exposes in the act the potential that has brought it into being: if it is a poem, it will expose in the poem the potential of language; if it is a painting, it will expose on the canvas the potential of painting (of looking); if it is an action, it will expose in the act the potential of acting. Only in this sense can one say that inoperativity is a poem of poetry, a painting of painting, a praxis of praxis. Rendering inoperative the works of language, the arts, politics, and economy, it shows what a human body can do, opens it to a new possible use.

Inoperativity as a specifically human praxis also allows us to understand in what way the concept of use here proposed (like that of form-of-life) relates to the Marxian concept of "form of production." It is certainly true that, as Marx has suggested, the forms of production of an epoch contribute in a decisive way to determine its social relationships and culture; but in relation to every form of production, it is possible to individuate a "form of inoperativity" that, while being held in close relationship with it, is not determined by it but on the contrary renders its works inoperative and permits a new use of them. One-sidedly focused on the analysis of forms of production, Marx neglected the analysis of the forms of inoperativity, and this lack is certainly at the bottom of some of the aporias of his thought, in particular as concerns the definition of human activity in the classless society. From this perspective, a phenomenology of forms of life and of inoperativity that proceeded in step with an analysis of the corresponding forms of production would be essential. In inoperativity, the classless society is already present in capitalist society, just as, according to Benjamin, shards of messianic time are present in history in possibly infamous and risible forms.

§ Intermezzo I

1. In a brief work published forty years after the death of Michel Foucault, Pierre Hadot, who had been acquainted with him and episodically associated with him since 1980, takes care to specify the "convergences" and "divergences" between his thought and his friend's, in the course of a dialogue that was interrupted all too soon. If, on the one hand, he claims to find in Foucault the same themes and interests, which converge in a conception of ancient philosophy—and of philosophy in general—as an "exercise" or "style of life," on the other hand, he firmly distances himself from his friend's theses:

> In this labor of the self on the self, in this exercise of the self I also recognize, for my part, an essential aspect of the philosophical life: philosophy is an art of living, a style of life that touches on all of existence. I would, however, hesitate to speak, as Foucault does, of an "aesthetics of existence," both in connection with Antiquity and, in general, as the task of the philosopher. Michel Foucault understands . . . this expression in the sense that our own life is the work of art that we must make. The term "aesthetics" indeed evokes, for us moderns, resonances very different from those that the word "beauty" (*kalon, kalos*) had in Antiquity. Moderns have the tendency to represent the beautiful as an autonomous reality independent of good and evil, while for the Greeks, by contrast, when the term referred to a human being, it normally implied a moral value. . . . For this reason, instead of speaking of a "cultivation of the self," it would be better to speak of transformation, of transfiguration, of "overcoming the self." To describe this state, one cannot avoid the term "wisdom," which, it seems to me, in Foucault appears rarely, if ever. . . . Curiously Foucault, who does do justice to the conception of philosophy as thera-

peutics, does not seem to notice that this therapeutics is above all intended to procure peace of the soul. . . . In Platonism, but also in Epicureanism and Stoicism, liberation from anxiety is obtained by means of a movement that causes us to pass from individual and impassioned subjectivity to the objectivity of a universal perspective. It is not a matter of the construction of a self, but on the contrary, of an overcoming of the I, or at least of an exercise by means of which the I is situated in the totality and has an experience of the self as part of this totality. (Hadot I, pp. 231–232)

2. At first glance, the opposition appears to be clear and seems to reflect a real divergence. As Hadot himself observes, what is in question is the "aesthetics of existence" that was Foucault's final conception of philosophy and that corresponded, moreover, in all probability with "the philosophy that he concretely practiced throughout his life" (Hadot I, p. 230). In an article that Hadot cites a little earlier in support of his diagnosis, Paul Veyne, a historian of antiquity to whom Foucault felt particularly close, seems, at least apparently, to move in the same direction:

The idea of styles of existence played a major role in Foucault's conversations and doubtless in his inner life during the final months of a life that only he knew to be threatened. *Style* does not mean distinction here; the word is to be taken in the sense of the Greeks, for whom an artist was first of all an artisan and a work of art was first of all a work. . . . The self, taking itself as a work to be accomplished, could sustain an ethics that is no longer supported by either tradition or reason; as an artist of itself, the self would enjoy that autonomy that modernity can no longer do without. (Veyne, p. 939/7)

3. The biography published in English by James Miller in 1993, with the meaningful title *The Passion of Michel Foucault*, contains ample sections on the private life of Foucault, in particular on his homosexuality and his regular visits to bathhouses and sadomasochistic gay bars (like the Hothouse in San Francisco) during his stays in the United States. But already a few years after Foucault's death, a young writer who had been close to him in his final years, Hervé Guibert, had related in two books (*Les secrets d'un homme* in 1988 and *À l'ami qui ne m'a pas sauvé la vie* in 1990) the childhood memories and secret traumas that Foucault is supposed to have communicated to him on his deathbed. Even earlier, during his first decisive stay in California, Simeon Wade, a young scholar who had accompanied the philosopher in a memorable excursion to Death Valley, had carefully taken down in handwritten notebooks his

reactions during an experiment with LSD, as though these were just as precious and important for the understanding of Foucault's thought as his works.

Certainly Foucault himself, who at a certain point had joined FHAR (Front homosexuel d'action révolutionnaire) and openly declared his homosexuality, despite being a reserved and discreet person according to his friends' testimony, never seems to draw sharp divisions between his public life and private life. In numerous interviews, he thus refers to sadomasochism as a practice of the invention of new pleasures and new styles of existence and, more generally, to the homosexual circles of San Francisco and New York as a "laboratory" in which one "tries to explore all the internal possibilities of sexual conduct from the perspective of the creation of new forms of life" (Foucault 2, p. 331/Rabinow, p. 151; cf. also p. 737/Rabinow, p. 164). It is therefore possible that precisely the Foucauldian idea of an art of existence, already clearly formulated at the beginning of the eighties, and his growing attention to practices through which human beings seek to modify themselves and to make their own life something like a work of art, may have authorized our interest in aspects of existence that usually are not considered pertinent for the understanding of an author's thought.

4. Hadot first of all understands the aesthetics of existence, which he attributes to Foucault as "his final conception of philosophy," according to its modern resonance, in which, as an "autonomous reality independent of good and evil," it is opposed to the ethical dimension. In this way, he in a certain way attributes to Foucault the project of an aestheticization of existence, in which the subject, beyond good and evil, more similar to Huysmans's Des Esseintes than to the Platonic Socrates, shapes his life as a work of art. A survey of the places where Foucault makes use of the expression "aesthetics of existence" instead shows beyond any doubt that Foucault resolutely and constantly situates the experience in question in the ethical sphere. Already in the first lecture of the 1981–82 course *The Hermeneutics of the Subject*, almost as though he had foreseen Hadot's objection in advance, he warns against the modern temptation to read expressions like "care of the self" or "concern with oneself" in an aesthetic and non-moral sense. "Now you are well aware," he writes, "that there is a certain tradition (or rather, several traditions) that dissuades us (us, now, today) from giving any positive value to all these

expressions . . . and above all from making them the basis of a morality. They . . . sound to our ears . . . like a sort of challenge and defiance, a desire for radical ethical change, a sort of moral dandyism, the assertion-challenge of a fixed aesthetic and individual stage" (Foucault 1, p. 14/12). Against this (so to speak) aestheticizing interpretation of the care of the self, Foucault instead underlines that it is precisely "this injunction to 'take care of oneself' that is the basis for the constitution of what have without doubt been the most severe, strict, and restrictive moralities known in the West" (ibid., p. 14/13).

5. The expression "aesthetics of existence"—and the theme of life as work of art that is joined with it—is always used by Foucault in the context of an ethical problematization. Hence in the 1983 interview with Dreyfus and Rabinow (to which Hadot also makes reference), he declares that "the idea of *bios* as material for an aesthetic piece of art is something that fascinates me"; but he adds immediately, to specify that what he has in mind is a non-normative form of ethics: "The idea also that ethics can be a very strong structure of existence, without any relation with the juridical per se, with an authoritarian system, with a disciplinary structure" (Foucault 2, p. 390/Rabinow, p. 260). In another interview, published in May 1984 with the editorial title "An Aesthetics of Existence," the expression is preceded by an analogous specification: "This elaboration of one's own life as a personal work of art, even if it obeyed collective canons, was at the center, it seems to me, of moral experience, of the moral will, in Antiquity; whereas in Christianity, with the religion of the text, the idea of God's will, and the principle of obedience, morality took much more the form of a code of rules" (Foucault 2, p. 731/Lotringer, p. 451). But it is above all in the introduction to the second volume of *The History of Sexuality* that the pertinence of the "aesthetics of existence" to the ethical sphere is clarified beyond any doubt. If Foucault here proposes to show how sexual pleasure was problematized in antiquity "through practices of the self that brought into play the criteria of an aesthetics of existence" (Foucault 3, p. 17/12), this takes place in order to respond to the genuinely ethical question: "why is sexual conduct, why are the activities and pleasures that attach to it, an object of moral solicitude?" (ibid., p. 15/10). The "arts of existence" with which the book is concerned and the techniques of the self through which human beings sought to make of their life "an *oeuvre* that carries certain aesthetic values and meets certain stylistic criteria" are in reality "intentional and

voluntary actions" through which human beings fix canons of behavior that serve a function that Foucault defines as "etho-poetic" (pp. 15–17/10–13). What is in question is not an improbable genealogy of aesthetics but a "new genealogy of morals" (Foucault 2, p. 731/Lotringer, p. 451). It is a matter of reintroducing into ethics "the problem of the subject that I had more or less left aside in my first studies . . . to show how the problem of the subject has not ceased to exist throughout this question of sexuality" (ibid., p. 705/Lotringer, p. 472). In fact, the care of the self for the Greeks is not an aesthetic problem; it "is ethical in itself" (p. 714/Rabinow, p. 287).

6. Hadot did not hide his belated acquaintance with the work of Foucault ("I must confess, with great shame, that, too absorbed in my own research, I had very poor knowledge of his work then [1980]," Hadot 1, p. 230). This can in part explain why the other "divergences" denounced by Hadot also seem to rest on imprecise data. When he writes that "instead of speaking of a 'cultivation of the self,' it would be better to speak of transformation, of transfiguration, of 'overcoming the self'" and that, to describe this state, "one cannot avoid the term 'wisdom,' which, it seems to me, in Foucault appears rarely, if ever"; and when he notes, finally, that "Foucault, who does do justice to the conception of philosophy as therapeutic, does not seem to notice that this therapeutic is above all intended to procure peace of the soul," each time and point by point it is a matter of factual inexactitude. The index of the course on *The Hermeneutics of the Subject*, which constituted, so to speak, the laboratory for the investigations on the care of the self, in fact shows that the term "wisdom" appears at least eighteen times, and the term "wise man" almost as many times. In the same course, one reads that, in the ambit of the spirituality that Foucault intends to reconstruct, "the truth enlightens the subject; the truth gives beatitude to the subject; the truth gives the subject tranquility of the soul. In short, in the truth and in access to the truth, there is something that fulfills the subject himself, which fulfills or transfigures his very being" (Foucault 1, p. 18/16). And just a little earlier, Foucault writes that spirituality "postulates that for the subject to have right of access to the truth he must be changed, transformed, shifted, and become, to some extent and up to a certain point, other than himself" (ibid., p. 17/15).

7. The divergences do not concern the displacement of the aesthetic sphere into the ethical or a simple difference in vocabulary so much as

the very conception of ethics and the subject. Hadot does not succeed in detaching himself from a conception of the subject as transcendent with respect to its life and actions, and for this reason, he conceives the Foucauldian paradigm of life as work of art according to the common representation of a subject-author who shapes his work as an object external to him. And yet in a celebrated piece from 1969, Foucault had intended to put precisely this conception into question. Reducing the author to a juridical-social fiction, he suggested that we see in the work not the expression of a subject anterior and external to it, but rather the opening of a space into which the subject never stops vanishing, and identified indifference with respect to the author as "one of the fundamental ethical principles of contemporary writing" (Foucault 4, p. 820/116). In this he was once again faithful to the teaching of Nietzsche, who in an aphorism of 1885–86 (to which Heidegger did not fail to call attention; qtd. in Heidegger 3, p. 222/180) had written: "The artwork, where it appears *without* an artist, e.g., as body [*Leib*], as organization (the Prussian officer corps [*preussisches Offizierkorps*], the Jesuit order). To what extent the artist is only a preliminary stage. The world as an artwork that gives birth to itself." In the same sense, in the interview with Dreyfus and Rabinow, Foucault specifies that speaking of life as a work of art implies precisely calling into question the paradigm of the exclusive artist-creator of a work-object: "What strikes me is the fact that, in our society, art has become something that is related only to objects and not to individuals or to life. That art is something which is specialized or done by experts who are artists. But couldn't everyone's life become a work of art? Why should the lamp or the house be an art object but not our life?" (Foucault 2, p. 392/Rabinow, p. 261).

8. How, then, are we to understand this creation of one's own life as a work of art? The problem, for Foucault, is inseparable from his problematization of the subject. The very idea of life as work of art derives from his conception of a subject that can no longer be separated out into an originary constituent position. "I think," he writes in the interview cited above, "that there is only one practical consequence of the idea that the subject is not given in advance: we have to create ourselves as a work of art. . . . [W]e should not have to refer the creative activity of somebody to the kind of relation he has to himself, but should relate the kind of relation one has to oneself to a creative activity" (Foucault 2, pp.

392–393/Rabinow, p. 262). The relation with oneself, that is to say, constitutively has the form of a creation of self, and there is no subject other than in this process. For this reason Foucault breaks with the conception of the subject as foundation or condition of possibility of experience. On the contrary: "experience is the rationalization of a process, itself provisional, which results in a subject, or rather in subjects" (Foucault 2, p. 706/Lotringer, p. 472). This means that properly there is not a subject but only a process of subjectivization: "I would call subjectivization the process through which results the constitution of a subject" (ibid.). And again: "I don't think there is actually a sovereign, founding subject, a universal form of subject that one could find everywhere. . . . I think on the contrary that the subject is constituted through practices of subjection, or, in a more anonymous way, through practices of liberation, of freedom . . ." (p. 733/Lotringer, p. 452).

9. It is clear that it is not possible here to distinguish between a constituent subject and a constituted subject. There is only a subject that is never given in advance, and the work to be constructed is the constructing subject itself. This is the paradox of the care of the self that Hadot does not manage to understand when he writes that "it is not a matter of the construction of a self, but on the contrary, of an overcoming of the I." "Self" for Foucault is not a substance nor the objectifiable result of an operation (the relation with itself): it is the operation itself, the relation itself. That is to say, there is not a subject before the relationship with itself and the use of the self: the subject is that relationship and not one of its terms (cf. part I, §3.2 above). In accordance with its essential pertinence to first philosophy, the subject implies an ontology, which, however, is not, for Foucault, that of the Aristotelian *hypokeimenon* nor that of the Cartesian subject. It is above all from this latter, probably following a suggestion from Heidegger, that Foucault takes his distance. The specific achievement of Descartes is, in fact, that "he succeeded in substituting a subject as founder of practices of knowledge for a subject constituted through practices of the self" (Foucault 2, p. 410/Rabinow, p. 278).

10. The idea that ethics coincides not with the relation to a norm but first of all with a "relationship with oneself" is constantly present in Foucault. It is this and nothing else that he uncovered in his studies on the *souci de soi* in the classical world: "Pour les Grecs, ce n'est pas parce qu'il est souci des

autres qu'il est éthique. Le souci de soi est éthique en lui-même" ("What makes it ethical for the Greeks is not that it is care for others. The care of the self is ethical in itself"; Foucault 2, p. 714/Rabinow, p. 287). Certainly every moral action entails "a relation to the reality in which one is inscribed or to a code to which one refers"; but it cannot be reduced to an act or to a series of acts in conformity to a rule, because it implies in every case "a certain relationship with oneself" (Foucault 2, p. 558). And this relationship, Foucault specifies, must not be understood simply as an "awareness of oneself" but rather as the "constitution of the self as moral subject" (ibid.). "It is the kind of relationship you ought to have with yourself . . . which determines how the individual is supposed to constitute himself as a moral subject of his own actions" (Foucault 2, p. 618/Rabinow, p. 263). Ethics is, for Foucault, the relationship that one has with oneself when one acts or enters into relation with others, constituting oneself each time as subject of one's own acts, whether these belong to the sexual sphere, the economic, the political, the scientific, etc. Thus, what is in question in *The History of Sexuality* is in no way a social or psychological history of sexual behaviors but the way in which the human being comes to the point of constituting himself or herself as a moral subject of his or her own sexual behaviors. And, in the same way, what was able to interest him in the experiments of the homosexual communities of San Francisco or New York was, once again, the relation with oneself that their novelty entailed and the consequent constitution of a new ethical subject.

11. In the last course at the Collège de France, *Le courage de la vérité* (*The Courage of Truth*), concluded a few months before his death, Foucault evokes, in connection with the Cynics, the theme of the philosophical life as true life (*alethes bios*).

In the résumé of the 1981–82 course *L'herméneutique du sujet*, in which the theme of the care of the self had been developed through a reading of Plato's *Alcibiades*, Foucault had written that "s'occuper de soi n'est pas une simple préparation momentanée à la vie; c'est une forme de vie" ("attending to the self is not therefore just a brief preparation for life; it is a form of life"; Foucault 1, p. 476/494). Now, in the paradigm of the philosophical life, he closely links the themes of truth and of mode of life. Cynicism, he writes, had raised an important question, which restores the radicality of the theme of the philosophical life: "la vie, pour être vraiment la vie de la vérité, ne doit-elle pas être une vie autre, une vie radicalement et paradoxalement autre?" ("for life truly to be the life of truth, must it not be an *other* life, a life which is radically and paradoxically other?"; Foucault 5, p. 226/245). That is to say, there are in the tradition of classical philosophy two different modalities of linking the practice of the self to the courage of truth: the Platonic one, which privileges *mathemata* and knowledge, and the cynical one, which instead gives to the practices of the self the form of a test (*épreuve*) and seeks the truth of being human not in a doctrine but in a certain form of life, which by subverting the current models of society makes of the *bios philosophikos* a challenge and a scandal (ibid., p. 243/265).

In the lineage of this Cynical model, Foucault also inscribes "militancy as bearing witness by one's life in the form of a style of existence" (Foucault 5, p. 170/184) in the tradition of revolutionary movements up through *gauchisme*, certainly very familiar to his generation. "La résurgence du gauchisme," he writes, using terms perhaps best fit to characterize Situationism, which is curiously never mentioned in his writings, "comme tendance permanente à l'intérieur de la pensée et du projet révolutionnaire européens, s'est toujours faite en prenant appui non pas sur la dimension de l'organisation, mais sur cette dimension du militantisme qui est la socialité secrète se manifestant et se rendant visible par des formes de vie scandaleuses" ("the resurgence of leftism as a permanent tendency within European revolutionary thought and projects has always taken place not by basing itself on the organizational dimension but on the dimension of militantism comprising a secret sociality or style of life . . . which manifests itself and makes itself visible in scandalous forms of life"; p. 171/185). Alongside this is the paradigm of the artist in modernity, whose life, "in the very form it takes, should constitute some kind of testimony of what art is in its truth" (p. 173/187).

In the analysis of the "theme of the life of the artist, so important throughout the nineteenth century" (ibid.), Foucault again finds the proximity between art and life and the idea of "an aesthetics of existence" that he had formulated in *L'usage des plaisirs*. If, on the one hand, art confers to life the form of truth, on the other hand, the true life is the guarantee that the work that is rooted in it is truly a work of art. In this way, life and art become indeterminate and art is presented as form of life at the very point where form of life appears as a work of art.

In any case, in the *bios* of the philosopher as much as in that of the artist, the practice of the self as constitution of an other form of life is the true theme of the course, which in the manuscript closes with the affirmation, which can perhaps be considered as a sort of last will and testament: "il ne peut y avoir de vérité que dans la forme de l'autre monde et de la vie autre" ("there can be truth only in the form of the other world and the other life"; p. 311/340).

12. To understand the peculiar ontological status of this subject that is constituted through the practice of the self, it may be useful to draw an analogy with a pair of categories drawn from the sphere of public law: constituent power and constituted power. Here also the aporia, which has paralyzed the theory of public law, arises from the separation of the two terms. The traditional conception places at the origin a constituent power, which creates and separates off from itself, in a ceaseless circularity, a constituted power. True constituent power is not that which produces a constituted power separated from itself, which refers back to constituent power as its unreachable foundation, which, however, has no other legitimacy than that which derives from having produced a constituted power. Constituent is, in truth, only that power—that subject—that is capable of constituting itself as constituent. The practice of the self is that operation in which the subject adequates itself to its own constitutive relation and remains immanent to it: "the subject puts itself into play in taking care of itself" (Foucault 1, p. 504/523). The subject, that is to say, is what is at stake in the care of the self, and this care is nothing but the process through which the subject constitutes itself. And ethics is not the experience in which a subject holds itself behind, above, or beneath its own life but that whose subject constitutes and transforms itself in indissoluble immanent relation to its life, by living its life.

13. But what does it mean to "constitute-oneself"? Here one has something like the "self-constituting as visiting" or the "walking-oneself" with which Spinoza (cf. above, part I, §2.5) exemplifies the immanent cause. The identity of active and passive corresponds to the ontology of immanence, to the movement of autoconstitution and autopresentation of being, in which not only does there fail every possibility of distinguishing between agent and patient, subject and object, constituent and constituted, but in which even means and end, potential and act, work and inoperativity are indeterminated. The practice of the self, the Foucauldian ethical subject, is this immanence: being subject as self-walking.

The being that is constituted in the practice of the self never remains—or should never remain—beneath or before itself, never separates—or should never separate—off from itself a subject or a "substance," but remains immanent to itself, is its constitution, and never stops self-constituting, self-exhibiting, and self-using as acting, visiting, walking, loving. Hence difficulties and aporias of every kind. The problem of the Foucauldian subject is the problem of the autoconstitution of being, and a correct understanding of ethics here necessarily entails a definition of its ontological status. When was something like a "subject" separated off and hypostatized in being in a constituent position? Western ontology is from the very beginning articulated and run through by scissions and caesurae, which divide and coordinate in being subject (*hypokeimenon*) and essence (*ousia*), primary substances and secondary substances, essence and existence, potential and act, and only a preliminary interrogation of these caesurae can allow for the comprehension of the problem that we call "subject."

14. Precisely because the theory of the subject entails an ontological problem, we find here the aporias that have marked from the very beginning its status in first philosophy. The relation with the self determines, as we have seen, the way in which the individual is constituted as subject of its own moral actions. The self, however, according to Foucault does not have any substantial consistency but coincides with the relationship itself, is absolutely immanent in it. But then how can this self, which is nothing but a relation, be constituted as subject of its own actions in order to govern them and define a style of life and a "true life"? The self, insofar as it coincides with the relationship with the self, can never be posited as subject of the relationship nor be identified with the subject that has been constituted in it. It can only constitute itself as constituent but never identify itself with what it has constituted. And yet, as constituted subject, it is, so to speak, the Gnostic or Neoplatonic hypostasis that the practice of the self allows to subsist outside itself as an ineliminable remainder.

What happens in the relationship between the self and the moral subject is something like what Sartre described in the relationship between consciousness and the ego: the self, which has constituted the subject, allows itself to be hypnotized and reabsorbed in it and by it. Or again, it is like what, according to Rudolf Boehm, happens in the Aristotelian scission between essence and existence: this pair, which was supposed to define the unity of being, in the last analysis splits it up into an inexistent essence and an inessential existence, which ceaselessly refer to one another and endlessly fall outside one another. That is to say that self and subject are circularly linked in a constituent relation, and at the same time, precisely for this reason they find themselves in an absolute impossibility of coinciding once and for all. The subject, which must govern and direct its actions in a form of life, has been constituted in a practice of the self that is nothing other than this very constitution and this form of life.

15. The ontological aporia is found in Foucault, as one could have foreseen, on the level of practice, in the theory of power relations and of the governance of human beings that is actualized in it. Power relations, unlike states of domination, necessarily entail a free subject, which it is a matter of "conducting" and governing and which, as free, stubbornly resists power. And yet, precisely insofar as the subject "freely" conducts and governs itself, it will inevitably enter into power relations, which consist in conducting the conduct of others (or allowing one's own to be conducted by others). The one who, by "conducting" his life, has been constituted as subject of his own actions, will thus be "conducted" by other subjects or will seek to conduct others: subjectivation into a certain form of life is, to the same extent, subjection to a power relation. The aporia of democracy and its governance of human beings—the identity of the governors and the governed, absolutely separated and yet to the same degree indissolubly united in an indivisible relation—is an ontological aporia, which concerns the constitution of the subject as such. As constituent power and constituted power, the relation with the self and the subject are simultaneously transcendent and immanent to one another. And yet it is precisely the immanence between self and subject in a form of life that Foucault persistently sought to think up to the end, tangling himself in ever more difficult aporias and, at the same time, forcefully pointing in the only direction in which something like an ethics could become possible for him.

16. In the interview given to *Les nouvelles littéraires* less than a month before his death and posthumously published on June 28, 1984, Foucault turns to the question of the subject and, in defining his final investiga-

tions, writes that in these latter for him it was a matter "of reintroducing the problem of the subject that I had more or less left aside in my first studies . . . to show how the problem of the subject has not ceased to exist throughout this question of sexuality" (Foucault 2, p. 705/Lotringer, p. 472). Immediately after, however, he specifies that in classical antiquity, the problem of the care of the self was forcefully posed, while a theory of the subject was entirely lacking:

> This doesn't mean that the Greeks didn't strive to define the conditions of an experience, but it wasn't an experience of the subject; rather, it was of the individual, insofar as he sought to constitute himself through self-mastery. Classical antiquity never problematized the constitution of the self as subject; inversely, beginning with Christianity, there is an appropriation of morality through the theory of the subject. Yet a moral experience centered essentially on the subject no longer seems to me satisfactory today. (Ibid., p. 706/Lotringer, p. 473)

If antiquity offers the example of a care and of a constitution of the self without the subject and Christianity that of a morality that entirely absorbs the ethical relation with the self into the subject, Foucault's wager is thus to keep hold of the reciprocal co-belonging of the two elements.

17. From this perspective, one can understand the interest that the sadomasochistic experience could take on in his eyes. Sadomasochism for Foucault is first of all an experiment in fluidifying power relations. "One can say," he declares in a 1982 interview,

> that S&M is the eroticization of power, the eroticization of strategic relations. What strikes me with regard to S&M is how it differs from social power. What characterizes power is the fact that it is a strategic relationship which has been stabilized through institutions. So the mobility in power relations is limited . . . the strategic relations of people are made rigid. At this point, the S&M game is very interesting because it is a strategic relation, but it is always fluid. Of course, there are roles, but everyone knows very well that those roles can be reversed. Sometimes the scene begins with the master and slave, and at the end the slave has become the master. Or, even when the roles are stabilized, you know very well that it is always a game. Either the rules are transgressed, or there is an agreement, either explicit or tacit, that makes them aware of certain boundaries. (Foucault 2, pp. 742–743/Rabinow, p. 169)

The sadomasochistic relation is, in this sense, entirely immanent to a power relation ("S&M is not the relationship between one who suffers and the one who inflicts suffering, but between a master and the one over whom the master exercises mastery"; ibid., p. 331/Rabinow, p. 151), which uses and transforms it into a function of power. "S&M is the utilization of a strategic relationship as a source of pleasure (physical pleasure)" (p. 743/Rabinow, p. 170).

If sadomasochism interests Foucault, this is because it shows that it is possible to act on these relations, whether in order to fluidify them and invert their roles or to displace them from the social level to the sexual or corporeal level, using them for the invention of new pleasures. But in any case, the power relation remains, even if it is opened in this way to a new dialectic, different from that between power and resistance whose structure Foucault had defined. The horizon of power relations and governmentality remains not only unsurpassable but also, in some way, inseparable from ethics ("la notion de gouvernementalité," he wrote in a long interview from January 1984, "permet de faire valoir la liberté du sujet et le rapport aux autres, c'est-à-dire ce qui constitue la matière même de l'éthique [the concept of governmentality makes it possible to bring out the freedom of the subject and its relationship to others—which constitutes the very stuff of ethics]," p. 729/Rabinow, p. 300).

Nevertheless, the transformation of power relations that occurs in sadomasochism cannot fail to entail a transformation on the level of ontology. The S&M relation, with its two poles in mutual exchange, is an ontological relation, for which the Foucauldian thesis according to which "the self with which one has the relationship is nothing but the relationship itself" holds in a paradigmatic way. Foucault did not unfold all the implications of the "ontological adequation of the self to the relationship," which he nonetheless caught a glimpse of. Certainly the subject, the self of which he speaks, cannot be inscribed into the tradition of the Aristotelian *hypokeimenon*, and yet Foucault—likely for good reasons—constantly avoided the direct confrontation with the history of ontology that Heidegger had laid out as a preliminary task.

What Foucault does not seem to see, despite the fact that antiquity would seem to offer an example in some way, is the possibility of a relation with the self and of a form of life that never assumes the figure of a free subject—which is to say, if power relations necessarily refer to a subject, of a zone of ethics entirely subtracted from strategic relationships, of an Ungovernable that is situated beyond states of domination and power relations.

PART II

An Archeology of Ontology

In the pages that follow we propose to ascertain whether access to a first philosophy, that is, to an ontology, is today still—or once again—possible. For reasons that we will seek to clarify, at least since Kant, this access has become so problematic that it is not thinkable except in the form of an archeology. First philosophy is not, in fact, an ensemble of conceptual formulations that, however complex and refined, do not escape from the limits of a doctrine: it opens and defines each time the space of human acting and knowing, of what the human being can do and of what it can know and say. Ontology is laden with the historical destiny of the West not because an inexplicable and metahistorical magical power belongs to being but just the contrary, because ontology is the originary place of the historical articulation between language and world, which preserves in itself the memory of anthropogenesis, of the moment when that articulation was produced. To every change in ontology there corresponds, therefore, not a change in the "destiny" but in the complex of possibilities that the articulation between language and world has disclosed as "history" to the living beings of the species *Homo sapiens*.

Anthropogenesis, the becoming human of the human being, is not in fact an event that was completed once and for all in the past: rather, it is the event that never stops happening, a process still under way in which the human being is always in the act of becoming human and of remaining (or becoming) inhuman. First philosophy is the memory and repetition of this event: in this sense, it watches over the historical *a priori* of *Homo sapiens*, and it is to this historical *a priori* that archeological research always seeks to reach back.

ℵ.   In the preface to *Les mots et les choses* (1966), Foucault uses the term "historical *a priori*" to define that which, in a determinate historical epoch, conditions the possibilities of the formation and development of knowledges. The expression is problematic, because it brings together two elements that are at least apparently contradictory: the *a priori*, which entails a paradigmatic and transcendental dimension, and history, which refers to an eminently factual reality. It is probable that Foucault had drawn the term from Husserl's *Origin of Geometry*, which Derrida had translated into French in 1962, but certainly not the concept, because while in Husserl the *historisches Apriori* designates a sort of universal *a priori* of history, it instead always refers in Foucault to a determinate knowledge and to a determinate time. And yet, if it does not in any way refer back to an archetypal dimension beyond history but remains immanent to it, its contradictory formulation brings to expression the fact that every historical study inevitably runs up against a constitutive dishomogeneity: that between the ensemble of facts and documents on which it labors and a level that we can define as archeological, which though not transcending it, remains irreducible to it and permits its comprehension. Overbeck has expressed this heterogeneity by means of the distinction, in every study, between prehistory (*Urgeschichte*) and history (*Geschichte*), where prehistory does not designate what we usually understand by this term—that is, something chronologically archaic (*uralt*)—but rather the history of the point of emergence (*Entstehungsgeschichte*), in which the researcher must settle accounts with an originary phenomenon (an *Urphänomen* in Goethe's sense) and at the same time with the tradition that, while it seems to transmit the past to us, ceaselessly covers up the fact of its emergence (It., *sorgività*) and renders it inaccessible.

One can define philosophical archeology as the attempt to bring to light the various historical *a prioris* that condition the history of humanity and define its epochs. It is possible, in this sense, to construct a hierarchy of the various historical *a prioris*, which ascends in time toward more and more general forms. Ontology or first philosophy has constituted for centuries the fundamental historical *a priori* of Western thought.

The archeology that attempts to reopen access to a first philosophy must nevertheless first of all settle accounts with the striking fact that, beginning from a moment for which the name of Kant can serve as a signpost, it is precisely the impossibility of a first philosophy that has become the historical *a priori* of the time in which we still in some way live. The true Copernican turn of Kantian critique does not concern the position of the subject so much as the impossibility of a first philosophy, which Kant calls *metaphysics*. As Foucault had intuited early on, "it is probable that we belong to an age of critique whose lack of a first philosophy reminds us at every moment of its reign and its fatality" (Foucault 6, pp. xi–xii/xv). Certainly Kant, at the very moment when he sanctioned the impossibility of metaphysics, sought to secure its survival by giving it refuge in the stronghold of the transcendental. But the transcendental—which in medieval logic designated what is always already said and known when one says "being"—necessarily entails a displacement of the historical *a priori* from the anthropogenetic event (the articulation between language and world) to knowledge, from a being that is no longer animal but not yet human to a knowing subject. Ontology is thus transformed into gnoseology and first philosophy becomes philosophy of knowledge.

Up to Heidegger, all or almost all post-Kantian professional philosophers had kept to the transcendental dimension as if it went without saying, and in this way, believing themselves to be saving the prestige of philosophy, they in fact enslaved it to those sciences and knowledges of which they thought they could define the conditions of possibility, precisely when these latter, projected toward a technological development without limits, demonstrated that they did not actually have any need of it. It fell to non-professional philosophers, like Nietzsche, Benjamin, and Foucault, and in a different sense a linguist like Émile Benveniste, to seek a way out of the transcendental. And they have done this by shifting the historical *a priori* back from knowledge to language: and in this, by not attending to the level of meaningful propositions but by isolating each time a dimension that called into question the pure fact of language, the pure being given of the enunciated, before or beyond their semantic content. The speaking being or enunciator has thus been substituted for Kant's transcendental subject, and language has taken the place of being as historical *a priori*.

This linguistic declension of ontology seems today to have reached its completion. Certainly language has never been so omnipresent and pervasive, superimposing itself in every sphere—not only in politics and communication but also and above all in the sciences of nature—over being, apparently without leaving any remainder. What has changed, however, is that language no longer functions as a historical *a priori*, which while remaining unthought, determines and conditions the historical possibilities of speaking human beings. In being totally identified with being, it is now put forward as a neutral ahistorical or post-historical effectuality, which no longer conditions any recognizable sense of historical becoming or any epochal articulation of time. This means that we live in a time that is not—or at least pretends not to be—determined by any historical *a priori*, which is to say, a post-historical time (or rather, a time determined by the absence or impossibility of such an *a priori*).

It is from this perspective that we are seeking to trace out—even if purely in the form of a summary sketch—an archeology of ontology, or more precisely, a genealogy of the ontological apparatus that has functioned for two millennia as a historical *a priori* of the West. If ontology is first of all a hodology, which is to say, the way that being always historically opens toward itself, it is the existence today of something like a *hodos* or a way that we seek to interrogate, by asking ourselves whether the track that seems to have been interrupted or lost can be taken up again or instead must be definitively abandoned.

§ 1 Ontological Apparatus

1.1. An archeology of first philosophy must begin from the apparatus of being's division that defines Aristotelian ontology. This apparatus—which divides and at the same time articulates being and is, in the last instance, at the origin of every ontological difference—has its locus in the *Categories*. Here Aristotle distinguishes an *ousia*, an entity or essence, "which is said most strictly, primarily, and first of all" (*kyriotata te kai protos kai malista legomene*) from the secondary essences (*ousiai dueterai*). The former is defined as "that which is not said of a subject [*hypokeimenon*, that which lies under, *sub-iectum*] nor in a subject" and is exemplified by the singularity, the proper name, and deixis ("this certain man, Socrates; this certain horse"); the latter are "those in whose species the essences called primary are present, as are the genera of these species—for example, 'this certain man' belongs to the species 'man' and the genus of this species is 'animal'" (*Categories*, 2a 10–15).

Whatever may be the terms in which the division is articulated in the course of its history (primary essence/secondary essence, existence/essence, *quod est/quid est*, *anitas/quidditas*, common nature/supposition, *Dass sein/Was sein*, being/beings), what is decisive is that in the tradition of Western philosophy, being, like life, is always interrogated beginning with the division that traverses it.

ℵ. We translate *hypokeimenon* with "subject" (*sub-iectum*). Etymologically the term means "that which lies under or at the base." This is not the place to show the turns and vicissitudes by means of which the Aristotelian *hypokeimenon* became the subject of modern philosophy. It is certain in any case that, by means of Latin translations, this passage of the *Categories* has decisively determined the vocabulary of Western philosophy. In the terminology of Aquinas, the Aristotelian articulation of being thus appears in this way:

> According to the Philosopher, substance is said in two ways. In a primary sense it means the *quidditas* of the thing, signified by its definition, and thus we say that the definition means the substance of a thing, which the Greeks call *ousia* and we call *essentia*. In a second sense, it is the subject [*subiectum*] or *suppositum* ["what is put under"] which subsists [*subsistit*] in the genus of substance. This can be expressed with a term that means intention and this is called *suppositum*. It is also called by three names signifying the thing: that is, a thing of a nature [*res naturae*], subsistence [*subsistentia*], and hypostasis [*hypostasis*]. For insofar as it exists in itself and not in another, it is called *subsistentia*, and insofar as it underlies some common nature, it is called a thing of a nature; as, for instance, "this man" is a thing of human nature. Finally, insofar as it is pre-supposed by the accidents [*supponitur accidentibus*], it is called hypostasis or substance. (Aquinas 2, I, q. 29, art. 2, Resp.)

Whatever may be the terms in which it is expressed at various times, this division of being is at the base of the "ontological difference" that, according to Heidegger, defines Western metaphysics.

1.2. The treatise on *Categories* or predications (though the Greek term *kategoriai* means "imputations, accusations" in juridical language) is traditionally classified among Aristotle's logical works. However, it contains, for example, in the passage in question, theses of an undoubtedly ontological character. Ancient commentators therefore debated over what was the object (*skopos*, end) of the treatise: words (*phonai*), things (*pragmata*), or concepts (*noemata*). In the prologue to his commentary, Philoponus writes that according to some (among them Alexander of Aphrodisias) the object of the treatise is only words, according to others (like Eustatius) only things, and according to others, finally (like Porphyry), only concepts. More correct, according to Philoponus, is the thesis of Iamblichus (which he accepts with some clarifications) according to which the *skopos* of the treatise is words insofar as they signify things by means of concepts (*phonon semainouson pragmata dia meson noematon*; Philoponus, pp. 8–9).

Hence the impossibility, in the *Categories*, of distinguishing logic and ontology. Aristotle treats here of things, of beings, insofar as they are signified by language, and of language insofar as it refers to things. His ontology presupposes the fact that, as he never stops repeating, being is said (*to on legetai . . .*), is always already in language. The ambiguity between logic and ontology is so consubstantial to the treatise that, in the history of Western philosophy, the categories appear both as classes of predication and as classes of being.

1.3. At the beginning of the treatise, immediately after having defined homonyms, synonyms, and paronyms (that is, things insofar as they are named), Aristotle specifies this onto-logical implication between being and language in the form of a classification of beings according to the structure of subjectivation or pre-supposition.

> Of beings, some are said of a subject [*kath' hypocheimenou*, lit.: "on the pre-supposition of a lying under"] but are not in any subject [*en hypocheimenoi oudeni*]. For example, "human" is said on the presupposition [subjectivation] of a certain human being but is not in any subject. . . . Others are in a subject but are not said of any subject. . . . For example, a certain grammatical knowing is in a subject, the soul, but is not said of any subject. . . . Still others are both said of a subject and in a subject. For example, knowledge is said of a subject, grammar, and is in a subject, the soul. Yet others are neither in a subject nor said of a subject: for example, a certain man or a certain horse. (*Categories*, 1a 20–1b 5)

The distinction between *saying* (to say of a subject) and *being* (to be in a subject) does not correspond to the opposition between language and being, linguistic and non-linguistic, so much as to the promiscuity between the two meanings of the verb "to be" (*einai*), the existentive and the predicative. The structure of subjectivation/presupposition remains the same in both cases: the articulation worked by language always pre-sup-poses a relation of predication (general/particular) or of inherence (substance/accident) with respect to a subject, an existent that lies-under-and-at-the-base. *Legein*, "to say," means in Greek "to gather and articulate *beings* by means of *words*": onto-logy. But in this way, the distinction between *saying* and *being* remains uninterrogated, and it is the opacity of their relation that will be transmitted by Aristotle to Western philosophy, which will take it in without the benefit of an inventory.

ℵ.   It is well known that in Indo-European languages the verb "to be" generally has a double meaning: the first meaning corresponds to a lexical function, which expresses the existence and reality of something ("God is," that is, exists), while the second—the copula—has a purely logico-grammatical function and expresses the identity between two terms ("God is good"). In many languages (as in Hebrew and Arabic), or in the same language in different epochs (as in Greek, in which originally the copulative function is expressed by a nominal phrase with no verb: *ariston hydor*, "the best thing is water"), the two meanings are, by contrast, lexically distinct. As Émile Benveniste writes,

> What matters is to see clearly that there is no connection, either by nature or by neces-sity, between the verbal notion of "to exist, to be really there" and the function of the "copula." One need not ask how it happens that the verb "to be" can be lacking or omitted. This is to reason in reverse. The real question should be the opposite; how is it that there is a verb "to be" which gives verbal expression and lexical consistency to a logical relationship in an assertive utterance? (Benveniste, p. 189/164)

Precisely the promiscuity between the two meanings is at the base of the many aporias and difficulties in the history of Western ontology, which has been con-stituted, so to speak, as a double machine, set on distinguishing and, at the same time, articulating together the two notions into a hierarchy or into a coincidence.

1.4. A little further down, apropos of the relation between secondary substances and primary substances, Aristotle writes:

> It is clear from what has been said that if something is said of a subject [*kath'hypokeimenou*, "on the pre-sup-position of a lying-under"], both its name and its definition are necessarily predicated [*kategoreisthai*] of the subject. For example, "man" is said on the subjectivation [on the pre-sup-position] of this certain man, and the name is of course predicated (since you will be predicating "man" of this certain man), and also the definition of "man" will be predicated of this certain man (since this certain man is also a man). Thus, both the name and the definition will be predicated of the subject. (*Categories*, 2a 19–25)

The subjectivation of being, the presupposition of the lying-under is there-fore inseparable from linguistic predication, is part of the very structure of language and of the world that it articulates and interprets. Insofar as, in the *Categories*, being is considered from the point of view of linguistic predica-tion, of its being "accused" (*kategorein* first of all means "to accuse" in Greek) by language, it appears "most properly, in the first place, and above all" in the form of subjectivation. The accusation, the summons to trial that lan-guage directs toward being subjectivates it, presupposes it in the form of a *hypokeimenon*, of a singular existent that lies-under-and-at-the-base.

The primary ousia is what is said neither on the presupposition of a sub-ject nor in a subject, because it is itself the subject that is pre-sup-posed—as purely existent—as what lies under every predication.

1.5. The pre-supposing relation is, in this sense, the specific potential of human language. As soon as there is language, the thing named is presupposed as the non-linguistic or non-relational with which language has established its relation. This presuppositional power is so strong that we imagine the non-linguistic as something unsayable and non-relational that we seek in some way to grasp as such, without noticing that what we seek to grasp in this way is only the shadow of language. The non-linguistic, the unsayable is, as should be obvious, a genuinely linguistic category: it is in fact the "category" par excellence—the accusation, the summons worked by human language, which no non-speaking living being could ever conceive. That is to say, the onto-logical relation runs between the beings presupposed by language and their being in language. What is non-relational is, as such, above all the linguistic relation itself.

It is in the structure of presupposition that the interweaving of being and language, ontology and logic that constitutes Western metaphysics is articulated. Called into question from the point of view of language, being is from the very beginning divided into an existentive being (existence, the primary *ousia*) and a predicative being (the secondary *ousia*, what is said of it): the task of thought will then be that of reassembling into a unity what thought—language—has presupposed and divided. The term "presupposition" indicates, that is to say, the subject in its original meaning: that which, lying before and at the base, constitutes the "on-which" (on the presupposition of which) one says and which cannot, in its turn, be said about anything. The term "presupposition" is etymologically pertinent: *hypokeisthai* is used, in fact, as passive perfect of *hypotithenai*, and *hypokeimenon* thus means "that which, having been pre-sup-posed, lies under." In this sense Plato—who is perhaps the first to thematize the presuppositional power of language that is expressed in language in the opposition between names (*onomata*) and discourse (*logos*)—can write, "The primary names, by which in some way other names are presupposed [*hypokeitai*], in what way do they manifest beings to us?" (*Cratylus*, 422d), or again: "by each of these names is presupposed [*hypokeitai*] a particular essence [*ousia*]" (*Protagoras*, 349b). Being is that which is a presupposition to the language that manifests it, that on presupposition of which what is said is said.

(It is this presuppositional structure of language that Hegel—hence his success and his limits—will seek at the same time to capture and to liquidate by means of the dialectic; Schelling, for his part, will instead attempt to grasp it by suspending thought, in astonishment and stupor. But even in this case, what the mind *as if astonished* contemplates without managing to neutralize it is the very structure of presupposition.)

ℵ.   Aristotle frequently expresses with perfect awareness the onto-logical inter-weaving of being and saying: "Those things are said in their own right to be that are indicated by the figures of the categories; according to the way in which it is said, such is the meaning of being" (*kath' autà de einai legetai osaper semanei ta schemata tes kategorias: osachos gar legetai, tosautachos to einai semanei, Metaphys-ics*, 1017a 22ff.). The ambiguity is after all implied in the celebrated formulation of *Metaphysics*, 1028a 10ff.: "Being is said in many ways . . . for in one sense it means that a thing is or is a 'this,' and in another sense it means that a thing is of a certain quality or quantity and each of the other things that are predicated in this way." Being is constitutively something that "is said" and "means."

1.6. Aristotle therefore founds the priority of the subjective determina-tion of *ousia* in these terms:

> All the other things are either said on the pre-sup-position [*kath' hypokeim-enou*, on subjectivation] of the primary *ousiai* or they are in the presupposi-tion of these. . . . For example, "animal" is predicated of the human being, and therefore also of this certain human being; for were it predicated of none of the individual human beings, it would not be predicated of the human be-ing at all. . . . So if the primary substances [*ousiai*] did not exist, it would be impossible for any of the other things to exist. Thus, all the other things are either said on the presupposition of their standing-under or presupposed in the latter. (*Categories* 2a 34–2b6)

This priority of the primary substance—expressed in language by a proper name or an ostensive pronoun—is confirmed a few lines after: "The primary *ousiai*, insofar as they are supposed [*hypokesthai*] by all the other things and all the others are predicated of them and are in them, are for this reason called *ousiai* par excellence" (*Categories*, 2a 15–17).

The primary essence is "most properly, in the first place, and above all" *ousia*, because it is the limit point of subjectivation, of being in language, that beyond which one can no longer name, predicate, or signify but only indicate. Thus, if "every substance seems to signify a certain 'this'" (*tode ti*), this is true in the proper sense only of primary substances, which always manifest "what is individual and one" (*atomon kai hen arithmoi*); secondary substances, for example, "man" or "animal," "by contrast signify a certain quality: the subject [the lying-at-the-base] is not in fact one, as in the primary substance, but 'man' is predicated of many things and also 'animal'" (3b 10–16).

1.7. It is because of the priority of this subjective determination of being as primary *hypokeimenon*, as the impredicable singularity that stands-under-and-at-the-base of linguistic predication, that in the tradition of Western philosophy the term *ousia* is translated into Latin with *substantia*. Beginning with Neoplatonism, in fact, the treatise on the *Categories* acquired a privileged place in the *corpus* of Aristotle's works and, in its Latin translation, it exercised a determinative influence on medieval culture. Boethius, in whose version the Middle Ages knew the *Categories*, despite perceiving that the more correct translation would have been *essentia* (*ousia* is a deverbal formed from the participle of the verb *einai*, and in his theological treatise against Eutyches and Nestorius, Boethius therefore has the term *essentia* correspond to *ousia* and reserves *substantia* for the Greek *hypostasis*), instead made use of the term *substantia* and thus in a decisive way oriented the vocabulary and the understanding of Western ontology. Being can appear as that which lies-under-and-at-the-base only from the point of view of linguistic predication, that is, starting from the priority of the subjective determination of *ousia* as primary *hypokeimonon* that stands at the center of Aristotle's *Categories*. The entire lexicon of Western ontology (*substantia*, *subiectum*, *hypostasis*, *subsistentia*) is the result of this priority of the primary substance as *hypokeimenon*, as lying-at-the-base of every predication.

1.8. In book VII of the *Metaphysics*, when he has asked the question "what is *ousia*?" and after he has distinguished four senses of the term, Aristotle refers explicitly to the subjective determination of being elaborated in the *Categories*.

> The *hypokeimenon*, the subject [that which lies-under-and-at-the-base] is that on the basis of which other things are said, while it is not said of others; for this reason it must be defined as primary, because the primary subject seems to be above all [*malista*] *ousia*. (1028b 35–1029a 1)

At this point, however, he seems to call into question the priority of the subject and in fact to affirm its insufficiency:

> We have now said in general [*typoi*, "as in a sketch"] what *ousia* is, namely, what is not (nor is said) on the basis of a subject, but is that on the basis of

which all (is and is said). But one must not define it only in this way, because
it is not sufficient [*hikanon*]: not only is it obscure [*adelon*], but in this way
material would be *ousia*. . . . (1029a 9–12)

From this moment, the priority of the subjective determination of being cedes its place to the other determination of *ousia* that Aristotle will
call *to ti en einai* (*quod quid erat esse* in the medieval translations). To
understand Aristotelian ontology means to correctly situate the relation
between these two determinations of *ousia*.

1.9. A student of Heidegger, Rudolf Boehm, dedicated a penetrating analysis to the problem of this apparent contradiction in Aristotle's
thought, which seems at the same time to affirm and to negate the priority of the subject. He critiques the traditional interpretation that, beginning in the Middle Ages, maintains the priority of the "lying-at-the-base"
(*das Zugrundeliegende*) and shows that Aristotle introduces the *ti en einai*
precisely to respond to the aporias implicit in that priority. The subjective
determination of essence in fact thinks *ousia* not in itself but insofar as
something else requires and demands it as that which stands-under-and-
at-the-base of itself. That is to say, the priority of the subject in Aristotle
is in agreement with the thesis according to which the question of *ousia*
has a sense only if it is articulated as a relation to another, that is, in the
form "by means of what is something predicated as something?" This
determination, however, introduces into being a fundamental division,
through which it is divided into an inexistent essence and an existent
without essence. Put differently, if one thinks being from the "lying-at-
the-base," one will have, on the one hand, an inessential existent (a "that
it is" without being, a *quod est* without *quidditas*) and, on the other, an
inexistent essence: "Essence [*Wesen*] and being [*Sein*] fall outside one another and, in this way, break with one another, in the twofold sense of
the term: they each break with the other and fall to pieces" (Boehm, R.,
p. 169).

By means of the concept *ti en einai*, then, Aristotle seeks to think the
unity and identity of existence and essence, of the existentive being of the
primary substance and the predicative being of the secondary substance,
but does it in such a way that, in the last analysis, the subject lying-at-
the-base turns out to be inaccessible and essence appears as something
non-existent. That is to say, the *ti en einai* expresses the irreducible reciprocal counterposition (*Widerspiel*) of being and existing, which Boehm,

from the perspective of his master Heidegger, in the last analysis refers back to the "wonder that the existing being is," whose sole adequate expression is the question: "why is there being rather than nothing?" (pp. 202–203).

1.10. A preliminary condition of every interpretation of the *ti en einai* is an analysis of its grammatical structure, which Boehm curiously leaves aside. This is so true that the same expression is translated in different ways by Boehm (*das Sein-was-es-war*, "being-what-it-was"), by Natorp (*das was es war sein*, "what it was to be"), by Aquinas and the medieval Scholastics (*quod quid erat esse*), by Ross and others (simply as "essence"). As long as the unusual grammatical structure of the expression—and the still more unusual presence of the past *en* ("was") in place of the present *esti*—has not been clarified, the passage to its philosophical interpretation is in no way possible.

In 1938, a young philologist who was to die in the war in 1942, Curt Arpe, devoted an exemplary study to an analysis of the *ti en einai* that is also grammatical. He shows that, to understand the sense of the *ti en einai*, it is necessary to mentally complete the formula with two datives, one pure and one predicative. In fact, Aristotle commonly expresses the essential predication with a predicative dative—thus, precisely in the passage in which one seeks the definition of the *ti en einai* (1029b 12–20): *toi soi einai*, "being yourself" (literally, "being to oneself"), *toi mousikoi einai*, "being cultured" (lit., "being to the cultured"), *toi epiphaneiai einai*, "being the surface," and elsewhere, *toi anthropoi einai*, "being human"— or "to the human." However, since Aristotle does not speak here only of being human in general but of the being human of this certain human being, it is necessary to insert into the formula a pure or concrete dative. "With this," writes Arpe, "one clarifies the grammatical form of the question *ti en einai*; to be understood, it requires completion by means of a pure dative and a predicative dative produced by assimilation. By putting the article *to* first, the formula takes on the meaning of a response to the question" (Arpe, p. 18).

That is to say, *to ti en einai* means (in the case of a human being): "what it was for X (for Socrates, for Emma) to be (Socrates, Emma)." The formula expresses the *ousia* of a certain entity by transforming the question "what is it for this certain being to be?" into the response "what it was for that certain being to be."

ℵ. That Arpe's suggestion is correct is also proven by the fact that in *Categories*, 1a 5, Aristotle writes: "if one is to say what it is for each [*ekateroi*, pure dative] of them [*scil.* the human being and the ox] to be an animal [*zooi*, predicative dative] . . ." Yet note that in the *Categories* the verb is still in the present (*ti esti*).

As we have seen, the formula *to ti en einai* allows two translations: "what it was to be" and "being what it was." Both are in a certain way to be maintained, because the formula expresses precisely the movement from the one to the other, without their ever being able to coincide. As has been noted, "with the two terms *hypokeimenon* and *ti en einai* are named the two meanings in which Aristotle uses the ambivalent term *ousia*" (Tugendhat, qtd. in Boehm, R., p. 25). And yet, "what it was to be for X" can never truly "be" what it was.

1.11. If in this way the grammatical structure and the sense of the formula are clarified, there remains the problem of the imperfect "was" (*en*): why must Aristotle introduce into the definition of essence a past tense, why "what it *was*" instead of "what it is"? This turns out to be the decisive problem that defines the ontological apparatus that Aristotle has left as an inheritance to Western philosophy.

Scholars have proposed explanations that, while correct in certain aspects, do not catch hold of the problem in its complexity. Arpe is thus in a favorable position when he rejects as Platonic the solution of Trendelenburg, according to whom the imperfect derives from the priority of the model in the mind of the artisan with respect to the work (Arpe, p. 15). But even Natorp's solution, which Arpe seems to share, however correct it is, does not exhaust the problem. According to Natorp, the *ti en einai* means "what from time to time for a certain subject 'was' or signified in every case the same thing, if one brings it alongside this or that predicate. It is possible that in the past tense 'was' there is hidden something more profound, but in the first place it means nothing more profound than the fact that the term, of which the definition must be given, is presupposed as already known through use and that even its denotation is presupposed as factually identical and that now this identity must be particularly put in relief and brought to one's awareness" (Arpe, p. 17). As for Boehm, he sees in the imperfect the expression of the unity and identity of being and essence, in the sense that the identity of being of an existing being with what it is necessarily entails "the identity of its being with what it already was": that is to say, it is a matter of securing the continuity of a certain being with itself. "The essential identity of being and essence is at the same time the ceaselessly reaffirmed identity of an autonomous being in general" (p. 171).

If Aristotle had wanted to express only the banal fact that the presupposed subject is necessarily already known or to affirm the identity with itself of every essential entity (and both things certainly correspond to his thought), he could have had recourse to more precise formulas than the simple imperfect *en*. What is in question here is, rather, the very structure of the Aristotelian ontological apparatus, which always divides being into existence and essence, into a presupposed subject on the basis of which something is said and a predication that is said of it. Once this division is posited, the problem becomes: how is it possible to say the primary substance, the *sub-iectum*? How can one grasp what *has been* presupposed in the form of the *hypokeimenon*, namely, the being Socrates of Socrates, the being Emma of Emma? If it is true, as Boehm's investigations have shown, that being has been divided into an inessential existent and an inexistent essence, how will it be possible to overcome this division, to cause the simple wonder "that something is" to correspond with "what it is to be this"?

The "what it *was* for this being to be" is the attempt to respond to this question. If, insofar as it has been presupposed, the individual can be grasped only as something past, the only way to catch hold of the singularity in its truth is in time. The past tense "was" in the formula *ti en einai* certainly expresses the identity and continuity of being, but its fundamental achievement, whether or not Aristotle was fully aware of it, is the introduction of time into being. The "something more profound" that "is hidden" in the past tense "was" is time: the *identity* of the being that language has divided, if one attempts to think it, necessarily entails *time*. In the very gesture with which it divides being, language produces time.

1.12. The question to which "what it was to be" must give a response is: given the scission between a *sub-iectum*, an inessential existent lying-at-the-base and an inexistent essence, how is it possible to grasp singular existence? The problem here is similar to the one Plato had posed in the *Theatatus*, when he has Socrates say that the primary, simple elements do not have a definition (*logos*) but can only be named (*onomasai monon*, 201a 1ff.). In the *Metaphysics* (1043b 24), Aristotle attributes this "aporia" to the followers of Antisthenes, who affirmed that one could only give a definition of composite substances and not of simple ones.

The problem is all the more important, insofar as the logical apparatus that, according to Aristotle, should orient every study is formulated
as follows: "The 'why' is always sought in this form: 'why something is
[or belongs to, *hyparchei*] something else" (1041a 11ff.). That is to say, it
is a matter of eliminating every question of the type: "why something is
something" by articulating it in the form "why something is (belongs to)
something else" (thus, not "why is an educated man an educated man"
but "by means of what is a human being a living being of this or that
type"; not "why is a house a house" but "by means of what are these materials, bricks and roofing-tiles, a house").

The apparatus runs up against a peculiar difficulty when a thing is not
predicated of something else, as when one asks, "what is a human being?"
In this case, in fact, we find ourselves before a simple expression (*haplos
legesthai*; 1041b 2), which is not analyzable into subject and predicates.
The solution that Aristotle gives to this problem shows that the *ti en einai*
is precisely what serves to grasp the being of a simple or primary substance. In this case as well, he suggests, the question—for example, "what
is a house?"—must be articulated in the form: "why are these things a
house?," and this is possible "because there is present [or belongs to them]
what *was* the being of the house" (*hoti hyparchei ho en oikiai einai*; 1041b
5–6). In the formula *ho en oikiai einai*, which explicitly recalls that of the
ti en einai, the past tense "was" certainly refers to the existence of the
house as something already known and evident (a little before, Aristotle
had written: *hoti hyparchei, dei delon einai*, "what exists must be evident";
1041a 22); but one does not understand the functioning of the apparatus
if one does not comprehend that the mode of this existence is essentially
temporal and entails a past.

1.13. If we now ask what type of temporality is in question, it is evident that it cannot be a question of a chronological temporality (as if the
preexistence of the subject could be measured in hours or days) but of
something like an operative time, which refers to the time that the mind
takes to realize the articulation between the presupposed subject and its
essence. For this reason, the two possible translations of the formula *to
ti en einai* are both to be maintained: "what it was for X to be" refers to
the presupposed *hypokeimenon*, and "being what it was" to the attempt to
catch hold of it, to make subject and essence coincide. The movement of
this coincidence is time: "being what it was for X to be." The division of

being worked by this apparatus serves to put being in motion, to give it time. The ontological apparatus is a temporalizing apparatus.

In the tradition of Western philosophy, this temporality internal to the subject will be thought, beginning with Kant, in the form of autoaffection. When Heidegger writes: "time as pure self-affection forms the essential structure of subjectivity" (Heidegger 7, §34), one must not forget that, through the implied dative and the past tense "was" of the *ti en einai*, Aristotle had already marked out in the *hypokeimenon*, in the *subiectum*, the logical place of what was to become modern subjectivity, indissolubly linked to time.

1.14. Aristotle does not explicitly thematize the introduction of time into being implied in the *ti en einai*. However, when he explains (*Metaphysics*, 1028a 30ff.) in what sense *ousia* is *protos*, primary and first of all, he distinguishes three aspects of this priority: according to the concept (*logoi*), according to knowledge (*gnosei*), and according to time (*chronoi*). According to the concept, insofar as in the concept of each thing is necessarily present that of *ousia*; according to knowledge, because we know something better when we know what it is. The explication of the third aspect of priority, the temporal, seems to be lacking. In place of this, Aristotle formulates the task of thought in these terms: *kai de kai to palai te kai nyn kai aei zetoumenon kai aei aporoumenon, ti to on, touto esti tis he ousia* ("and indeed the question that, both now and of old, has always been raised, and always been the subject of doubt, is what *ousia* is"). If, according to the logical sequence, this sentence should be read as a clarification of the temporal sense of the *protos*, then it cannot refer solely to a chronological time. Here Aristotle implicitly cites a passage from Plato's *Sophist*, which Heidegger was to use as the epigraph of *Being and Time*: "you have long known what you meant when you said 'being'; we, by contrast, at one time [*pro tou*] knew it, but now we have fallen into an aporia [*eporekamen*]" (Plato, *Sophist* 244a). Being is that which, if one seeks to catch hold of it, divides itself into a "before" (*palai*), in which one believed one could comprehend it, and a "now" (*nyn*) in which it becomes problematic. The comprehension of being, that is to say, always entails time. (Heidegger's posing again of the problem of being is a revival of Aristotelian ontology and will remain up to the very end in solidarity with its aporias.)

1.15. In the ontological apparatus that Aristotle leaves as an inheritance to Western philosophy, the scission of being into essence and existence

and the introduction of time into being are the work of language. It
is the subjectivation of being as *hypokeimenon*, as that-on-the-basis-of-
which-one-says, that puts the apparatus in motion. On the other hand,
as we have seen, the *hypokeimenon* is always already named by means of a
proper name (Socrates, Emma) or indicated by means of a deictic "this."
The *ti en einai*, the "what it was for Emma to be Emma," expresses a relation that runs between the entity and its being in language.

By abstracting itself from predication, the singular being recedes into
a past like the *sub-iectum* on the presupposition of which every discourse
is founded. The being on-the-basis-of-which-one-says and that cannot
be said is always already pre-supposed, always has the form of a "what it
was." In being presupposed in this way, the subject maintains at one and
the same time its priority and its inaccessibility. In the words of Boehm,
it is inaccessible due to—and at the same time, despite—its priority and
has its priority despite—and at the same time due to—its inaccessibility
(Boehm, R., pp. 210–211). But as Hegel comprehends in the dialectic of
sense certainty that opens the *Phenomenology*, this past is precisely what
allows one to grasp in language the immediate "here" and "now" as time,
as "a history." The impossibility of saying—other than by naming it—
singular being produces time and dissolves into it. (That Hegel thought
the absolute as subject and not as substance means precisely this: that
the presupposition, the "subject" as *hypokeimenon* has been liquidated,
pushed into the background as presupposition, and at the same time captured, by means of the dialectic and time, as subject in a modern sense.
The presuppositional structure of language is thus revealed and transformed into the internal motor of the dialectic. Schelling will instead
seek, without success, to arrest and neutralize linguistic presupposition.)

1.16. Now one can understand what we meant when we affirmed that
ontology constitutively has to do with anthropogenesis and, at the same
time, what is at stake in the Aristotelian ontological apparatus—and
more generally, in every historical transformation of ontology. What is
in question, in the apparatus as in its every new historical declination, is
the articulation between language and world that anthropogenesis has
disclosed as "history" to the living beings of the species *Homo sapiens*.
Severing the pure existent (the *that it is*) from the essence (the *what it is*)
and inserting time and movement between them, the ontological apparatus reactualizes and repeats the anthropogenetic event, opens and defines

each time the horizon of acting as well as knowing, by conditioning, in the sense that has been seen as a historical *a priori*, what human beings can do and what they can know and say.

According to the peculiar presuppositional structure of language ("language," according to Mallarmé's precise formulation, "is a principle that develops itself through the negation of every principle"—that is, by transforming every *archè* into a presupposition), in anthropogenesis the event of language pre-supposes as not (yet) linguistic and not (yet) human what precedes it. That is to say, the apparatus must capture in the form of subjectivation the living being, presupposing it as that on the basis of which one says, as what language, in happening, presupposes and renders its ground. In Aristotelian ontology, the *hypokeimenon*, the pure "that it is," names this presupposition, the singular and impredicable existence that must be at once excluded and captured in the apparatus. The "it was" (*en*) of the *ti en einai* is, in this sense, a more archaic past than every verbal past tense, because it refers to the originary structure of the event of language. In the name (in particular in the proper name, and every name is originally a proper name), being is always already presupposed by language to language. As Hegel was to understand perfectly, the precedence that is in question here is not chronological but is an effect of linguistic presupposition.

Hence the ambiguity of the status of the subject-*hypokeimenon*: on the one hand, it is excluded insofar as it cannot be said but only named and indicated; on the other hand, it is the foundation on the basis of which everything is said. And this is the sense of the scission between "that it is" and "what it is," *quod est* and *quid est*: the *ti en einai* is the attempt to overcome the scission, by including it in order to overcome it (in the medieval formula *quod quid erat esse*, this attempt to hold together the *quod est* and the *quid est* is obvious).

ℵ. According to the axiom formulated by Aristotle in the *De anima* 415b 13 ("Being for the living is to live," *to de zen tois zosi to einai estin*), what holds on the level of being is transposed in a completely analogous way onto the level of living. Like being, so also "living is said in many ways" (*pleonachos de legomenou tou zen*; ibid., 413a 24), and here as well one of these senses—nutritive or vegetative life—is separated from the others and becomes a presupposition to them. As we have shown elsewhere, nutritive life thus becomes what must be excluded from the city—and at the same time included in it—as simple living from politically qualified living. Ontology and politics correspond perfectly.

1.17. The ontological paradigm in Plato is completely different. He is the first to discover the presuppositional structure of language and to make this discovery the foundation of philosophical thought. This is the passage—as celebrated as it is misunderstood—from the *Republic* (511b) in which Plato describes the dialectical method:

> Then also understand the other subsection of the intelligible, I mean that which language itself [*autos ho logos*] touches on [*haptetai*] with the potential of dialoguing [*tei tou dialegesthai dynamei*]. It does not consider these presuppositions [*hypotheseis*, etymologically, "that which is placed under, at the foundation"] as first principles [*archai*] but truly as presuppositions—as stepping-stones to take off from, enabling it to reach the non-presupposed [*anypotheton*] toward the principle of everything and, having touched on it [*hapsamenos autes*], it reverses itself and, keeping hold of what follows from it, comes down to a conclusion without making use of anything visible at all but only of ideas themselves, moving on from ideas to ideas and ending in ideas.

The power of language is that of transforming the principle (the *archè*) into a presupposition ("hypothesis," what the word presupposes as its referent). It is what we do in every non-philosophical discourse, in which we take it for granted that the name refers to something non-linguistic that we therefore treat as a given, as a principle from which we can start in order to acquire knowledge. The philosopher, by contrast, is someone who, conscious of this presuppositional power of language, does not treat hypotheses as principles but rather as presuppositions, which are to be used only as footholds to reach the non-presupposed principle. Contrary to a recurrent equivocation, it is important to understand that the method that Plato describes has nothing to do with a mystical practice but is situated rigorously within language (as he says beyond all possible doubt, what is in question is what "language itself touches on with the potential of dialoguing"). That is to say, it is a matter, once we have recognized the presuppositional power of the *logos*—which transforms the reality that thought must reach into the given referent of a name or a definition—of recognizing and eliminating the presupposed hypotheses (Plato also calls them "shadows"—*skiai*—and "images"—*eikones*; *Republic* 510e) by making use of language in a non-presuppositional, which is to say non-referential, way (for this reason, when it is a question of confronting decisive problems, Plato prefers to have recourse to myth and joking).

This is to say that the philosopher frees language from its shadow and, instead of taking hypotheses for granted, seeks to ascend from these latter—namely, from denotative words—toward the non-presupposed principle. The idea is this word freed from its shadow, which does not presuppose the *archè* as given but seeks to reach it as what is not a presupposition to name and discourse. Philosophical discourse always and only moves by means of these non-presuppositional words, emancipated from their sensible referent, which Plato calls ideas and which, significantly, he always expresses by means of the name in question preceded by the adjective *autos* ("itself"): the circle itself (*autos ho kyklos*; *Epistle* VII, 342a–b), the thing itself. The thing itself, which is in question here, is not an obscure non-linguistic presupposition of language but what appears when, once we have taken note of its presuppositional power, language is liberated from its shadow. The "circle itself" is the word "circle" insofar as it signifies not simply the sensible circle but itself insofar as it signifies it. Only by extinguishing the presuppositional power of language is it possible for it to let the mute thing appear: the thing itself and language itself (*autos ho logos*) are in contact at this point—united only by a void of signification and representation. (A word can signify itself only by means of a representative void—hence the metaphor of "touching": the idea is a word that does not denote but "touches." That is to say, as happens in contact, it manifests the thing and at the same time also itself—recall, in *De anima* 423b 15, the definition of touching as that which perceives not "through a medium" [*metaxy*] but "at the same time [*ama*] as the medium.")

In this sense, Kojève is right to say that philosophy is the discourse that, in speaking of something, also speaks of the fact that it is speaking about it. It goes without saying, however, that this awareness does not exhaust the philosophical task, because with this starting point, different and even opposed perspectives are possible. While according to Plato thought must seek to reach the non-presupposed principle by eliminating the presuppositional power of language, Aristotle—and Hegel after him—by contrast put at the basis of their dialectic precisely the presuppositional power of the *logos*.

1.18. Ontology thinks being insofar as it is said and called into question in language, which is to say that it is constitutively *onto-logy*. In the Aristotelian apparatus, this is manifested in the scission of being into a *hypokeimenon*, something lying-at-the-base (the being named or indicated of a singular existent, insofar as it is not said of a subject but is a presupposition for every discourse) and that which is said on the presupposition of it. In the *ti en einai* Aristotle seeks to think their identity, to articulate together what had been divided: being is what *was* always presupposed in language and by language. That is to say: existence and identity coincide—or can coincide by means of time.

In this way, the task that the apparatus, as historical *a priori*, opens up for the history of the West is both speculative and political: if being is divided in the *logos* and nevertheless not irreducibly split, if it is possible to think the identity of the singular existent, then upon this divided and articulated identity it will also be possible to found a political order, a city and not simply a pasture for animals.

But is there really such an articulation of being—at once divided and unitary? Or is there not rather in the being so conceived an unbridgeable hiatus? The fact that unity entails a past and demands time in order to be realized renders it no less problematic. In the *ti en einai*, it has the form: "what it *was* each time for this existent to be (or live)." The past measures the time that necessarily insinuates itself between the existentive determination of being as *hypokeimenon* (this existent, the *tode ti*, the first subject) and its persevering in being, its being identical to itself. Existence is identified with essence by means of time. That is to say, *the identity of being and existence is a historical-political task.* And at the same time, it is an archeological task, because what must be grasped is a past (a "was"). History, insofar as it seeks to gain access to presence, is always already archeology. The ontological apparatus, insofar as it is chronogenic, is also "historicogenic"; it produces history and preserves it in motion, and only in this way can it be preserved. Politics and ontology, ontological apparatuses and political apparatuses are in solidarity, because they have need of one another to actualize themselves.

ℵ.   In this sense, being and history are in solidarity and inseparable. Here the Benjaminian axiom holds according to which there is a history of everything of which there is a nature (which is to say, being). Taking up once more the Aristotelian thesis according to which "nature is on its way toward itself," one can say that history is the way that nature takes toward itself (and not, as in the ordinary conception, something separate from it).

1.19. At the end of *Homo Sacer I*, the analogy between the epochal situation of politics and that of ontology had been defined on the basis of a radical crisis, which assails the very possibility of distinguishing and articulating the terms of the ontologico-political apparatus:

> Today *bios* lies in *zoè* exactly as essence, in the Heideggerian definition of Dasein, lies (*liegt*) in existence. Schelling expressed the outermost figure of his thought in the idea of a being that is only what is purely existent. Yet how can a *bios* be only its own *zoè*, how can a form of life seize hold of the very *haplos* that constitutes both the task and the enigma of Western metaphysics? (Agamben 4, pp. 210–211/188)

Existence and essence, existentive being and copulative being, *zoè* and *bios* are today completely pulled apart or have just as completely collapsed into one another, and the historical task of their articulation seems impossible to carry out. The bare life of the *homo sacer* is the irreducible hypostasis that appears between them to testify to the impossibility of their identity as much as their distinction: "what it was for X to be or live" is now only bare life. In the same way, the time—at once chronological and operative—in which their articulation was achieved, is no longer graspable as the *medium* of a historical task, in which being could realize its own identity with itself and human beings could secure the conditions of their human, which is to say, political, existence. The Aristotelian ontological apparatus, which has for almost two millennia guaranteed the life and politics of the West, can no longer function as a historical *a priori*, to the extent to which anthropogenesis, which it sought to fix in terms of an articulation between language and being, is no longer reflected in it. Having arrived at the outermost point of its secularization, the projection of ontology (or theology) onto history seems to have become impossible.

ℵ. For this reason, Heidegger's attempt to grasp—in perfect coherence with precisely his Aristotelian model—being as time could not but fail. In his interpretation of Kant, Heidegger affirms that time, as form of internal sense and pure autoaffection, is identified with the I. But precisely for this reason, the I cannot grasp itself in time. The time that, with space, was to render experience possible is itself inexperienceable; it only measures the impossibility of self-experience. Every attempt to grasp the I and time therefore entails a discrepancy. This discrepancy is bare life, which can never coincide with itself, is always in a certain sense missed and never truly lived. Or, if one prefers, to live is precisely this impossibility of self-experience, this impossibility of making one's existing and one's being coincide. (This is the secret of James's novels: we can live only because we have missed our life.)

The precept "become what you are," in which one could express the intention of the Aristotelian apparatus (with the slight correction: "become what you were"), insofar as it entrusts to time a task that it can never bring to an end, is contradictory. According to Kojève's suggestion, it should rather be reformulated in this way: "become what you can never be" (or "be what you can never become"). It is only at the price of madness that Nietzsche, at the end of the history of metaphysics, believed he was able to show in *Ecce Homo* "*wie man wird, was man ist,*" "how one becomes what one is."

§ 2   Theory of Hypostases

2.1. An epochal change in the ontology of the West happens between the second and third century of the common era and coincides with the entry into the vocabulary of first philosophy of a term almost completely unknown to classical thought (completely absent in Plato, in Aristotle it appears only in the originary sense of "sediment, remainder"): *hypostasis*. In a study devoted to the semantic history of the term, Dörrie has shown how this word, which appears for the first time in Stoic ontology, beginning with Neoplatonism progressively spread as a true and proper *Modewort* (Dörrie, p. 14) in the most diverse philosophical schools to designate existence, in place of the classical *ousia*. In its character as a "fashionable term," it constitutes a striking antecedent of the analogous diffusion of the term "existence" in twentieth-century philosophies. At the end of the ancient world, there is a proliferation of hypostasis in the philosophico-theological vocabulary just as, in the philosophical discourse of the twentieth century, there will be a proliferation of existence. But while in twentieth-century existentialism a priority of rank of existence over essence corresponds to the lexical priority, in late-ancient thought the situation of hypostasis is more ambiguous: indeed, the presupposition of the term's diffusion is an inverse process through which being persistently tends to transcend existence. To the displacement of the One beyond being there thus corresponds an equal heightening of its being given existence and manifesting itself in hypostases. And to this change of the historical *a priori* there corresponds, in every sphere of culture, an epochal transformation whose importance—insofar as we perhaps still live under its sign—we are still not in a position to measure. Being (as is obvious today) tends to exhaust itself and disappear, but in disappearing, it leaves in its place the residual pure effectiveness of hypostasis, bare existence as such. Heidegger's thesis according to which "essence lies [*liegt*] in existence" is, in this sense, the final—almost sepul- chral—act of hypostatic ontology.

2.2. The originary meaning of the term *hypostasis*—alongside that of "base, foundation"—is "sediment" and refers to the solid remainder of a liquid. Thus, in Hippocrates *hyphistamai* and *hypostasis* designate, re- spectively, the depositing of urine and the sediment itself. In Aristotle the term appears only in this sense, to signify the sediment of a physiological process (*On the Parts of Animals*, 677a 15) and excrement as the remainder of nourishment (ibid., 647b 28, 671b 20, 677a 15). We must reflect on the fact that it is precisely a term that originally meant "sediment" or "re- mainder" that became the key term or *Modewort* to express a fundamen- tal ontological concept: existence. In an exemplary article, Benveniste has suggested that in the presence of identical morphemes provided with completely different meanings, one must seek out above all whether there exists a use of the term able to lead back to unity the apparent diversity of the meanings (in this way, as we will see, he was able to explain the two apparently irreconcilable meanings of *trepho*: "to nourish" and "to curdle"; Benveniste, pp. 290–293/249–253).

It will thus be opportune to ask ourselves from this perspective which meaning of *hyphistamai* and *hypostasis* allows one to make sense of an ap- parently incomprehensible semantic development of the term. In reality, the diversity of meanings is easily explained. Once one considers that, if the verb originally means "to produce a solid remainder"—and thus, "to reach the solid state, to be given a real consistency"—the development toward the meaning of "existence" is perfectly natural. Existence here ap- pears—with a radical transformation of classical ontology—as the result of a process by means of which being is reified and given consistency. Not only does the originary meaning not disappear in the new one, but it al- lows us to understand how a school of thought, namely, Neoplatonism, which persistently sought to displace the One beyond being, could never conceive existence except as "hypostasis," that is, as the material remain- der and sediment of that transcendent process.

2.3. While the *hypokeimenon*, the simple existent, was for Aristo- tle the first and immediate form of being, which had no need for a foundation because it was itself the first (or ultimate) subject, on the presupposition of which every comprehension and every predication becomes possible, already the Stoics had instead made use of the terms *hyphistasthai* and *hypostasis* to define the passage from being in itself to existence. Thus, they designated with the verb *hyphistasthai* the mode of being of incorporeals, like the "sayable," time, and the event, while they made use of the verb *hyparchein* in reference to the presence of bodies. There is an incorporeal dimension of being, which has the nature of a process and an event, and not of a substance. Further developing this tendency, hypostasis now becomes something like an operation—conceptually if not genetically second—by means of which being is actualized in existence. For this reason Dio of Prusa can write: "every being has a hypostasis" (*pan to on hypostasin echei*; Dörrie, p. 43). Being is distinct from existence, but this latter is at the same time something (once again the image of sediment is illuminating) that being produces and that moreover necessarily belongs to it. There is no other foundation of existence than an operation, an emanation, or an effectuation of being.

א.   That the new hypostatic terminology, which takes form beginning with the Stoics, was initially hardly comprehensible, is clearly shown in a passage from Galen, in which he defines as "pedantry" the distinction that some philosophers make between being and hypostasis: "I say that it is pedantry [*mikrologia*] to distinguish according to category being and hypostasis [*to on te kai to hyphestos*]" (Galen 2, II, 7). But that this "pedantry" instead corresponds to a real change in the way of conceiving being appears just as clearly if one compares two occurrences—distant from one another and, moreover, symmetrically inverse—of the new terminology. Philo, who as always anticipates tendencies that will be confirmed only with Neoplatonism and Christian theology, thus writes that "only God exists [or subsists] in being" (*en toi einai hyphesteken*); Alexander of Aphrodisias by contrast, to define the mode of existence of single beings as opposed to categories and ideas, makes frequent use of the expression "to be in hypostasis [in existence]" (*einai en hypostasei*; Dörrie, p. 37). Beings are in the mode of hypostasis, of existence, but there is also a non-hypostatic being. On the one hand, there is the God of Philo, in whom it is not possible to distinguish being and existing (or, to paraphrase a modern expression, whose existence lies in his essence); on the other hand, there are the multiple beings in which being lies and remains in existence. "To exist in being" and "to be in existence": here begins the process that will lead to an ever greater pulling apart of being from existence and of the divine from the human.

2.4. If it is true that Plotinus is the creator of the Neoplatonic doctrine of hypostases (Dörrie, p. 45), it was Porphyry who technicalized the term "hypostasis" in his teacher's thought, already in the titles that he gives to essays 1 ("On the Three Principal Hypostases") and 3 ("On the Cognitive Hypostases") of the fifth *Ennead*.

Neoplatonic ontology seeks to combine the Aristotelian apparatus of scission and articulation of being with the genuinely Platonic impulse toward a beyond of being. The result is that being becomes a field of forces held in tension between a principle beyond being and its realizations (or emanations) in existence, called precisely hypostases. For the horizontality of Aristotelian ontology there is substituted a decisively vertical conception (high/low, transcendence/hypostasis). In Plotinus and his disciples, the term "hypostasis" thus designates the intellect, the soul, and all things that gradually proceed from the One and the hypostases that it has produced: "So it goes from the beginning to the last and lowest, each remaining behind in its own place, and that which is generated taking another, lower rank with respect to its generator" (V, 2, 2).

The use of the expressions "to have a hypostasis" (*hypostasin echein*, eighteen occurrences) or "to take a hypostasis" (*hypostasin lambanein*, at least six occurrences) in the *Enneads* is significant. Existence is not the originary given but something that is "taken" or produced ("Hypostases are generated [*hai hypostaseis ginontai*] while remaining immobile and invariant principles"; III, 4, 1). But it is precisely the relationship between the principle beyond being and the multiplicity of hypostases that emanate from it that constitutes the problem that Plotinian ontology never manages to unravel.

In essay 4 of the fifth *Ennead*, which bears the title "How Things That Are from the First Are after It, or on the One," the problem displays its most aporetic formulation. On the one hand, there is an immobile and immutable principle, and, on the other, there are the "existences" that proceed from it by means of an enigmatic *proodos*, a "going out" that is not yet a creation and that therefore does not correspond in any way to an act or movement of the One:

> If, then, something comes into being while the One abides in itself, it comes into being from it when it is most of all what it is. When, therefore, the One abides in its own proper way of life [*en toi oiekeioi ethei*], that which comes into being does come into being from it, but from it as it abides unchanged. . . . But

how, when the One remains unchanged, is something generated in act [*ginetai energeia*]? There is, on the one hand, the being in act of being [*ousias*] and, on the other, the being in act [which derives] from the essence of each thing. The first is each being insofar as it is in act, and the second derives from the first and must in everything be a consequence of it and be different from it. As in fire there is a heat which is the fullness of its essence and a heat that is generated from it when the fire exercises the activity that is native to its essence in abiding unchanged as fire. So it is also for the principle, abiding in its own proper way of life, a being in action [*energeia*] that is generated by its perfection, having taken a hypostasis [*hypostasin laboua*] from a great power, indeed the greatest of all, adds to the being and the essence [*eis to einai kai ousian elthen*]. For that principle is beyond being [*epekeina ousias*]. (V, 4, 2, 21–39)

2.5. Perhaps never as in this passage does the impossibility of expressing the new hypostatic paradigm with the vocabulary of Aristotelian ontology appear so obvious. The Aristotelian apparatus of the division of being (being/existence, potential/act) is still standing, but the relation between the two counterposed terms changes completely. While in Aristotle essence was what resulted from a question turned toward grasping existence (what it was for X to be), existence (hypostasis) is now in some way a performance of the essence.

The *hypokeimenon*, the subject lying at the base in the Aristotelian apparatus, which had to be taken up by means of the *ti en einai* as the being that it *was*, is now separated and enters into an infinite process of flight: on the one hand, an ungraspable and unsayable principle, which tends to proceed or regress beyond being; on the other hand, its hypostatic emanations into existence. Aristotelian ontology has been irrevocably damaged: between the presuppositional subject in flight beyond being and language and the hypostatic multiplicities there does not seem to be any passage.

It is this contradictory tension—which is also that between Platonic eternity and Aristotelian time—that Plotinus and Porphyry's theory of hypostases tries in vain to unravel. The introduction of time into being, implicit in the Aristotelian apparatus, thus takes the form of a circular movement of hypostases that come out of being (*proodos*) in order to make a return to it (*epistrophè*).

א. In the *Elements of Theology*, Proclus systematizes the Plotinian hypostatic ontology. On the one hand (Proclus 1, prop. 27), he forcefully emphasizes that the productive principle does not produce the hypostases because of a lack or by means of a movement (it is significant that Proclus here uses the expression "to confer a hypostasis"—*ten hypostasin parechetai*—but *parecho* means etymologically "to have alongside") but only due to its fullness and superabundance. On the other hand, he seeks to find a *medium* or a common element between the producer and the hypostases by means of the concepts of similarity (*homoiotes*; prop. 28–29), participation (*metexis*; prop. 23–24, 68–69), and irradiation (*ellampsis*; prop. 81). "For if the participant is separate [from the participated], how can it be participated by that which contains neither it nor anything from it? Accordingly a potential or irradiation, proceeding from the participated to the participant, must link the two" (ibid.). Here one clearly sees how the Neoplatonic attempt to reconcile a genuinely Platonic conceptuality (participation, similarity) with the categories of Aristotelian ontology necessarily produces aporias, which the concepts of irradiation and procession vainly seek to resolve.

ℵ. The concept of hypostasis has a particular importance in Gnosticism. Plotinus reproved the Gnostics for multiplying hypostases (*Ennead* II, 9, 2 and 6). In effect, in the testimonies that have been preserved, according to the Gnostics, from preexisting principles, also called "Abyss" or "Protofather," there gush forth a multiplicity of "existences" or hypostases, which seem to parody or disseminate the three Plotinian hypostases. What defines the Gnostic hypostases is that they are in some way incarnate in a personal entity, which is inscribed in a genealogy and of which something like a myth is recounted. Thus, one of the hypostases, Sophia (which corresponds to the soul, according to some; Hadot 2, p. 214) suffers a "passion" and falls, departing from the Father. According to what Hippolytus recounts, from the passion of Sophia are produced "hypostatic substances" (*ousias hypostatas*; "from fear, the psychical substance, from pain the material, from aporia the demonic, from conversion and supplication the return"). Here we can obviously see that the hypostases are the place of a subjectivization, in which an ontological process that goes from the preexistent to existences finds something like a personal figure. In the Gnostic hypostases, the Aristotelian "subject" (the *hypokeimenon*) enters into a process that will lead to its being transformed into the modern subject.

2.6. The Neoplatonic doctrine of the hypostases attains its decisive development in trinitarian theology. Although the term *hypostasis* had been used by the Arians to emphasize the difference between the Son and the Father, it prevailed—in a definitive way only from the time of Athanasius—as a way to express the ontological relation implicit in the doctrine of the Trinity: "one God in three hypostases" (*heis theos en trisin hypostasesin*). In this context, the term *hypostasis*, up until then often confused with *ousia*, is clearly distinguished from the latter: the three hypostases or existences refer to one sole substance.

From this moment, the history of the concept of hypostasis is entangled with that of the burning conflicts in which a terminological divergence was transformed into heresy, a lexical scruple into an anathema. Through an alternating succession of disputes and councils, secessions and condemnations, the formula that emerged in the end to designate the Trinity against Arians and Sabellians, Nestorians and Monophysites is: *mia ousia, treis hypostaseis.*

The problem was complicated because the Latin West (which had used the term *substantia* to translate *ousia*) preferred to speak of "persons" rather than hypostases—in the decisive formulation of Tertullian: *tres personae, una substantia.* Thanks also to the patient mediating work of the Chalcedonian fathers, the contrast between the Latin Church and Greek Church was resolved with the First Council of Constantinople. The distinction between hypostasis and person was recognized as purely terminological. "We Greeks," writes Gregory of Nazianzus,

> piously say one *ousia* in three hypostases, the first word expressing the nature of divinity and the second the triplicity of the individuated properties. The Latins think the same, but due to the restrictions of their language and the poverty of their vocabulary, they cannot distinguish the hypostasis from the substance and hence make use of the term "person.". . . This slight difference of sound was taken to indicate a difference of faith . . . they had the same sense, and were in no way different in doctrine. (Gregory Nazianzen, Oration 21, 35)

‎‎ℵ.‎ That the trinitarian hypostases must not be understood simply as potentials or habits in the single divine substance but as hypostatic existences is clearly affirmed by Gregory of Nyssa. In the trinitarian economy, he writes, what are in question are not simply faculties or potentials of God (his word—*logos*—or his wisdom), but "a potential that has been given hypostatic existence according to the essence" (*kat' ousianyphestosa dynamis*; Gregory of Nyssa, p. 273). The Neoplatonic word is here transferred immediately to the trinitarian hypostases, something of which the Eastern fathers like Cyril were perfectly aware: "When the Platonists acknowledge three principal hypostases and affirm that the divine substance extends to three hypostases or when at times they use the same term 'trinity,' they are in agreement with the Christian faith and nothing would be amiss for them if they wanted to apply the term 'consubstantiality' to the three hypostases to conceive the unity of God" (Picavet, p. 45).

2.7. Dörrie has observed that in Athanasius the term *hypostasis* does not mean simply "reality" but rather "realization" (*Realisierung*): "it expresses an act, not a state" (Dörrie, p. 60). God is one unique being, one sole *substantia*—in itself unknowable, like the One of Plotinus—which gives itself reality and existence in three singularly determinate hypostases, three aspects (*prosopa*) or manifestations (which, as we have seen, will become three "persons" in the Latin West).

In the West, starting with Boethius's definition, which was to meet with enormous success, the concept of person was defined as *naturae rationalis individua substantia*, "individual subsistence of a rational nature" (*natura*, on the other hand, was *unamquemque rem informans differentia specifica*, "the specific difference that informs any singular thing whatsoever," according to Boethius). In this way, the problem of the trinitarian persons or hypostases was conjoined with the philosophical problem of individuation, of the way in which the divine nature as much as the creaturely become an *individua substantia*, individuate or "personify." (The "personal" character of the modern subject, this concept that has proven so determinative in the ontology of modernity, has its origin in trinitarian theology and, by means of the latter, in the doctrine of the hypostasis, and it has never truly emancipated itself from it.)

In this way, hypostasis—which in Neoplatonism seemed to imply, even if only apparently, a priority of essence over existence—enters into a slow process of transformation that in modernity will ultimately lead to a priority of existence. In the Latin formula *tres personae, una substantia*, person (*prosopon*, mask and at the same time face) entails, as we have seen, that the divine substance manifests itself, gives itself form and effective reality in an individuated existence. In the foreground here is the *oikonomia*, the activity by means of which the divine nature is revealed in this way to itself and to creatures. That Christian ontology—and thus modern ontology, which derives from it—is a hypostatic ontology means that it is eminently effectual or operative: as Dörrie reminds us, *hypostasis* means not so much reality as realization.

While in the Aristotelian apparatus singular existence was the presupposed given, in hypostatic ontology it is now something that must be achieved or effectuated. In the *Isagoge*, Porphyry had systematized the Aristotelian doctrine of the categories from the logical point of view in the form of a tree or scale (*klimax*) that descended from the highest genus—substance—through generic and specific differences down to the individual. It has been suitably observed that, while the Eastern Fathers entered into the tree from the bottom, that is, by starting from the concrete existent individual to ascend toward species and genus and finally to substance, the Latin Fathers entered into the tree from above and then proceeded *per descensum* from the general to the individual, from substance to genus to species to finally touch upon singular existence. By starting from the universal, they are for that reason drawn to then seek the formal reason or the principle that is added to essence to determine its individuation. The suggestion—certainly useful to understand the two different mental attitudes with regard to the problem of existence— is inexact to the extent that the relation between essence and existence (at least in the theological model) entails or should always imply both movements. But what is essential is that ontology now becomes a field of forces held in tension between essence and existence, in which the two concepts, in themselves theoretically inseparable, tend nevertheless to pull apart and draw back together according to a rhythm that corresponds to the growing opacity of their relation. The problem of individuation—which is the problem of singular existence—is the place where these tensions reach their greatest point of stretching apart.

2.8. In Augustine's reflections, the problem of the relation between essence and existence appears as the problem of the relation between the Trinity in itself and the singular divine persons. In book VII of the *De Trinitate* he thus asks whether the name God and the attributes like "good," "wise," or "omnipotent" should be referred to the Trinity in itself (*per se ipsam*) or rather to each singular divine person (*singula quaeque persona*; Augustine 2, VII.1). As has been observed (Beckmann, p. 200), the true problem here is how it is possible to reconcile the unity of the essence with the plurality of the three persons. It is in order to respond to this difficulty that Augustine pronounces a thesis that has determined for centuries the way in which we have thought relation: "Every essence that is called something by way of relationship is also something besides the relationship" (*Omnis essentia quae relative dicitur est etiam aliquid excepto relativo*). To prove this thesis, he has recourse to the example—also decisive for the history of philosophy—of the relationship between master and slave. If a man is defined as "master," this entails that he is in relation with a slave (and vice versa). But the essence of this man is not exhausted in any way in his being-master but presupposes first of all his essence as a man. Only insofar as the master is a man can he enter into the master/slave relation and be said in a relative mode. As being-human is the substantial presupposition of being-master, so being-God, the Trinity in itself—such seems to be the implication—is the essential presupposition of the singular divine persons.

The analogy is imperfect, however, because the trinity of the persons inheres originally in the Christian God and it is therefore not possible, as in the case of the man with respect to the master, to think a God who was not always triune. Hence the decisive importance of the formula *excepto relativo*: it is to be read according to the logic of the exception that we have defined in *Homo Sacer I* (Agamben 4, pp. 21–22/17–19): the relative is at once included and excluded in the absolute, in the sense that—according to the etymology of the term *ex-ceptio*—it has been "captured outside," which is to say, included by means of its exclusion. The relativity and the singularity of the persons have been captured in the unitary essence-potential of God, in such a way that they are both excluded and included in it. Hence the disputes, contradictions, and aporias that have so profoundly marked the history of the Church and that trinitarian theology has never managed to resolve. In order to achieve this, it would have to abandon the conceptuality of Aristotelian and Neoplatonic ontology with an eye toward another ontology.

‎‭‮ℵ‬.   In Heidegger the difference between essence and existence, thematized as the "ontological difference" between Being and beings, becomes the crucial problem of philosophy. The ninth section of *Being and Time*, to which we owe the characterization of Heidegger's thought as an "existentialism," claims: "The essence of Dasein lies in its existence" (Heidegger 1, p. 42/67). Even if Heidegger insistently emphasizes that the concept of existence that is in question here is not that of traditional ontology, he himself speaks, with regard to Dasein, of a "priority of existence" (ibid., p. 43/68).

In later works, metaphysics is defined by means of the forgetting of the ontological difference and the priority of beings over Being. In the outline of the history of metaphysics contained in §259 of the *Beiträge zur Philosophie* (published in 1989 but composed between 1936 and 1938), metaphysics is defined by means of the priority of beings: it is "the thinking that thinks Being as the Being of beings, departing *from beings* and returning *back to them*" (Heidegger 9, p. 426/336). The final phase of the history of metaphysics is characterized by the retreat from and abandonment by being (*Seinsverlassenheit*):

> Beings then appear in that way, namely as objects and as things objectively present, as if Being were not . . . the abandonment of beings by being means that Being con-

ceals itself in the manifestness of beings. And Being itself is essentially determined as this self-withdrawing concealment. . . . Abandonment by Being: the fact that being is abandoning beings, is leaving them to themselves, and thus is allowing them to become objects of machination. (Ibid., pp. 112–115/88–91)

Here Aristotelian ontology is declined toward a hypostatic ontology. Beings, abandoned by Being, are something like a Neoplatonic or Gnostic hypostasis that, incapable of *epistrophe* toward the One that has produced it, now occupies the stage of the world alone.

We owe to Levinas a coherent and explicit development of Heideggerian ontology in a hypostatic direction. In *De l'existance à l'existant,* forcing the concept of Dasein, he defines as a hypostasis the passage from the impersonality of the "there is" (*il y a*) to the emergence of a simple individual existence, which is not yet a subject or a consciousness (Levinas 2, p. 75/65).

Here, in a decidedly hypostatic ontology, the connection that unites essence to existence and Being to beings seems, as in Gnosticism, to break. Heidegger's thought starting from the *Beiträge zur Philosophie* is the attempt—grandiose but certainly unsuccessful—to reconstruct a possible unity and, at the same time, to think beyond it. But the only way to resolve the aporias of hypostatic ontology would have been the passage to a modal ontology. It is an ontology of this type that we will seek to develop in the pages that follow.

§ 3   Toward a Modal Ontology

3.1. Perhaps never as in the correspondence between Leibniz and Des Bosses did the inadequacy of the Aristotelian apparatus in accounting for singularity emerge with such clarity. What is in question in the correspondence is the problem of how one can conceive the unity of composite substances, in such a way that this or that body does not seem to be only an aggregate of monads but can be perceived as a substantial unity.

"If a corporeal substance," writes Leibniz in response to the announcement of a dissertation *De substantia corporea* that Des Bosses is about to send him, "is something real over and above monads, as a line is taken to be something over and above points, we shall have to say that corporeal substance consists in a certain union, or rather in a real unifier superadded to monads by God [*uniente reali a Deo superaddito monadibus*]." Leibniz calls this absolute principle (*absolutum aliquid*) that confers its "unitive reality" on monads, and without which bodies would be mere appearances and only the monads would be real, a "substantial bond" (*vinculum substantiale*). "If that substantial bond of monads were absent, then all bodies with their qualities would be only well-founded phenomena, like a rainbow or an image in a mirror—in a word, continuous dreams that agree perfectly with one another" (Leibniz I, pp. 435–436/225–227; letter of February 15, 1712).

In the text attached to the letter, Leibniz seeks to specify the nature of the substantial bond, defining it as a "more perfect relationship" that transforms a plurality of simple substances or monads into a new substance:

> God not only considers single monads and the modifications of any monad whatsoever, but he also sees their relations, and the reality of relations and truths consists in this. Foremost among these relations are duration (or the

order of successive things), situation (or the order of co-existing), and inter-course (or reciprocal action). . . . But over and above these real relations, a more perfect relation can be conceived through which a single new substance arises from many substances. And this will not be a simple result, that is, it will not consist in true or real relations alone; but, moreover, it will add some new substantiality, or substantial bond [*aliquam novam substantialitatem seu vinculum substantiale*], and this will be an effect not only of the divine intel-lect but also of the divine will. This addition to monads does not occur in just any way; otherwise any scattered things at all would be united in a new substance, and nothing determinate would arise in contiguous bodies. But it suffices that it unites those monads that are under the domination of one monad, that is, that make one organic body or one machine of nature [*unum corpus organicum seu unam Machinam naturae*]. (Ibid., pp. 438–439/233)

3.2. What is in question in the substantial bond is the problem of what allows one to consider as one sole substance such and such a "natural machine," this "horse" or that "dog" (p. 457/269), this or that human body, independently of the union of the body with the soul. The problem becomes more complicated, moreover, since the Jesuit theologian Des Bosses is interested above all in understanding how one can understand the unity of the body of Christ that is in ques-tion in eucharistic transubstantiation (*hoc est corpus meum*). The idea of the natural bond allows Leibniz to propose an elegant solution of the problem.

If what defines the singular existence of the body is the substan-tial bond, it will not be necessary for transubstantiation to destroy the monads of the bread and wine. It will be sufficient that the bond of the body of Christ eliminates and substitutes for the prior bond that defined the aggregate of those substances. The phrase "this is my body" therefore does not designate the monads but the bond that actualizes their unity:

> I think that your transubstantiation can be explained by retaining monads (which seems to agree better with the reason and order of the universe), but with the substantial bond of the body of Christ added by God to unite the monads of the bread and wine substantially, while the former substantial bond is destroyed, and with it its modifications or accidents. Thus there will remain only the phenomena of the monads of the bread and wine, which would have been there, if no substantial bond had been added to their monads by God. (p. 459/273)

Against Des Bosses, who persists in conceiving what makes up the unity of the singular substance as a special form of accident, which he calls "absolute accident" or "substantial mode," Leibniz affirms that the singularity of the composite substance does not result from a modification of the monads nor can it be something like a mode or accident that would exist in them as in a subject. The bond, though not a preexisting form, constitutes the unity of the body as a substantial reality.

3.3. It is certainly not by chance that Leibniz has recourse to the term "bond" to express what the ontological vocabulary called the unity of substance. The Franciscans, who from the start had affirmed that the living body is already given in the embryo in its unity and perfection, even before the soul is united to it, had called this principle *forma corporeitatis*. With respect to the term *forma*, so closely linked to Aristotelian ontology, the term *vinculum* emphasizes the fact that Leibniz was seeking to think something different, even if (or perhaps precisely for this reason) he is constrained to add the adjective "substantial." It has been observed that Leibniz uses the term "bond" in his minor mathematical work to designate a sign that combines numerical or algebraic symbols into a unity. If in certain cases the union is contingent and the bond can be dissolved, in others, like the square root of two, it is indissoluble from the quantities that it modifies, which therefore exist solely by means of the bond. But the term *vinculum* had behind it other traditions well known to Leibniz as well, like those of law and magic, in which the bond is an active potential, which indissolubly joins what in nature is divided.

In every case it is certain that the terminological choice, just like the tenacity with which Des Bosses opposes it, corresponds to the attempt, which as we will see is not always successful, to think in a new way the categories of the Aristotelian ontology.

3.4. What is at stake in the debate is at this point clear: how to think the unitary nature of corporeal singularity not as an appearance but as something real. For Des Bosses, the unity of the body (such and such a horse, such and such a boy: the primary substance in Aristotle) is nothing but a mode or an accident emanating from the substantial form. For Leibniz, it is by contrast a question of a new principle that is still of the order of substance but that obliges us to rethink substance in unheard-of terms, even at the risk of contradicting its traditional definition.

Just as in the *Monadology* the relation of the monads among themselves was expressed with the metaphor of a "living mirror" (every monad is *un miroir vivant* of the whole universe), the image that progressively clears a path for Leibniz to define the peculiar nature of the bond is the acoustico-musical one of an echo. The letter that closes the exchange is, in this sense, a sort of miniature treatise that seeks to define, not without difficulties and contradictions, a new vocabulary for ontology.

Des Bosses insisted on conceiving the substantial bond as a mode. Leibniz affirms that it cannot be a mode, because it neither alters nor modifies the monads ("sive ponas, sive tollas, nihil in monadibus mutatur"; p. 516/367). Furthermore, even though both the substantial form and the material of the composite are contained in the bond, this latter does not link the monads in an essential way (*essentialiter*) but solely in a natural way (*naturaliter*). In Leibnizian vocabulary, this means that the bond "demands [*exigit*] the monads, but does not essentially imply [*involvit*] them, because it can exist without the monads and vice versa." Hence the appropriateness of the metaphor of the echo: just as the soul is the echo of external things and is nonetheless *independent* of them, so also "it is an echo of monads, according to its constitution, with the result that once posited it demands monads, but does not depend on them [*exigit monades, sed non ab iis pendet*]" (p. 517/369).

What the image of the echo seeks to express is this curious intimacy and, at the same time, exteriority between the bond and the monads. If the body were something other than an exterior echo of the monads, it would be a different substance and not their bond; if it were something inherent to them, it would be one of their accidents or a modification. And yet the idea of an echo as something substantial is certainly paradoxical. Indeed, if it is possible to conceive of sounds (monads) without an echo, we cannot see how it is possible to think an echo without the sounds that precede it. For this reason Leibniz is constrained to hypothesize something like an "originary echo" (*echo originaria*; p. 519/375), or an echo that is a "source of modifications" (*fons modificationum*; p. 504/351). And to the objection that an echo cannot be a principle of action, he responds that "a body returning an echo is a principle of action" (p. 503/349).

And when Des Bosses suggests that in saying "this body," as Christ does in the Eucharist, the demonstrative pronoun does not necessarily refer to the individuality of the substance (*individualitatem substantiae*) but to that of appearances (p. 454/261), Leibniz responds that "when it is said, 'this is my body'. . . we do not designate monads by either 'this' or 'body'. . . but the substance arising or composed through substantial bonds" (p. 459/273). What constitutes the unmistakable singularity of such and such a body is not appearance but reality; it is not only a mode but a substance—and yet a substance that does not have any consistency other than the purely acoustical one of an echo. But it is an echo that is, so to speak, active, which demands the monads but does not depend on them and in fact acts on them as something originary that harmonizes and constitutes them into a unity.

3.5. Many times in the dispute the two interlocutors give the impression that their divergence is more terminological than real ("Whether one can call beings modes or accidents is a question of words," p. 453/259; "You are free to call the bond that gives reality to the composite a substantial mode," p. 515/363). But in truth, what is at stake concerns precisely the way in which one must understand the fundamental concepts of scholastic ontology. For the Jesuit, who firmly holds to the traditional concept, what Leibniz understands as the unity of the singular body can only be a mode or an accident, even if of a special type (for this reason defined, through forcing the concept, as "substantial"); for Leibniz, bodies are neither modes nor accidents but substances (Boehm, A., p. 32); it is, however, a matter of forcing the traditional concept of substance in an unforeseen direction. On the one hand, what he wants to grasp is still the Aristotelian prime substance, "what it was for X to be." On the other hand, this no longer appears to him as a presupposition but as an active force, which results almost *a posteriori* from the monads as an echo and therefore cannot be easily subsumed under the concept of substance, of something that lies beneath and at the base.

It has been proposed that we interpret the novelty of Leibniz's conception by means of a primacy of relation over being (Fremont, p. 69). This means, however, on the one hand, diminishing the novelty, because Scholastic theology had already unreservedly affirmed the priority of the trinitarian relation (the "economy") over substance in God. On the other hand, it contradicts what Leibniz actually says, which, in the letter that concludes the correspondence, seems to distinguish the bond from the relations that run between the monads: "The orderings," he writes, "or relations that join two monads are not in one monad or the other, but in both equally and at the same time; that is, really in neither, or only in the mind thinking this relation, unless you add a real bond, or something substantial, which is the subject of the common predicates and modifications, that is, those joining them together" (Leibniz 1, p. 517/371). If the bond is a relation, however, it does not, like a mode, have a subject in which it inheres: it is "something absolute, and therefore substantial" (*absolutum aliquid adeoque substantiale*; ibid., p. 433/227).

3.6. In the stubbornness with which the Jesuit holds to his "substantial mode" and the philosopher to his "bond," what was really going on was a difficulty concerning the historical situation of ontology. The philosophy that in the background for Leibniz was late Scholasticism, which had found perhaps its most complete expression in Francisco Suárez's *Disputationes metaphysicae* (it has been rightly said that Suárez is the "manual" in which Leibniz reads the *Schola Peripatetica*). Here the tradition that identified the object of metaphysics in the *ens qua ens* had reached a point at which the relation between essence and existence, which Aristotle believed he had resolved in the *ti en einai*, had become the central problem of ontology. If in God essence and existence coincided, in creatures—and markedly in bodies and composite substances—it was rather a matter of thinking their relation, which was anything but taken for granted. While in his investigation of *ousia* Aristotle began with a primacy of the *hypokeimenon*, which is to say, of the singular existent, Scholasticism by contrast, developing a Neoplatonic gesture, began with a primacy of essence, from which it was a matter of deducing existence. But once the being of creatures was defined starting from essence, the principle that worked out its determination in singular existence became extremely problematic. Singular existence remains the *experimentum crucis* of philosophy, which it cannot avoid and in which it unceasingly threatens to make shipwreck.

3.7. It is in the attempt to define the relation between essence and existence that philosophers and theologians run aground in a series of distinctions as subtle as they are inconclusive. These reach their critical mass in the problem of the principle of individuation. In the Scholastic tradition from Aquinas and Scotus up to Cajetan and Suárez, everyone conceded that individual existence added something to essence: the divergences concerned how to define their difference and their relation. Two positions here seem to be definitively opposed: the first, represented by Henry of Ghent, denies every real difference between essence and existence (or, as it is also expressed in Scholastic theology with regard to individuation, between common nature and the supposition). The other, exemplified by Thomas Aquinas, affirms that in material creatures essence and existence, nature and supposition differ *realiter*.

Between these two positions, a third progressively imposed itself, which, developing one of Scotus's theses, found perhaps its most complete formulation in Suárez. According to this doctrine, in created things the individual adds to the common nature something really distinct from it, and yet singular existence is not distinct from essence like one thing is distinct from another (*ut res a re*). Already Aquinas, despite affirming that existence really differs from essence, specified that "just as we cannot say that running itself runs, so we cannot say that existence exists" (Aquinas 6, *lectio* 2). If singular existence cannot be simply reduced to essence, it can never be separated from this latter like one thing from another, one essence from another essence. It is to define this peculiar status of singular existence that the concepts of "mode" and "modal difference" arise.

3.8. The theory of modes finds its first thematic elaboration in Giles of Viterbo. Already in his early treatise on *The Degrees of the Forms*, Giles observed that in extended matter, extension (which admittedly belongs to the category of quantity) is not some other thing with respect to the matter (which belongs to the category of substance) but only its mode of being (*modus se habendi*):

> Others believe that the extension of matter differs from extension as quantity and is a certain different thing from matter, in such a way that matter and its extension would be two really [*realiter*] different things. . . . It is, however, preferable to say that the passive extension of which they speak is not a category in itself but falls into the essence of the matter and is a certain mode of being [*quendam modum se habendi*], which belongs to the matter insofar as it is conjoined to quantity. (Trapp, pp. 14–15)

The same concept of mode is used by Giles to explain eucharistic transubstantiation, in which the accidents of the bread and wine that remain as such after transubstantiation, deprived of substance, acquire the mode of a substance, while the human nature of Christ, insofar as it is united to the divine Word, despite being a substance, acquires the mode of an accident:

In the sacrament of the Eucharist, since the accidents are here without substance . . . what here according to the thing is an accident, has a certain mode of substance [*habet quendam modum substantiae*], insofar as it belongs to them to exist for themselves; and in the human nature of Christ, the nature, although according to the thing it is a substance, nevertheless insofar as it inheres to the Word in its entirety, acquires the mode of an accident [*habet quendam modum accidentis*]. (Trapp, p. 17)

According to Giles, "being for itself" (*per se esse*) and "inhering" (*inesse*) do not express the essence of substance and accident but only a mode of their being ("Inhering does not mean the very being of the accident but a certain mode of its being [*modus essendi eius*], just as being for itself does not mean the very being of substance but a certain mode of being of substance"; p. 18). "Being for itself" and "being in another" (*esse in alio*), these two fundamental terms of Aristotelian ontology, differ modally (*modaliter*) and not essentially. The Spinozan definition of substance as "what is in itself" (*quod in se est*) and of mode as "what is in another" (*quod in alio est*) becomes more comprehensible if one places it against the background of Giles's conception of modal difference.

It is in the treatise *On the Composition of the Angels* that the concept of mode finds its proper place in the context of the problem of individuation as a means of defining the relationship between common nature (essence) and supposition (singular existence). Against Henry of Ghent, Giles maintains that nature and supposition really differ (otherwise *homo* and *humanitas* would be the same thing) but that this difference has a modal and not essential character (*suppositum non dicit essentiam aliam a natura*); otherwise we could not predicate, as we in fact do, the humanity of the human being. The common nature (humanity) differs from the supposition (the singular human) like potential from act, like a *res* not yet modified differs from the same *res* once modified (pp. 24–25).

In accordance with an ambiguity that will durably mark the concept of mode, the difficulty here concerns the very status of mode, which is both logical and ontological. Nothing is more instructive, from this perspective, than the tenacious polemic concerning Giles's concept of mode that takes place between Godfrey of Fontaines and Thomas of Argentina. According to the former, that something really differs from another and is nonetheless not another thing is logically contradictory. "If mode," writes Godfrey, is a nothing [*nihil*] or absolutely non-existent [*absolute non ens*], then by means of it one thing cannot differ from another, not only really but not even according to reason. If it is instead something, it will be a certain being. If it is a being, or is such only in the mind, then it cannot constitute any real difference with respect to the thing outside the mind. Or else it is a true being for itself outside the mind, and in this case, either it is perfectly identified with the nature and then, since the nature is that mode, it is not possible that it constitutes a difference; or else it is a being different from the nature, absolutely, and then it can only be really or relatively composed with it, and then the relation between substance and its accidents will be something real, which is false. . . . (p. 36)

Thomas of Argentina's response constitutes perhaps the most subtle attempt to define the peculiar place of mode between being and nothing, between the logical and the ontological:

The mode is nothing, but it is something that expresses the nature itself: and thus a thing, which is to say a nature. And moreover, mode and nature do not mean the nature AND something [*natura et aliquid*] but the nature itself diversified BY MEANS OF something [*per aliquid*], which is a real mode, because it really follows on a variation made in the nature itself. (Ibid.)

℘. Eucharistic transubstantiation produces the paradox of accidents without substance (the bread and wine under transubstantiation are accidents without substance) and of a substance without accidents (the body of Christ). It is a matter of a problem that radically calls into question the categories of ontology and, by obligating him to rethink the traditional definition of accident, suggests to Giles his recourse to the notion of mode.

3.9. Between real distinction—which is in things—and that of reason—which is in the mind—Scotus had introduced the formal distinction, which was something less than a real distinction and more than a distinction of reason. Scotus's disciples had inscribed in this category the distinction between essence and existence, nature and supposition, quantity and substance. Picking up on a tradition that had been in the process of consolidating from Giles to Cajetan, Suárez calls this distinction modal and constructs upon it a true and proper theory of modes:

I maintain that there is, in created things, a distinction—which is actual and corresponds to the nature of things before any operation of the mind—that is not as great as that which intervenes between two things or completely distinct essences. It can be called real, because it derives from things and not from an extrinsic intellectual denomination; yet to better distinguish it from the real distinction, we can call it . . . more properly a modal distinction, because it always runs between a thing and its mode. (Suárez 2, p. 255)

The modal distinction entails that the reality of created things is defined not only by the entity, which Suárez calls substantial or radical, but also by "real modes, which are something positive and grasp entities by themselves, conferring on them something that is outside essence in its totality, insofar as it is individual and existent in nature" (ibid.). Among these real modes, Suárez lists the inherence to substance of a quantity or quality, the union of substantial form with matter (this is Leibniz's problem in the correspondence with Des Bosses) and "existence or personhood with respect to the common nature" (p. 256).

Mode is therefore an affection of the thing, "which determines its ultimate state and its reason for existing, without, however, adding to it a new essence but only by modifying it" (ibid.). Once again, it is a question of defining a paradoxical state of being, insofar as it is totally deprived of an essence of its own and yet is really distinct from that to which it adheres as a mode, namely, by modifying it.

> Thus this mode as we have defined it is really distinguished from the thing of which it is a mode . . . but is not properly distinguished from that of which it is a mode like one thing from another thing [*ut res a re*]; it is distinguished by a lesser distinction, which is more properly called modal. Lesser, both because mode, considered in itself, is not properly a thing or entity and therefore cannot be distinguished as one thing from another; and also because this mode is thus intimately [*intimite*] joined to the thing of which it is a mode, which no power could ever make to exist without the latter, as if its conjunction implied an identity. . . . (p. 257)

The idea of mode was invented to render thinkable the relation between essence and existence. These are distinct and at the same time absolutely inseparable. Their relation is, however, asymmetrical, because, as Suárez specifies a little later, in the modal distinction, "the separation of one element from the other is not reciprocal, which means that one extreme can remain without the other, but not vice versa . . . and this defines modal being, which cannot subsist by itself nor be separated from that of which it is a mode" (p. 263). That is to say, in the distinction a hierarchy is implied that, if one conceives existence as a mode, entails a reversal of the

Aristotelian priority of the *hypokeimenon* in favor of essence. Precisely this priority of essence, however, renders individuation, which is to say, the passage from essence to existence, incomprehensible. If one conceives singular existence as the mode of a preexistent essence—which Suárez avoids doing—individuation becomes incomprehensible. If existence is in fact absolutely inessential and adds to essence nothing but a modification, if essence can be without its mode, why and by virtue of what is essence to be brought into existence or be modified?

3.10. The elegance with which Scotus resolves the problem of individuation found its legendary form in the concept of haecceity. Scotus conceives individuation as the addition to common nature or form not of another form or essence but of an *ultima realitas*, an ultimacy of the form itself. Singular existence does not, that is to say, add anything to the common form other than a haecceity (or ecceity [It., *eccoità*]—as one, thinking of the Christological *ecce homo*, could translate Scotus's ingenious term *haecceitas*). "Ecceity" is not something other than the essence but only its ultimate reality, in which it can be offered up for display (for this reason Suárez will see in it a mode). In form or mode there is not a principle *by virtue* of which it is individuated: here one has only an ultimacy *of* form, the extreme modification that allows one to say: behold the man, or else: this is my body. But for this reason it is necessary, according to Scotus, that the common form or nature be in itself indifferent to any singularity whatsoever or, as Scholastics will repeat after him, that "it is not repugnant to it to be supposed with any singularity."

Here one clearly sees that once essence and existence have been divided (or, as happens in Christian theology, their coincidence is admitted only in God), it is then necessary to seek in essence what permits—or at least does not prevent—its individuation. This is the meaning of the indifference or non-repugnance of which Scotus speaks. As Avicenna had already said, *equinitas est equinitas tantum*, horsehood is only horsehood; it is indifferent to both generality and singularity and has in itself nothing that is opposed to being individuated in haecceity.

Radicalizing and at the same time critiquing Scotus's position, Suárez affirms that essence does not need any ulterior principle to be individuated. Certainly it is possible to distinguish individual existence from common essence, but this difference is not modal, as for Scotus, but purely a difference of reason, and it does not have a foundation in the thing distinct from its essence. For this reason, to the question whether "being this or that being (that is, singular existence) adds some mode . . . distinct from the being itself, so that this certain being, or substance, according to the nature of the thing is formally distinguished, insofar as the substance adds a mode, which is not included in the concept of being" (p. 82), Suárez responds negatively. The essence of a singular being already contains its possible individuation and does not have need of any real supplement, not even the inessential adjunct that is mode.

3.11. Even if one thinks the relation between essence and singular existence on the model of the Aristotelian relation between potential and act, possible and actual, individuation remains problematic. What drives the possible to produce itself in ecceity, to actually realize itself in act in this or that singularity?

In a famous passage from Book Theta of the *Metaphysics* (1047a 24–25), Aristotle laid out (but not resolved) the problem in the enigmatic formulation according to which: "That is potential for which, if the act of which it is said to have potential is verified, nothing will be potential not to be." If essence and existence have been divided like potential and act, nothing is more problematic than their relation.

For this reason, just as Scotus had to suppose in essence an indifference or non-repugnance to singularity, so also Suárez must postulate in essence or common nature an *aptitudo* to being produced in a certain singular existence. "The intrinsic principle from which the individual difference of a substantial form derives is the very essence of the form, to the extent to which it has a certain aptitude to inform matter" (p. 185). In the same sense, insofar as it is possible, essence "has a certain aptitude, or non-repugnance, to being produced in a certain being" (Courtine, p. 302). "The aptitude of possible things to exist is nothing other than a certain non-repugnance on their part and, on the part of the cause, signifies a potential to produce them" (ibid., p. 319).

Aptitude is certainly more than indifference or non-repugnance; but what it can consist in, what inclines or disposes an essence to individuation, is not easy to explain once one thinks, as does Suárez, that it already contains all it needs and that the difference between essence and existence is only one of reason. When Leibniz, several decades later, defines existence as a "demand" of essence and, in the correspondence with Des Bosses, writes that the bond that defines the existence of composite substances "demands the monads, but does not essentially entail them," it is with this same problem that he is seeking to contend.

It is not surprising, then, that in another passage of the *Disputations*, Suárez must have recourse to the concept of expression to somehow account for the conceptual difference between essence and existence. The determination of being in singular existence, he affirms, must not be understood according to the mode of a composition but only as a more expressive mode of conceiving the entity (*per modum expressioris conceptionis*). Essence and singular existence are not, that is to say, two really separate concepts, but they differ only "insofar as one is more determinate than the other [*unus est magis determinatus quam alio*] . . . insofar as in one the thing is conceived more expressively [*per unum expressius concipitur res*]" (Suárez, p. 101).

What this supplement of expressivity is with respect to Scotus's haecceity or Giles's mode, Suárez does not specify. But it is certain that this passage is like a passing of the baton that announces the decisive gesture with which Spinoza will write that particular things "are nothing but modes wherein the attributes of God find expression in a definite and determinate way" (Spinoza 2, 1, prop. 25, cor.).

3.12. At this point we can better understand what is at stake in the correspondence between Leibniz and Des Bosses with which we began. The stakes are genuinely ontological. It is a matter of thinking the singular existence of a body, that is, of something that the development of ontology had rendered problematic. Des Bosses takes up the position, for him more reassuring, of the modal tradition: existence is not an entity but a mode of being, which does not add to the essence anything but a modification. He agrees with Leibniz that the monads on their own can only constitute an aggregate and that they are therefore in need of a bond: but this bond is only a mode of the dominant monad (that which gives form to the body, the essence), and not, as Leibniz maintains, something absolute and substantial. Against this modalistic conception of the unity of an existent body, another tradition had reacted, which objected to the *modistae* that "it is absurd that there should be any formally distinct entity by means of which form is united to matter; therefore, it is absurd that there should be a modal union" (Boehm, A., p. 51).

Leibniz—who had made his debut in 1663 with a dissertation *On the Principle of Individuation*, in which he had made his own the thesis of

Suárez according to which "every individual is individualized by means of the totality of its essence"—now introduces, in order to explain the unity of composite substance, something more substantial than a mode or a difference of reason, which, taking up again a concept already widely used by the Scholastics, he calls *vinculum substantiale*, substantial bond. But what is in question here is not whether the principle of individuation is a mode or a substantial bond so much as a transformation of the fundamental concepts of ontology. What is decisive, from this perspective, is the concept of demand, which Leibniz had already elaborated at the end of the 1680s in his text *De veritatis primis*. The bond is an active principle, which "demands the monads," just as, in the text on the first truths, existence is defined as "a demand of essence." The "nonrepugnance" of Scotus and the "aptitude" of Suárez have now become a demand. Existence is not a mode of essence or a difference of reason alone: it is a demand.

It is this transformation of ontology that we will seek to follow and to develop from a new perspective.

3.13. Some decades before the years in which the correspondence unfolded, the model of a modal ontology had been elaborated by a philosopher with whom Leibniz maintained a relation that has rightly been defined as "a mixture of admiration and repugnance" (Friedmann, p. 277): Spinoza. And it is certain that this aspect of Spinoza's thought seemed to the majority of his contemporaries just as unacceptable as his supposed atheism, if Bayle, subjecting him to ridicule, could write that "in Spinoza's system, those who say that the Germans killed ten thousand Turks express themselves badly, unless they mean: God, modified in the Germans, killed God modified in ten thousand Turks" (ibid., p. 187). In any case, whether Bayle was right or wrong, the problem of the relation between substance and the modes is one of the cruxes of Spinozan hermeneutics.

Spinoza's radical ontological thesis is well known: "Nothing exists except substance and modes" (*praeter substantias et modos nihil existit*; Spinoza 2, 1, prop. XV, proof.). It has been stated that Spinoza's novelty does not consist in the definition of substance but in that of modes; and nevertheless, even though in the *Cogitata* (1, 1) he had distinguished modes from accidents ("The accident is only a mode of thought and exists solely with respect to thought, while the mode is something real"; Spinoza 3, p.

120), the definition of the modes closely follows the traditional definition of accidents: the modes are "affections of substance; that is, that which is in something else and is conceived through something else" (*in alio est, per quod etiam concipitur*; Spinoza 2, 1, def. 5). (With a significant variation, the corollary of proposition XXV defines particular things as "affections of the attributes of God; that is, modes wherein the attributes of God find expression in a definite and determinate way.")

One of the problems with which Spinoza's interpreters must always contend is the fact that substantially new thoughts are expressed in the terminology of the philosophy of his time. As we have seen, the latter, which derived from the Scholastic tradition, distinguished between essence and existence and between common nature and individual supposition and made use of the concept of mode to think these differences. It has quite appropriately been noted that in Spinoza the problem of the principle of individuation is never mentioned (Wolfson, p. 392). This means that the substance/modes relationship is posed for him in an entirely different way from the way that Scholasticism had thought the passage from common nature to the individual supposition or from potential to act. He most likely chose the term "mode" because, without simply signifying a difference of reason, it implied the least possible difference with respect to substance. Modes are in the substance, are in God (*quod omnia in Deo sint*; Spinoza 2, 1, app.), and yet the relation, at once of identity and of difference, between the multiple, particular, finite things and the unique substance remains problematic, at least as long as we are constrained to think it in terms of the concepts of traditional ontology.

In point of fact, in what sense is one to understand the affirmation that modes "are in another," if they are only affections and modifications of substance? Is it here a question of a real difference or of a logical difference? The human being (Spinoza 2, 2, prop. X and cor.) is a mode, and as such it is in God and expresses God's nature. The human being's nature "is constituted by definite modifications of the attributes of God," and yet "the being of substance does not pertain to the essence of the human being." The interweaving of reality and mode of thinking, of ontological and logical, which Spinoza proposed to clarify, here reaches its greatest density. Are the modes affections of God or of God's attributes (the attributes are—as per definition 4, part 1—"that which the intellect perceives of substance as constituting its essence")? Precisely with respect to the substance/modes relationship, one could say that Spinoza did not manage to resolve the ambiguity between ontological and logical that the Aristotelian apparatus had left as a legacy to Western philosophy.

ℵ. The concept of mode—insofar as it seeks to think the coincidence or indifference of essence and existence, potential and act—carries with it an ambiguity, so that in the history of philosophy, it is presented now as a logical concept (one prefers to speak then of "modality" or modal logic), now as an ontological concept. The ambiguity is still evident in Kant, according to whom the categories of modality express the relation of an object with our faculty of knowing and yet "do not have only a logical meaning . . . but are to pertain to things and their possibility, actuality, or necessity" (*Critique of Pure Reason*, A219, B627). It is possible to see in this dual nature of modalities something more than an echo of the peculiar nature of the formal distinction according to Scotus (which is more than a distinction of reason and yet less than a real distinction) and of mode according to Suárez, which is real, but not like a thing (the modes *non sunt formaliter entia*). The undecidability of logic and ontology is, in this sense, consubstantial with the concept of mode and must be brought back to the constitutive undecidability of Aristotelian onto-logy, inasmuch as the latter thinks being insofar as it is said. This means that the ambiguity of the concept of mode cannot be simply eliminated but must rather be thought as such.

It is possible that the dispute between philosophy inappropriately defined as continental and analytic philosophy has its root in this ambiguity and can therefore be resolved only on the terrain of a rethinking of the theory of modes and of the categories of modality.

3.14. A possible paradigm to explain the relationship between substance and modes, between *natura naturans* and *natura naturata*, is the emanationist paradigm. Scholars have shown the analogies between the Spinozan model and that which the Neoplatonic tradition had transmitted to philosophers and Jewish Kabbalists. God is cause of the modes not through an act of creation but through the very necessity according to which, in the emanationist model, the intellects and hypostases emanate from the first cause. The analogy is misleading, however. In the emanationist paradigm, that things proceed from God means that they really go out from God and become separated from God. In Spinoza, by contrast, the modes remain in God:

There is no such thing as the procession of the finite from the infinite in Spinoza. God or substance is to him an infinite logical crust which holds together the crumbs of the infinite number of the finite modes, and that crust is never broken through to allow the crumbs to escape or to emanate. Infinite substance by its very nature contains within itself immediate infinite modes, and the immediate infinite modes contain within themselves mediate infinite modes, and the mediate infinite modes contain within themselves the infinite number of finite modes. . . . (Wolfson, p. 398)

Bayle's ironic observation that God modified in the Germans kills God modified in ten thousand Turks, with the pantheistic implication that it suggests, was perhaps not so impertinent.

3.15. The problem of the ontological meaning of the difference between being and modes emerges with particular clarity in the relationship between *En-sof* and *sefiroth* in the Kabbalah. Scholem has brought to light the connections and divergences between Plotinus's One and the Kabbalists' *En-sof* (the "without end" or "Infinitely," given the originary adverbial character of the expression). But he saw with just as much clarity that the crucial question here is that of the identity or difference between the *En-sof* and the *sefiroth* (which correspond to Plotinus's hypostases). Like Plotinus's One, so also the *En-sof* is absolutely deprived of determinations or attributes (as such, it is called *belimah*, literally "without which," by the Kabbalists). What happens, then, in the passage from this "infinitely without which" to the *sefiroth*, each of which represents, like the hypostases in Plotinus, a property and a determination? The problem is made more pressing—the decisive leap or fracture is in fact situated here—in the relation between the *En-sof* and the first *sefirah* (which according to some is thought and according to others is will). If the *En-sof* and the first *sefirah* (or, more generally, the ensemble of the ten *sefiroth*) are essentially different, then between God and his emanations or words (as the Kabbalists also call them) an abyss is thrown open; if they are identical, the risk is the fall into pantheism.

Hence the strategic meaning of the nothing in the Jewish (and Christian) conception of creation ex nihilo: between the *En-sof* and the *sefiroth* there is the nothing (*'ayin*) and, in the words of the Kabbalist Azriel, in producing being from the nothing, God "has made his Nothing into his Being" (Scholem 1, p. 424). The problem reproduces itself, however, at this point as the problem of the relation (of identity or difference) between the *En-sof* and the nothing.

One could say that the early Kabbalists, who wanted to establish between the *En-sof* and the *'ayin* a difference that would be in name but not in nature, thereby in fact struck the first act out of the drama of the universe, which contains the dialectical exposition of the Whole. Hence the theory of the identity between the two terms gave rise to a pantheistic reversal: the creation out of nothing is only a cipher of the essential unity of all things with God. (Scholem 2, pp. 78–79)

The relation between the *En-sof* and the *sefiroth* seems always on the point of making shipwreck in an absolute identity or of shattering into a difference every bit as absolute.

א.   Herrera, in his treatise *The Gate of Heaven*, expresses this difficulty by saying that it is just as contradictory to affirm that the *En-sof*, as first cause, produces what it already is and contains in itself, as to affirm that it produces what it is not and does not possess:

> But if the First Cause contains everything in itself, because it is infinitely perfect, I wonder if, in the universal production of all things, it has given and communicated that which it is and has in itself, or that which it is not and does not have. If they should answer me claiming that it gave that which it is and has, I would argue that this cannot be, because that which it is and has is infinite and most simple, but everything that it gave is limited and somehow composite, and also because that which it is and has, because it is unproduced and unproducible, cannot be produced, and because nothing can or does produce the being and existence that it already has, because production is a passage from non-being to being. . . . But if they should say that it gave that which it is not and does not have, it would appear that there is something that the supremely and infinitely perfect one is not or does not have in itself, which is against what reason properly shows us. . . . It is left for us, then, to conclude, fitting together and in effect reconciling these two extremes and mediating between them like the prince of the Peripatetics who introduced potential between nothing and being in act, that the First Cause in a particular fashion produces what it is and has, and somehow produced what it is not and does not have. . . . (Herrera, p. 292)

It clearly results that the problem cannot be resolved from within the categories of traditional ontology and demands instead the passage to a different conceptuality.

3.16. What is in question here is nothing less than the metaphysical problem of the ontological difference between Being and beings. In the relationship between the *En-sof* and the *sefiroth*, between the One and the hypostases, it is a question of the ontological difference that, according to Heidegger, defines the metaphysics of the West. As sometimes happens, the cruciality and the difficulty of the decision is attested in Heidegger in an easily overlooked textual detail: the correction of one word in a sentence of the *Nachwort* added in 1943 to the fourth edition of *What Is*

Metaphysics? Where in the 1943 text we read: "It belongs to the truth of Being that Being certainly [*wohl*] is without beings, and that by contrast beings are never without Being," the fifth edition (1949) corrects the "certainly" into "never": "It belongs to the truth of Being that Being is never without beings and that beings are never without Being" (Heidegger 10, p. 102/233). While in the first version the connection between Being and beings is broken from the side of Being, which consequently appears as nothing, the second edition affirms that Being can never be separated from beings and is in some way identified with them, as the manifestation and unveiling of something is not essentially other with respect to what it manifests. Does the ontological difference mean a separation and a hiatus between Being and beings, or is what is in question here instead the unveiling and veiling of one and the same thing? What are beings for Being and Being for beings, if they can never be separated? The correction, left without a motivation, seems to indicate an oscillation and an uncertainty.

The problem is resolved—here as for the relationship between the *Ensof* and the *sefiroth* and between the One and its hypostases—if one poses it in terms of a modal ontology (assuming that one can still speak of an ontology in that case). Between being and modes the relationship is neither of identity nor of difference, because the mode is at once identical and different—or, rather, it entails the coincidence, which is to say the falling together, of the two terms. In this sense, the problem of the pantheistic risk is poorly posed. The Spinozan syntagma *Deus sive nature* does not mean "God = nature": the *sive* (whether it derives from the conditional and concessive *si* or the anaphoric *sic*) expresses the modalization, which is to say, the neutralization and disappearance of identity as much as difference. What is divine is not being in itself but its *sive*, its always already modifying itself and "naturing itself"—being born [It. *nascere*]—in the modes.

At this point, the problem is that of finding the concepts that allow us to correctly think modality. We are accustomed to think in a *substantival* mode, while mode has a constitutively *adverbial* nature, it expresses not "what" but "how" being is.

3.17. In Spinoza, there is a concept that furnishes the key for understanding the substance/modes relation beyond the contradictions of traditional ontology. It is that of the immanent cause, over which we have already had occasion to linger. Proposition XVIII of the first part states it in this way: "God is the immanent, not the transitive, cause of all things," which the demonstration states precisely by specifying that "there can be no substance external to God, that is, a thing which is in itself external to God. . . . Therefore God is the immanent, not the transitive, cause of all things." The reference to the Aristotelian concept of internal cause (*enyparchon*) as opposed to external (*ektos*; *Metaphysics*, 1070b 22) is pertinent, but it adds nothing to what seems to be a tautological explanation (God is internal or immanent cause, because there is nothing outside God).

We have shown (cf. above, part 1, §2.5) how Spinoza furnished a decisive indication on how one should understand this concept in the *Compendium grammatices linguae hebraeae*, in connection with a special form of the infinitive noun (the infinitive in Hebrew is declined like a noun), which expresses an action referred at once to the agent and the patient (which he exemplifies with the expressions "to constitute-oneself as visiting" or "to walk-oneself"). This form of the Hebrew verb corresponds exactly to the middle voice of the Greek or Latin verb, which we have evoked in connection with use (cf. above, part 1, §2.3).

The immanent cause is therefore an action in which agent and patient coincide, which is to say, fall together. This means that, in the modes, substance, to paraphrase Spinoza's example, "constitutes itself as existing" (or living, if, as is written in the *Cogitata*, ch. 6, God is life), "walking-itself" into existence. But this also means that, in order to think the substance/modes relationship, it is necessary to have at our disposal an ontology in the middle voice, in which the agent (God, or substance) in effectuating the modes in reality affects and modifies only itself. Modal ontology can be understood only as a medial ontology, and Spinozan pantheism, if it is a question of pantheism, is not an inert identity (substance = mode) but a process in which God affects, modifies, and expresses Godself.

In the first part of this book, we have called "use" a medial process of this kind. In a modal ontology, being uses-itself, that is to say, it constitutes, expresses, and loves itself in the affection that it receives from its own modifications.

א. The relation of immanent cause entails that the active element not cause the second but rather "express" itself in it. The concept of expression, to which

Gilles Deleuze quite fittingly drew attention and which we have seen to appear already in Suárez and Thomas of Argentina, runs through the whole of Spinoza's *Ethics,* and it refers both to the relationship between attributes and substance (every attribute "expresses eternal and infinite essence"; Spinoza 2, 1, def. 6) and to that between the modes and God ("Whatever exists expresses God's nature or essence in a definite and determinate mode"; prop. XXXVI, proof.). From the perspective that interests us here, the expression acts as a principle of transformation and neutralization of the concept of cause that, by abandoning all hierarchy between cause and effect, affirms the immanence of the expressed in the one expressing and of the passive in the active.

3.18. A correct understanding of the being/modes relationship allows us to resolve, or rather to transform into euporias, the aporias of the Aristotelian apparatus, above all that of the fundamental relation between being and language. What is at stake in the *ti en einai* was the identity-relation of a thing with itself, the relation between Emma and her being Emma ("what it was for Emma to be Emma"). But this relation is thinkable only because the entity has been named, only because Emma has a name, has been called Emma (cf. above, part 2, §1.15). That is to say, the ontological relationship runs between the entity and its being named, between Emma and her being-called Emma, between Emma and her "sayability" (this is what the Stoics called *lekton,* "sayable," and conceived as an attribute that is neither mental nor linguistic but ontological).

It is this relation that is also in question—without his being able to become aware of it, nor even less to resolve it—in Scotus's formal distinction. What he calls formal being or *formalitas*—distinguishing it from both real being and mental being—is, in truth, being-said. Such a being-said is not to be in any way conceived as a being in the mind, dependent on the knowing relation of a subject: it is instead the quality or character that the entity receives insofar as it is said, insofar as it has always already received a name and, as such, has always already been presupposed. Here the name is an ontological attribute of the thing and not an exterior label.

In developing in a new direction the Augustinian thesis according to which the relation exists in itself independently of the relative, Scotus defines the being of the relation as a form and the ontological status of this form as an *ens debilissimum.* The relation is something existent, but it is among all beings the weakest, because it consists solely in the mode of being of two entities ("relatio inter omnia entia est ens debilissimum, cum sit sola habitudo duorum"; *Sup. Praed.*, q. 25, 10; qtd. in Beckmann, p. 45). Precisely for this reason it is difficult to know ("et ita minimum cognoscibile in se"; ibid.): if we seek to grasp it—if we seek to grasp the being-said—it slips away between our hands. The *ens debilissimum* is being-said, is the name.

The error that Scotus repeats in Augustine's trail is that of conceiving essence in itself as something that must be a presupposition to its being said relatively and that can, as such, be considered and enjoyed independently of the relative. In the case of God's trinitarian essence, it is thus possible, according to Scotus, to desire and enjoy it without reference to one of the divine persons: "I affirm that it is possible for the human being in this world to enjoy the divine essence without enjoying the person [*frui essentia divina non fruendo persona*] and the proof is that, according to Augustine, if the essence is said in a relative way, it is not an essence, because every essence that is said in a relative way is something excluding the relative" (*Ox.*, 1, d. 1, p. 1, q 2., 31; qtd. in Beckmann, p. 205).

This would mean—and the error is in this way immediately refuted—that it is possible to love God without loving Christ or—if we translate it into the terms that interest us here—that it is possible to love Emma's identity with herself (her essence) without loving the singularity that is called Emma (her existence).

The whole problem of the relation between essence and existence, between being and relative being appears in a new light if it is placed in the context of a modal ontology. Essence cannot be without the relative nor being without the entity, because the modal relation—granted that one can speak here of a relation—passes between the entity and its identity with itself, between the singularity that has the name Emma and her being-called Emma. Modal ontology has its place in the primordial fact—which Aristotle merely presupposed without thematizing it—that being is always already said: *to on legetai . . .* Emma is not the particular individuation of a universal human essence, but insofar as she is a mode, she is that being for whom it is a matter, in her existence, of her having a name, of her being in language.

ℵ. It is from this perspective that it is necessary to consider Benjamin's intuition that, in an aphorism of *Short Shadows*, defines Platonic love as the love that "preserves and guards the name of the beloved" and for which "the existence of the loved one proceeds from her name like rays from a glowing nucleus" (Benjamin 2, p. 369/268). In this sense, love is a category of ontology: it is the care of that *ens debilissimum* that is the relation between a thing and its name, the assumption without reserve of the relation between the entity and its being in language.

3.19. Our goal here is not the interpretation of Spinoza or Leibniz's thought but the elaboration of categories that escape from the aporias of the ontological apparatus. Alongside the immanent cause, another precious concept from this perspective is that of demand, which we have already encountered in Leibniz. A rethinking of the categories of modality is not possible without a definition of the concept of demand. Not only existence but also possibility and contingency are transformed and modified through demand. That is to say, a definition of demand implies as a preliminary task a redefinition of the fundamental ontological categories, above all those of modality.

Leibniz thought demand as an attribute of possibility: *omne possibile exigit existere* ("everything possible demands to exist"; Leibniz 2, p. 176). What the possible demands is to become real, the potential—or essence—demands existence. For this reason Leibniz defines existence as a demand of essence: "Si existentia esset aliud quiddam quam essentiae exigentia, sequeretur ipsam habere quandam essentiam, seu aliquid novum superadditum rebus, de quo rursus quaeri potest, an haec essentia existat, et cur ista potius quam alia" (ibid.). Existence is not a *quid*, a something other with respect to essence or possibility; it is only a demand contained in essence. But how should we understand this demand? In a fragment from 1689, Leibniz calls this demand *existiturientia* (a term formed from the future infinitive of *existere*), and it is by means of it that he sees to render comprehensible the principle of reason. The reason why something exists rather than nothing "consists in the prevalence of reasons to exist [*ad existendum*] over those not to exist, that is, if it is permissible to say it with one word, of the demand to exist of essence [*in existiturientia essentiae*]" (Leibniz 3, pp. 1634–1635). The ultimate root of this demand is God ("for the demand of essences to exist [*existuritionis essentiarum*] it is necessary that there be a root *a parte rei* and this root can be nothing but the necessary entity, foundation [*fundus*] of essences and source [*fons*] of existences, namely God . . . if not in God and through God, essences could never find a way to existence [*ad existendum*]"; ibid.).

3.20. Demand is therefore a category of ontology. But this must entail a redefinition of the ontological categories that Leibniz refrained from undertaking. Thus, he attributes the demand to essence (or potential) and makes existence the object of the demand. That is to say, his thought still remains a tributary of the ontological apparatus, which divides essence and existence, potential and act in being, and sees in God their point of indifference, the "existificating" (*existificans*) principle, in which essence is made always already existent. But what is a possibility that contains a demand? And how are we to think existence, if it is nothing other than a demand? And what if demand is more original than the very distinction between essence and existence, potential and act? If being itself is to be thought starting from a demand, of which the categories of modality (possibility, contingency, necessity) are only the inadequate specifications, what must be decisively called into question?

3.21. According to Leibniz, the nature of demand is defined by the fact that it does not logically entail its object. That is to say, one says that a thing demands another, when if the first is, the other will also be, however, without the first logically implying it or containing it in its own concept and without it obliging the other to be. Demand is not a logical category. Thus, Leibniz can write in the correspondence with Des Bosses that "the substantial bond demands [*exigit*] the monads, but does not essentially entail [*involvit*] them, since it can exist without the monads and they can exist without it." To demand (*exigere*) is not to entail (*involvere*). (In the same sense Benjamin can write that the life of Prince Myshkin demands to remain unforgettable even when no one remembers it.) But what does it mean to demand that something be, without it necessarily being? Hence the peculiar ontological status of demand: it is not of the order of essence (it is not a logical implication contained in the essence), but neither does it coincide with actual reality. In the onto-logical, it consists of the threshold—the hyphen—that unites and at the same time separates the ontic and the logical, existence and essence.

Thus, demand is the most adequate category to think the ambiguity of logic and ontology that the Aristotelian apparatus has left as an inheritance to Western philosophy. It corresponds neither to language nor to the world, neither to thought nor to the real, but to their articulation. If ontology thinks being insofar as it is said, demand corresponds to the *insofar* that at once separates and unites the two terms.

The problem, however, is precisely that of how one is to think this articulation. It cannot be something like a substantial connection. For this reason it is at the same time real and not factual, neither simply logical nor completely real. If language and world stand opposite one another without any articulation, what happens between them is a pure demand—namely, a pure *sayability*. *Being is a pure demand held in tension between language and world*. The thing demands its own sayability, and this sayability is the meaning of the word. But in reality there is only the sayability: the word and the thing are only its two fragments.

3.22. An essence that becomes a demand is no longer a simple possibility or potential but something else. One could say that demand, in the sense that we have in mind, is a mode of potential. One would nevertheless therefore repeat the error of the Scholastics, who sought to reconcile mode with a conceptuality that is, in the last analysis, alien to it. Not only are possibility and essence transformed by demand; act and essence as well, invested with demand, lose their fixity and, contracting themselves on potential, demand to be possible, demand their own potential. *If existence becomes a demand for possibility, then possibility becomes a demand for existence.* Leibniz's posing of the problem of demand is here reversed: the possible does not demand to exist, but rather, it is the real that demands its own possibility. Being itself, declined in the middle voice, is a demand, which neutralizes and renders inoperative both essence and existence, both potential and act. These latter are only the figures that demand assumes if considered from the point of view of traditional ontology.

3.23. The problem of the *vinculum substantiale* must at this point be completely rethought. Being does not preexist the modes but constitutes itself in being modified, is nothing other than its modifications. One can then understand why Leibniz could write, in his still contradictory vocabulary, that the bond is something like an echo, "which once posited demands the monads." This proposition becomes intelligible only if one restores to the concept of demand its full ontological meaning. If demand and not substance is the central concept of ontology, one can then say that being is a demand of the modes just as the modes are a demand of being, on condition that we specify that demand here is neither a logical entailment nor a moral imperative. And this is also the only sense of the doctrine of the transcendentals: the being that is always already its modifications; it demands to be *unum, verum, bonum seu perfectum,* demands truth, justice, and perfection in the same sense in which Benjamin affirmed that justice is not a virtue but a state of the world.

3.24. It is here that the concept of *conatus* finds its proper place. When Spinoza defines essence as *conatus*, as "the force by which it endeavors to persist in its own being" (Spinoza 2, III, prop. 7: *Conatus, quo unaquaeque res in suo esse perseverare conatur, nihil est praeter ipsius rei actualis essentia*), he thinks something like a demand (in the scholium it says: *potentia sive conatus—conatus* is potential insofar as it is, in truth, a demand). The oxymoron "actual essence" shows the inadequacy of the categories of traditional ontology with respect to what is to be thought here.

The fact that the verb *conor* is in the middle voice shows once again its pertinence to the ontology that we are seeking to delineate here. If we propose to translate *conor* with "to demand" and *conatus* with "demand" ("The demand by means of which each thing demands to persevere in its being"), it is on the condition of not forgetting the medial nature of the process that is here in question: the being that desires and demands, in demanding, modifies, desires, and constitutes itself. "To persevere in its being" means this and nothing else.

א. In Plotinus's footsteps, in his treatise, Herrera identifies being (*ser*) and desiring (*querer*): "And as Plotinus learnedly proves, [the first Cause] is in itself no less what it wants than it wants what it is in itself" (Herrera, p. 264). On the other hand, to show how in the *En-sof* something like an impulse toward creation can be produced, he thinks this first movement as a delight, which he calls *sha'ashu'a*, "deleytable alteración": "And this emergence from itself, which is infinite, toward another which is finite, as it should be, is the *sha'ashu'a* or virtual movement by which (although in itself and entirely the same as the Cause) it appears to differ from itself and in effect be directed and inclined toward another . . . ." (ibid., p. 294). *Conatus* is in its most intimate nature desire and pleasure.

3.25. An adequate category for thinking *conatus* is that of *ductus*, which is defined as *tenor sub aliqua figura servatus*, "a tension preserved under a certain figure." This concept, which in some sense recalls the Stoic notions of *plege* and *tonos* (Cleanthes had spoken of a "*tonos* in the substance of all things"; *SVF*, fr. 497), which designate the internal tension of being, found an early application in the vocabulary of graphology, in which it designates the tension that guides the hand's gesture in the formation of letters.

It is according to this graphological paradigm that we can represent to ourselves the relationship between the demand—or tension—of substance and its modes. The modes are the figures in which substance preserves its demand (its *ductus*). Just as, in a line of writing, the hand's *ductus* passes continually from the common form of the letters to the particular traits that identify their singular presence, without it being possible at any point to draw a real boundary between the two, so also, in a mode—for example, a certain human face—human nature crosses over into existence in a continuous way and precisely this incessant emergence constitutes its expressivity. Common nature and singularity, essence and existence are only the two appearances generated by the incessant *ductus* of substance. And singular existence—the mode—is neither a substance nor a precise fact but an infinite series of modal oscillations, by means of which substance always constitutes and expresses itself.

3.26. In the formula that expresses the theme of ontology: *on he on, ens qua ens,* "being as being," thought has lingered on the first *ens* (existence, that something is) and on the second (essence, what something is) and has left unthought the middle term, the *qua,* the "as." The proper place of mode is in this "as." The being that is here in question is neither the *quod est* nor the *quid est,* neither a "that it is" nor a "what" but an *as.* This originary "as" is the source of modifications (the Italian *come,* "as," derives etymologically from *quo-modo*). Restoring being to its *as* means restoring it to its *com-moditas,* namely, to its just measure, to its rhythm and its ease (*commodus,* which in Latin is both an adjective and a proper noun, has precisely these meanings, and *commoditas membrorum* designates the harmonic proportion of the parts of the body). One of the fundamental meanings of "mode" is in fact the musical one of rhythm, just modulation (*modificare* means, in Latin, to modulate harmonically: it is in this sense that we have said that the "as" of being is the source of modifications).

Benveniste has shown that "rhythm" (*rhythmos*) is a technical term of pre-Socratic philosophy that designates form, not in its fixity (for this, Greek prefers to use the term *schema*) but in the moment in which it is assumed by what is moving, what is mobile and fluid (Benveniste, p. 33/286). Plato applies this term to the ordered movements of the body: "Order in movement is called 'rhythm,' and order in the vocal sounds—the combination of high and low notes—is called 'harmony'; and the union of the two is called 'a performance by a chorus'" (*Laws*, 665a). In this sense, the term is also used, particularly by lyric poets, to define the proper form and character of each individual: "know what rhythm governs human beings" (*gignoske d' oios rhythmos anthropous echei*; Archilocus), "do not praise a man before knowing his sentiment, his rhythm, and his character" (*orgen kai rithmon kai tropon*; Theognides).

Mode expresses this "rhythmic" and not "schematic" nature of being: being is a flux, and substance "modulates" itself and beats out its rhythm—it does not fix and schematize itself—in the modes. Not the individuating of itself but the beating out of the rhythm of substance defines the ontology that we are here seeking to define.

Hence the peculiar temporality of mode, on which it is appropriate to reflect. The adverb *modo* means in Latin "a short time ago, just now, recently." This indicates, in the "now," a small temporal gap, which is not a chronological past so much as a non-coincidence of the moment with itself, which obligates it to stop and take itself up again. We could say, then, that the temporal form of mode is neither the past nor the present nor even less the future: it is the *modern*, on condition of restoring to this discredited word its etymological meaning from *modo* and *modus* (present to some extent even in the related Italian term *moda*, "fashion").

Since its first appearance in a letter of Gelasius I, which distinguishes the *admonitiones modernae* from *antiquae regulae*, the term *modernus* always implies a tension with regard to the past, as if the present could grasp and define itself only in a gap with respect to itself. That is to say, the modern is intimately historical and archaic, because it has need of the ancient to refer and, at the same time, to oppose to itself. Analogously, the temporality of mode is not actuality: it is, in present existence or in the actual, the gap that impedes their coinciding with themselves—the operative time in which the flux of being pulsates and stops, takes itself up and repeats itself and, in this way, modulates itself in a rhythm. Insofar as it demands to preserve itself in its being, substance disseminates itself in the modes and can thus take form in time. The "being that it was" and its resumption in thought, existence and essence, substance and modes, past and present are only the moments or the figures of this rhythm, of this music of being: *ductus sub aliqua figura servatus*.

The person who is properly modern, in this sense, is not the one who opposes the ancient so much as the one who understands that only when something "has done its time" does it become truly urgent and actual.

Only at this point can the rhythm of being be known and grasped as such. Today we are in this extreme epochal situation, and yet it seems that human beings do not manage to become aware of it and continue to be cut and divided between the old and the new, the past and the present. Art, philosophy, religion, politics have done their time, but only now do they appear to us in their fullness, only now can we draw from them a new life.

ℵ.   Developing the Neoplatonic idea of emanation, Avicenna conceives of being as a flux (*fayd*). The first principle acts neither by will nor by choice but simply exists and, from its existence, accomplishes and "flows into" the world. The fact that in the image of flux what is in question is a tendential neutralization of the concept of cause, in the sense of the reciprocal immanence between causing and caused, is implicit in the way in which Albert the Great takes up this idea: "Only that can flow in which flowing and that from which it flows are of the same form, as the river has the same form as the source from which it flows . . . ." (Lizzini, pp. 10–11). If one maintains the image of flux, then the most adequate form for thinking mode is that of conceiving it as a vortex in the flux of being. It has no substance other than that of the one being, but, with respect to the latter, it has a figure, a manner, and a movement that belong to it on its own. The modes are eddies in the boundless field of the substance that, by sinking and whirling into itself, disseminates and expresses itself in singularities.

3.27. In order to correctly think the concept of mode, it is necessary to conceive it as a threshold of indifference between ontology and ethics. Just as in ethics character (*ethos*) expresses the irreducible being-thus of an individual, so also in ontology, what is in question in mode is the "as" of being, the mode in which substance is its modifications. Being demands its modifications; they are its *ethos*: its being irreparably consigned to its own modes of being, to its "thus." The mode in which something is, the being-thus of an entity is a category that belongs irreducibly to ontology and to ethics (which can also be expressed by saying that in mode they coincide). In this sense, the claim of a modal ontology should be terminologically integrated in the sense that, understood correctly, a modal ontology is no longer an ontology but an ethics (on the condition that we add that the ethics of modes is no longer an ethics but an ontology).

Only at this point does a confrontation with Heideggerian ontology become possible. If the difference between essence and existence becomes a crucial problem in *Being and Time*, in the sense that "the essence of

Dasein lies in its existence" (Heidegger 1, p. 42/67), the characteristics of this entity are not, however, to be conceived according to the model of traditional ontology as "properties" or accidents of an essence but "always and only as possible modes [*Weisen*] of being." Therefore, "when we designate this entity with the term 'Dasein,' we are expressing not its 'what' (as if it were a table, house, or tree) but its being" (ibid.).

Heidegger emphatically emphasizes that the concept of existence that is in question here is not that of traditional ontology, which is founded on the clear distinction of essence and existence. The reference to the "modes of being" and the specification "every being-thus [*Sosein*] of this entity is primarily being" (ibid.) should have made us understand that the ontology of Dasein, even if Heidegger does not pronounce it explicitly, is a radical form of modal ontology, even if not a clearly thematized one. The lectures of the summer semester of 1928 at Marburg, which contain such precious comments on passages from *Being and Time*, suggest this unreservedly: Dasein "designates the being for which its own proper mode of being [*seine eigene Weise zu sein*] in a definite sense is not indifferent" (Heidegger 8, p. 171/136). Dasein is not an essence that, as in Scotus and the scholastics, is indifferent to its modifications: it is always and only its mode of being, which is to say, it is always radically mode (paraphrasing the Scholastic motto according to which "horseness is only horseness," Dasein is mode and nothing more). Dasein is the mode of a being that coincides completely with mode.

It is not possible here to specify the reasons that drove Heidegger not to make the modal character of his ontology explicit. It is probable that it was precisely his prolonged adherence to the Aristotelian apparatus that did not allow him to understand that the ontological difference must be completely resolved into the being-modes relation. In any case, it is a matter of the same difficulty that constrained him to avoid up to the end a confrontation with the philosophy of Spinoza.

§ Intermezzo II

1. In the latter half of the thirties, while he was writing and compiling the remarks that come together in the notebook *Beiträge zur Philosophy* (*Contributions to Philosophy*, inappropriately designated by the editors of the *Gesamtausgabe* as one of his *Hauptwerke*), Heidegger insistently returns to his concept of Dasein (which he now always writes as Da-sein), and in revisiting the existential analytic that he had sketched in *Being and Time*, he newly defines the relationship between the human being and what that term was to designate. In *Being and Time*, he suggests, the concept was still thought in too anthropological a way, which could allow for equivocations. The term does not mean the human being or a characteristic or structural property of the human being (precisely this is what still seems to him to lend itself to "easy misunderstandings" in *Being and Time*): it is, rather, something that one must assume and "take up" (*übernehmen*; Heidegger 9, p. 297/235) and in which one must "be steadfast" (ibid., p. 319/252–253). As such, it indicates "a possibility of the human being to come," the "ground of a determinate future being of the human being, not the ground of 'the' human being as such" (p. 300/237), that is, of the human being who "endures being the *Da*, the 'there'" and conceives himself as the "steward of the truth of being" (p. 297/235). Dasein does not mean "presence in some place or another" or simply "turning up" (*Vorkommen*) but rather "steadfast enduring [*inständige Ertragsamkeit*] as grounding the 'there'" (p. 298/235), "persistence [*Beständnis*; *bestehen* means "to tenaciously overcome a test"] in the truth of Being [*Seyns*]" (p. 311/246). In the 1929–30 course *Fundamental Concepts of Metaphysics*, Dasein is defined still more figuratively as a "burden" that the human being must take upon himself.

Let us reflect on the terminology with which Heidegger seeks to define Da-sein: "taking up" (*übernehmen*), "possibility," "steadfast endurance," "persistence." That is to say, we are dealing not with something that is always already present in the human being and which the human can have at its disposal but instead with a task or a test that the human being must take up and endure—and it is an arduous task, if it is true that, as the title for §5 reads, it remains reserved for the "few and rare" (*Für die Wenigen—Für die Seltenen*).

Da-sein here seems to be not a substance but something like an activity or a mode of existing that the human being must assume in order to approach the truth (his own and that of being)—something that he therefore can also possibly miss. But how can that in which the very truth of being is in question remain entrusted solely to the uncertainty and contingency of a "test" or a "task"?

2. Here Heidegger is coming up against a difficulty that was already present in *Being and Time*. There the circular ontological constitution of Dasein, that is, of the entity for which being itself is at issue in its being, entails a "priority" (*Vorrang*; Heidegger 1, p. 13/34) and a "distinctiveness" (*Auszeichnung*; p. 11/32) of Dasein, which in its very structure—insofar as it "has a relation of being with its being"—is "in itself ontological" (p. 13/34). In this sense, Dasein is the "ontico-ontological condition for the possibility of any ontology" (p. 13/34). At the beginning of §4, the relation between Dasein and the human being had, however, been defined by Heidegger, at least in a hurried way, in these words: "As ways in which the human being behaves, sciences have the manner of being [*Seinsart*] this entity—the human being itself—possesses. This entity we grasp terminologically [*fassen wir terminologisch*] as 'Dasein'" (p. 11/32).

What is thematically confronted in the *Beiträge zur Philosophie* is precisely the problem of this "terminological grasp." Is it the human being who, in assuming its *Da*, is the "projector of Being" (*Entwerfer des Seins*; p. 299/236), who opens its clearing and safeguards its truth, or is it, rather, Being that "uses" (p. 318/251) the human being to this end? That is to say, is Being, the open, a performance of the human being as Dasein, or is Dasein (and the human being it entails) a performance of Being?

3. In the *Beiträge*, these questions never stop resonating, and it can be said that *Ereignis* (understood etymologically as "appropriation") is the ap-

paratus through which Heidegger seeks to resolve the aporia that is expressed in them. This is clearly confirmed in the explanation of the title that opens the book: what is in question here is "to let oneself be appropriated in appropriation [*Er-eignis*], which is equivalent to a transformation of the human being: from 'rational animal' (*animal rationale*) to Da-sein. The fitting rubric is therefore *Of* [*von*] *Ereignis*" (Heidegger 9, p. 3/5).

The paragraphs of section V, which bear the title "The Grounding," return constantly to the problem of the relation between Dasein and the human:

> Who is the human being? The one used [*gebraucht*] by Being for the sake of withstanding the essence [*Wesung*] of the truth of Being.
>
> As so used, however, humans "are" humans only inasmuch as they are grounded in Da-sein, i.e., inasmuch as they themselves, by creating, become the ones who ground Da-*sein*.
>
> Yet Being is also grasped here as appropriation [*Er-eignis*]. Both belong together: the grounding back [*Rückgrundung*] into Da-sein and the truth of Being as appropriation-event [*Ereignis*].
>
> We grasp nothing of the direction of the questioning that is opened up here if we casually base ourselves on arbitrary ideas of the human being and of "beings as such" instead of putting into question at one stroke both the "human being" and Being (not simply the being of the human being) and keeping them in question. (Ibid., p. 318/252)

Ereignis is what allows one to think the co-belonging and reciprocal foundation of human being and Dasein and of Dasein and Being. If the relation of co-belonging between Being and Dasein (the *Da*, the "there" as opening of Being) is already in *Being and Time* and even more in the *Beiträge* in some way analyzed and defined, that of the human being and Dasein and the transformation of the living human being, of the *animal rationale* into Da-sein that is in question in it remain, by contrast, problematic to the end. Being is "grounded back" into Dasein, but whether Dasein in turn needs a foundation or a place (a *Da*) in the human being is left vague. In what way does Dasein entail the human being in itself, so that Being, in appropriating Dasein to itself, can also appropriate to itself the human being? And what happens, in the event of appropriation, to the living human being as such?

4. Benjamin once defined Heidegger's style as "angular," in the sense that it betrayed the philosopher's fear of running up against a corner, that is, problems that he had not been able to get to the bottom of. That

Heidegger does not manage to get to the bottom of the co-belonging of the human being and Da-sein, that the problem of the living human being remains in some way unresolved, is obvious in the obscurity and vagueness that characterize the style of the *Beiträge* every time Heidegger comes up against this theme. Paragraph 175 is among those in which the question is precisely invoked. The question here is that of exceeding "the first reference to Da-sein as the grounding of the truth of Being" that in *Being and Time* had been achieved by means of asking about the human being, conceived as "the projector of Being [*der Entwerfer des Seins*] and thus as detached from all 'anthropology'" (p. 299/236). And yet what is equivocal here is that it seems that Dasein can be understood only with reference to the human being. Instead, when thought starting from the truth of Being, "Da-sein moves . . . away from the relation to the human being and reveals itself as the 'between' which is developed by Being itself so as to become the open domain for the beings that protrude into it, a domain in which beings are at the same time set back on themselves. The 'there' is appropriated and made to happen [*ereignet*] by Being itself. The human being, as steward of the truth of Being, is subsequently appropriated and thus belongs to Being in a preeminent and unique way [*in einer ausgezeichneten einzigen Weise*]" (ibid.). How this "preeminent and unique" appropriation of the human being on the part of Being can happen is not in any way explained, unless it is with the word "subsequently," which remains all the more problematic insofar as Dasein has just been moved away from any reference to the human being.

At this point it is not surprising that the paragraph concludes with a sentence in which the angular stylistics are neutralized and leave the problem entirely unresolved: "The question of what the human being is possesses now for the first time the openness of a path which nevertheless runs amid the uncovered and upon which the storm of Being is thus allowed to rage" (p. 300/237).

5. The central problem of the *Beiträge* and, in a certain sense, of the whole of Heidegger's thought is therefore precisely the one that every first-year philosophy student immediately sees and just as immediately lets drop: the relation between the living human being and Da-sein. If Dasein—as Heidegger never stops repeating—consists solely in being-the-there, in offering the clearing and opening for the truth of Being, where does the "there" come from and where is it situated, this "there"

that Dasein is and has to be? Only a rereading of §28 and §29 of *Being and Time*, devoted to the analysis of being-there as mood or state-of-mind, allows one to single out the starting point from which a response becomes possible.

Mood or state-of-mind "reveals Dasein in its being consigned [*Überantwortetsein*] to the 'there'" (p. 134/173). That is to say, Dasein is "always already disclosed as that entity to which it is consigned in its Being; and in this way it has been consigned to the Being which, in existing, it has to be"; and yet precisely the "whence and whither" (*das Woher und das Wo*) of this "there" remain obstinately in darkness (*im Dunkel*; ibid.). It is this characteristic of Dasein, of being veiled in its whence and its where and, nevertheless and precisely for this reason, "disclosed all the more unveiledly," that Heidegger calls the being-thrown of Dasein in "its 'there'" (*in sein Da*; p. 135). A few lines later, the foreignness and obscurity of the "there" are affirmed even more forcefully: "mood or attunement brings Dasein before the 'that-it-is' of its 'there,' which as such stares it in the face with the inexorability of an enigma" (p. 136/175).

And yet, in the same context, the "there" is defined, with respect to Dasein, as "its own," and a little before, we read that "Dasein from the very beginning [*von Hause aus*] brings its 'there' along with it" (p. 133/171). It is this original belonging, this character of "itsness" that must here be interrogated and called into question. Why is Dasein "consigned" to its "there" like an inexorable enigma, and why, in being its own "there," is it always already disposed to a certain mood or attunement? Where does this character of veiling and foreignness of the "there" come from? Why does the "there" remain so impenetrable for Dasein?

The only possible response is that the "there" is foreign, veiled, and emotionally disposed because it does not originarily belong to Dasein but to the human being, to the living being who offers to Dasein the place that this latter needs in order to find "its" "there." The involvement of the human being and Dasein takes place in the "there"; the "there" is the place of an originary conflict, of an expropriation and an appropriation, in which the living human being is abolished and suspended so that Dasein may have a place. The "gigantomachy concerning Being" that *Being and Time* proposes to renew presupposes a preliminary gigantomachy over the "there," which unfolds between the living human being and Dasein.

The "there" of Dasein takes place in the non-place of the living human being. And nevertheless, this conflict—or this reciprocal being-opened—that in *Being and Time* is not thematized as such and in the *Beiträge* appears only as a demand for a "transformation of the human being into Dasein," remains covered over and absorbed by the relation between Dasein and Being. In this way, the "there" is the object of a game of dialectical sleight of hand between Dasein and the human being, in which the "there," which can only come from the human being, is made proper to Dasein as if it were always already "its own" and is then appropriated by Being as its own clearing.

6. The presupposition of the living being as the anthropophoric element that functions, so to speak, as a substrate for the human being is a constant trait in modern philosophy. What is in question here is the problem—a strictly archeological one—of all the definitions—like that of the human being as *animal rationale*—that consist in adding a qualificative determination to an element that functions as foundation. If the human being is truly such only when a simply living being becomes rational, then one would have to presuppose an animal-human that is not yet truly human. In the same way, if the human being is truly such only when, in becoming Dasein, it is opened to Being, if the human being is essentially such only when "it is the clearing of Being," this means that there is before or beneath it a non-human human being that can or must be transformed into Dasein.

In the *Letter on Humanism*, Heidegger seems somehow aware of this dilemma. Metaphysics, he writes, "thinks the human being on the basis of its *animalitas* and does not think in the direction of his *humanitas*" (Heidegger 10, p. 155/246–247). What one must ask above all is "whether the essence of the human being primordially and most decisively lies in the dimension of *animalitas* at all," whether we can grasp this essence, as long as we define the human being as one living being (*Lebewesen*) among others. The error of biologism is not yet overcome insofar as one adds to the corporeity of the human being the soul, and to the soul the spirit. The human being dwells in its essence only insofar as it is claimed by Being, it ek-sists ecstatically "in the clearing of Being" (*in der Lichtung des Seins*), and this ek-sistence "can also never be thought as one specific modality of living creature among others." From this perspective, "even what we attribute to the human being as *animalitas* on the basis of the comparison with 'beasts'" must be thought starting from its ek-sistence (ibid.).

"The human body," Heidegger writes at this point, "is something essentially other than an animal organism" (ibid., p. 155/247). This enigmatic thesis, advanced hurriedly and yet unreservedly, could perhaps have constituted the germ of a different conception of the relationship not only between *animalitas* and *humanitas* but also between the human being and Dasein. What is in question here, as with the body of the slave in Aristotle, is nothing less than the possibility of another body of the human being. Nevertheless, in the text of the *Letter*, it is not taken up again or further developed. On the contrary, a few pages later, the relation between the human being and Dasein is evoked in terms that, despite the attempt to take a distance from them, seem to fall back into the aporia of a living being who becomes truly human only by accepting the claim of Being:

> But the essence of the human being consists in his being more than merely human [*mehr als der blosse Mensch*], if this is represented as "being a rational creature." "More" must not be understood here additively, as if the traditional definition of the human being were indeed to remain basic, only to be elaborated by means of an existentiell postscript. The "more" means: more originally and therefore more essentially in terms of his essence. But here something enigmatic manifests itself: the human being is in thrownness. This means that the human being, as the ek-sisting counterthrow [*Gegenwurf*] of being, is more than *animale rationale* precisely to the extent that he is less bound up with the human being conceived from subjectivity. The human being is not the lord of beings. The human being is the shepherd of Being. Human beings lose nothing in this "less"; rather, they gain in that they attain to the truth of Being. They gain the essential poverty of the shepherd, whose dignity consists in being called by Being itself into the preservation of being's truth. The call comes as the throw [*Wurf*], from which the thrownness of Dasein derives. (pp. 172–173/260–261)

Here we see how first philosophy is always above all the thought of anthropogenesis, of becoming human. But what is thrown here? If Dasein is what is generated as a repercussion of the call of Being, something like an animality or non-humanity is still a presupposition to the truly human, to the Dasein that, pro-jected into its "there," arrives in the truth of Being. Certainly the repercussion, according to a dialectical scheme that Hegel has rendered familiar to us, is more originary than the presupposition, namely, the *animal rationale*. But the presupposition here conceals the fact that the dialectical operation leaves a remainder that is still un-interrogated. The anthropogenetic event of appropriation on the part of Being can be produced only in a living being, whose destiny cannot fail to be in question in Dasein. Only a conception of the human that not only does not add anything to animality but does not supervene upon anything at all will be truly emancipated from the metaphysical defini-tion of the human being. Such a humanity nonetheless could never be thought as a task to be "taken on" or as the response to a call.

7. In §10 and §12 of *Being and Time*, the relation between Dasein and life had been briefly treated and resolved in the direction of an ontic and ontological priority of Dasein over the simply living. "Life," we read,

> is a particular mode of Being; but essentially it is accessible only in Dasein. The ontology of life is accomplished by way of a privative interpretation; it determines what must be the case if there can be anything like still-only-life [*Nur-noch-leben*]. Life is not a mere being-available, nor is it Dasein. In turn, Dasein is never to be defined ontologically by regarding it as life (in an onto-logically indefinite manner) plus something else. (p. 50/75)

Clearly any definition of what precedes thought and language—the un-derstanding of Being proper to Dasein—can only be presupposed by them and a presupposition to them. The event, the appropriation of the human being on the part of Being by means of Dasein, is something that presupposes the living being to which and in which the event has pro-duced itself. Heidegger knows perfectly well that what contemporary lan-guage and the natural sciences call life is, like sense certainty in Hegel, a presupposition that, as such, is obtained only in a privative way starting from Dasein, to return to which it is then necessary to add back in what has been taken away. But what is in question is precisely the status of this presupposition—in this case, the "still-only-life"—and it cannot be sim-ply set aside. Heidegger suggests that life is not a "simple being-available" (*pures Vorhandensein*; ibid.), but neither does it have the structure of Da-sein. Nevertheless, the modality of being of life is not subsequently inter-rogated in *Being in Time*, and Heidegger limits himself to confirming that the ontological constitution of life can be determined (for example, by biology) by way of privation only starting from the ontological struc-ture of Dasein: "Ontically as well as ontologically, the priority belongs to Being-in-the-world as taking care" (p. 58/85). But being-in-the-world (*In-der-Welt-sein*) as originary structure of Dasein is not the same thing as the animal environment (*Umwelt*).

8. In the winter semester of 1929–30, two years after the publication of *Being and Time*, Heidegger devoted an entire course to the animal and the human, the text of which, published in 1983 under the title *Fundamental Concepts of Metaphysics*, is certainly one of his major works (cf. above, Part I, §8.8). Here the relationship between the human being and the animal (and, even if Heidegger does not mention it explicitly, between the living human being and Dasein) is posed in the much more radical way than the critique of the dialectic of privation and addition that is implicit in the metaphysical definition of the *animal rationale*. The animal's mode of Being here appears, with respect to that of the human being, as closer and at the same time more difficult to think. The course opens by opposing the "world-forming" (*weltbildend*) human being and the ontological status of the animal with its "poverty of world" (*Weltarmut*), the open of human being-in-the-world and the non-open of the animal's relation with its environment (which is only the sum of its disinhibitors).

As soon as the analysis is developed and deepened, however, things become more complicated and the opposition loses its clarity. For the animal, who is captured by its disinhibitors and remains captivated (*benommen*) in them, the environment is not simply closed. On the contrary, it is open (*offen*), and perhaps more forcefully than the world can ever be open for the human being; and yet it is not revealed (*offenbar*) in its Being:

> In its captivation [*Benommenheit*], beings are not manifest, are not disclosed, but neither are they closed off. Captivation stands outside this possibility. As far as the animal is concerned we cannot say that beings are closed off from it. . . . But the captivation of the animal places the animal essentially outside the possibility that beings could be disclosed to it or closed off from it. To say that captivation is the essence of animality means: the animal as such does not stand within a revealedness [*Offenbarkeit*] of beings. (Heidegger 5, p. 361/248)

That is to say, if we attempt to define the ontological status of the animal's relation to its environment as it follows from the course, we must say that the animal is at the same time open and not open—or better, that it is neither one nor the other: it is open in a non-unveiling that, in one respect, captivates and captures it with unheard-of vehemence in its disinhibitor and, in another respect, never reveals as a being what holds it so fascinated and enchanted. Heidegger here seems to oscillate between two opposed poles, which in a way recall the paradoxes of mystical unknowing. On the one hand, animal captivation is a more intense opening than any human awareness (Heidegger can thus write that "life is a domain which possesses a wealth of openness with which the human world may have nothing to compare"; ibid., p. 371/255). On the other hand, insofar as it is not in a position to unveil and perceive its own disinhibitor as such, it is enclosed in a total opacity. Like human ek-sistence, captivation is in this sense also a form of ecstasy, in which "the animal in its captivation finds itself essentially exposed to something other than itself, something that can indeed never be manifest to the animal either as a being or as a non-being, but that . . . brings an essential disruption [*wesenhafte Erschütterung*] to the essence of the animal" (p. 396/273). It is not surprising, however, that, perhaps with a tacit illusion to the dark night of mysticism, Heidegger feels the need to evoke, in connection with the captivation of the living being with its disinhibitor, one of the most ancient symbols of the *unio mystica*, the moth that, out of love, lets itself be consumed by the flames, to which Debord was to compare his life many years later.

9. In the course, what corresponds to animal captivation in the human being and brings the open of the world into "the closest proximity" (p. 409/282) to the neither-open-nor-closed of the environment is profound boredom. The lengthy section that Heidegger devotes to the analysis of this "fundamental mood or attunement" has the strategic function of defining the metaphysical operator in which the passage from animal to human, from poverty of world to world, is carried out. In profound boredom, in fact, just as in animal captivation, the human being is stunned and consigned to "beings as a whole," which now stand before it in absolute opacity. "Beings as a whole," writes Heidegger,

> do not disappear, however, but show themselves precisely as such in their indifference. . . . This means that through this boredom Dasein finds itself set in place precisely before beings as a whole, to the extent that in this boredom the beings that surround us offer us no further possibility of acting and no further possibility of our doing anything. . . . Dasein thus finds itself delivered over to beings' telling refusal of themselves as a whole. (pp. 208–210/138–139)

In profound boredom, Dasein regresses, so to speak, to an animal condition: it is consigned to something that refuses itself to it, exactly as the animal in its captivation is captured and exposed in a non-unveiling. For this reason Heidegger can write that profound boredom is the human phenomenon to which "captivation, as precisely the essence of animality, apparently belongs in the closest proximity" (p. 409/282). But it is precisely in this "being-held-in-suspense" (*Hingehaltenheit*) of the human being with respect to the things that encircle it, in this self-refusal of beings as a whole, that something like a possibility—the possibility of Dasein—is produced in the human being. And this is precisely what the animal, captivated in its disinhibitor, cannot do, because its relation to the environment is constituted in such a way that a suspension and a possibility can never manifest themselves.

The human being thus appears as a living being that, in suspending its relations to things, grasps beings in their self-refusal as possibility. It is an animal that, in becoming bored, has awoken from and to its own captivation and can now grasp it as such, a moth that, while the flame is consuming it, notices the flame and itself for the first time. This means that Dasein is an animal that has grasped its animality and has made of this the possibility of the human being. But the human being is void, because it is only a suspension of animality.

10. Nowhere does Heidegger clearly pronounce a similar thesis, and it is in fact possible that at a certain point he retreated before it. And yet perhaps only such a thesis could allow us to understand why the clearing of Dasein is a burden that it is necessary to take up, why mood or attunement reveals Dasein in its being consigned and thrown into the "there." The "there" that the human being is and has to be and that stands before it as an implacable enigma has no concrete content, because what is grasped in it through its suspension is only animal captivation. This latter, which is something like an *Ur-Stimmung* and the ultimate source of every human mood or attunement, is the dark jewel set in the clearing of being, the black sun shining in the open.

For this reason, in the *Beiträge*, the fundamental attunement of the human being to come is defined as "die Verhaltenheit," re-straint, which is to say the "readiness for the refusal as gift" (Heidegger 9, p. 15/14), and "das Erschrecken," the dismay that withdraws before something that is veiled and, at the same time, holds Dasein enchanted with itself. And in the 1934–35 course on Hölderlin, it is the same factical situation, the same being irrevocably thrown into a given condition that presents itself as a task: "the historical vocation is always that of transforming the already-given [*das Mitgegebene*] into what is given-as-task [*das Aufgegebene*]" (Heidegger 11, p. 292/264). And if one wanted to name something like the fundamental attunement or mood, the *Grundstimmung* that dominates all of Heidegger's thought, one would have to define it as being obstinately consigned to something that just as tenaciously refuses itself, or being consigned to something unassumable. But this unassumable is nothing other than animal captivation, the "essential shock" that arises out of the living being from its being exposed and captured in a non-revelation. The living being is not simply a presupposition, which can be dialectically overcome and conserved, but something unassumable and obscure that remains in suspense in the very heart of Being.

11. This feeling of being implacably consigned to something that nevertheless must be taken up—being-thrown as task—was perhaps at the root of the "petty-bourgeois radicalism" and "will to destruction" in Heidegger that so irritated Löwith and Leo Strauss, and by which they partly explained his support of National Socialism. And perhaps this also explains why, at the end of the eighties in Paris, when Levinas, knowing of my participation in the seminars of Le Thor, had asked about my impressions of Heidegger, he was so surprised that I had found him "gentle." Like Löwith, Levinas, who had known him in the thirties, remembered him as strong and decisive, as someone who sought precisely to assume a task that he did not manage to carry through.

I remember the moment of his arrival at Le Thor in September 1966. I met him in the garden of the small hotel—it was called "Le chasselas," named after a vintage of the region—where he was also going to stay and suddenly his eyes struck me, so lively, bright, and penetrating, with nothing at all downcast about them, as in Löwith's recollection. The expression on his face was at once severe and gentle, of the kind of gentle severity that I had seen on the face of Tuscan peasants. He was, or so it seemed to me, self-conscious and yet seemed to suddenly forget himself to abandon himself to a smile, as when I showed him the photograph that I had just taken of him with a Polaroid (in those years it was still a novelty) and he exclaimed with surprise: "Sie sind ein Zauberer!" ("You are a magician!"). But he had impulses of anger that were just as sudden, as when, toward the end of the seminar on Heraclitus, he said, staring at Jean Beaufret: "You have constantly kept me from bringing the seminar to a conclusion."

He stopped for a long time to watch bocce players in the village, commenting on their moves with a sort of participatory, cheerful skill. And in the company of René Char or in Madame Mathieu's house, he showed a comfortable familiarity with the quality of the grape or wine. But when, near Aix, after a long hike in the woods we reached the point where Cézanne placed his easel to paint, he remained motionless for almost an hour, silent and as though struck dead before the stupendous vision of Ste. Victoire. Perhaps, even if the history of Being had now reached an end and the fundamental mood or attunement was by this time *Gelassenheit*, he still sought to assume the "there," to remain in the clearing of Being, in suspended animality.

12. If the interpretation of the genesis of the human being from animality that we have delineated here is correct, then possibility is not one modal category among others but is the fundamental ontological dimension, in which Being and the world are disclosed by the suspension of the animal environment. And it is because Being reveals itself above all in the form of the possible that Heidegger can write that "the human being, which as existent transcendence is thrown before in possibility, is a being of distance" (Heidegger 10, p. 131/135). The human being is a being of distance because it is a being of possibility, but insofar as the possibility to which it is assigned is only the suspension of the immediate relation of the animal with its environment, it contains the nothing and non-being as its essential traits. And precisely because being-human is given to it only as possibility, the human being is continually in the act of falling back into animality. The privilege of possibility in Heideggerian ontology is indissoluble from the aporia that assigns humanity to the human being as a task that, as such, can always be mistaken for a political task.

13. In 1929 at Davos, during the encounter—or clash—between Cassirer and Heidegger, the young Emmanuel Levinas, who was attending with other companions among whom was Franz Rosenzweig, resolutely took the side of Heidegger. It is recounted that that evening, while they were discussing and celebrating together the victory of the new thought against the old academic philosophy, Levinas, putting a white wig on his

head, had caricatured the neo-Kantian philosopher, with his imposing, premature white hair. All the more striking, then, is the fact that some of the central categories of the early Levinas can be read, without forcing, as caricatures (in the etymological sense of an "affected [It., *caricata*] figure," whose traits have, that is to say, been exaggerated) of Heideggerian notions, particularly of being-thrown.

In the essay *De l'évasion* (cf. above, part I, §8.4), Levinas pushes the opacity of *Geworfenheit* to the extreme, to the point of making of the brute fact of the "there is" (*il y a*), to which the human being is always consigned and "nailed down" (*rivé*), the fundamental characteristic of his ontology. In the experience of the "there is," which is revealed in insomnia, "when there is nothing to watch and despite the absence of any reason for remaining watchful," we are delivered over to an anonymous and oppressive presence, from which we cannot flee: "one is held by being, held to be" (Levinas 2, p. 75/65).

That what is in question here every time is nothing other than a heightening of the Heideggerian being-thrown is not doubtful; but while in Heidegger it is a matter precisely of assuming the "there" that Dasein is and has to be, by contrast, for Levinas, by means of a caricatured exaggeration of the emotive situation, of which he has highlighted the dreadful and shameful traits, it is a question of running away from the experience of "being consigned," from which—Levinas seems to suggest—Heidegger never seems to have managed to liberate himself. And the fact that the parodic intention here had a decisively critical function is confirmed beyond any doubt by the brief text *On the Philosophy of Hitlerism* written a year before, in which the same category of "being nailed down" serves to define the Nazi conception of corporeity.

14. Oskar Becker, one of the most gifted of Heidegger's early students, had also sought to find a way out of the master's thought by means of an exaggeration of the category of being-thrown. But while in Levinas it was a matter of a caricature of excess, Becker seems to practice a sort of caricature of defect or antiphrasis. To the Heideggerian pathos of being consigned, there corresponds here the adventurousness and lightness of a mode of existing from which every weight and every having-to-be seem to have disappeared.

The parodic intent is so little concealed that Becker, in opposition to the Heideggerian ek-sistence, can call the "hyperontological" experience that he seeks to analyze "paraexistence," and in the same sense, he can place a *Dawesen* precisely alongside *Dasein*.

One of the spheres in which Becker seeks to put what can be defined as his "counter- or para-analytic of Dasein" to the test is the existence of the artist. Heideggerian being-thrown, he argues in a 1929 essay, is not sufficient to account for the peculiar Dasein of the genius in all its aspects. Here the "character of weight" that defines Dasein in its being consigned and thrown into the "there" disappears. The artist's mode of existence, which is not simply historical but "adventurous and eventful," needs a new ontological category to be grasped, which can be approximately designated as "quasi-existential or para-existential." The "paraexistential" that is in question appears as something symmetrically inverse with respect to the existentials that Heidegger calls "being-thrown" and "projected." For this reason Becker calls it "being carried" (*Getragensein*; Becker, passim).

Taken literally, Becker argues, the expression could be misunderstood, as if one still had to do with a weight that must be supported. "With being-carried (*vehi, pheresthai*), one must rather think the peculiar weightless mobility of the firmament in the ancient conception (not Newtonian mechanics, according to which, by contrast, gravitation and centrifugal force uninterruptedly drag the stars along in the heavens)."

That is to say, we are dealing with a being carried without there being anything that supports us, with a condition in which what carries us is not—as in Heideggerian being-thrown or persuasion in Michelstaedter—the weight to which we are consigned but precisely the opposite, our absolute lack of weight and lack of a task. This does not mean that the artist lives in complete unconsciousness or outside history: instead, the peculiar "adventurousness" of his existence is situated "at the midpoint between the extreme insecurity of the projected-thrown and the absolute security of being-carried, between the extreme problematicity of everything historical and the absolute 'no problem' of every natural being" (ibid., pp. 31–32).

In this sense, being-thrown and being-carried define the two poles between which the various grades and modalities of existence are deployed and articulated. And as the form par excellence of being-carried, the inspiration of artistic existence—"heedless and not menaced by guilt and death" (p. 36)—is the opposite of the anguished and decisive being consigned to a task. And yet it is, at the same time, exposed in a fragility and caducity that being-thrown does not know.

15. Nothing compares to the condition described by Becker like the amorous experience, and the best testimony of being-carried is not found in the writings and working notes of artists but in the diary of a woman in love: Helen Grund Hessel.

Even though the events narrated in this diary are known from other sources and inspired a very celebrated film in the sixties, the edition published in 1991, almost ten years after the author's death, constitutes an exceptional document, in which, beyond the extraordinary amorous events that are narrated there, a form of life testifies of itself with an absolutely incomparable intensity and immediacy.

The diary covers three months, from August to October 1920. The existence that is described there in all its particulars, including intimate details, is never exhausted in a series of deeds and episodes, and thus it does not in any way constitute anything like a biography. Helen's life is "carried" to such a point that nothing can be isolated in it and acquire a factual consistency: everything flows and passes ceaselessly into vision (the diary is strewn with such moments in which the account breaks into a vision). And her being-carried is not something individual but drags along with itself the existence of the persons who surround her, from her lover Henri-Pierre Roché to her husband Franz Hessel, from her sons Uli and Stéphane to her sister Bobann and her friends Thankmar von Münchhausen, Herbert Koch, and Fanny Remak. The life that Helen lives and the life through which she lives are identified without remainder, and what appears in this coincidence is no longer a presupposed life but something that, in life, ceaselessly surpasses and overtakes it: a form-of-life.

PART III

Form-of-Life

§ 1   Life Divided

1.1. A genealogy of the concept of *zoè* must begin from the recognition—not initially to be taken for granted—that in Western culture "life" is not a medical-scientific notion but a philosophico-political concept. The fifty-seven treatises of the *Corpus Hippocraticum*, which gather the most ancient texts of Greek medicine, composed between the last few decades of the fifth century and the first few of the fourth century BCE, fill ten quarto volumes in the Littré edition. But an examination of the *Index Hippocraticum* shows that the term *zoè* occurs there just eight times, and never in a technical sense. That is to say, the authors of the *Corpus* were able to describe in minute detail the humors that compose the human body and whose equilibrium determines health and sickness; consult one another on the nature of nourishment, on the growth of the fetus, and on the relation between modes of life (*diaitai*) and health; describe the symptoms of acute maladies; and, finally, reflect on the medical art, without the concept "life" ever assuming an important role and a specific function. This means that to construct the *techne iatrike* (medical art), the concept "life" is not necessary.

א.   Of the eight texts of the *Corpus* in which the word *zoè* appears, three ("The Letter to Damagete," "The Discourse at the Altar," "The Discourse at the Embassy of Thessaly") do not have a medical character and are certainly apocryphal. Of the other five occurrences, three refer to the patient's duration of life in relation to imminent death: *On Joints*, 63, "life in such cases lasts only a few days" (*zoè oligomeros toutoisi ginetai*); *On Affections*, 23: "there is no hope of life" (*zoes oudemia elpis*); *Precepts*, 9: "they depart this life" (*metallassousi tes zoes*). In two, finally, the sense could be relevant, but it is left entirely indeterminate: *On the*

Heart, 7: "These ventricles are the fountains of a person's being, and rivers pass from them through the body to water its frame; these rivers carry life to a person [*ten zoen pherousi toi anthropoi*]"; *Nutriment*, 32: "Potential is one and not one, by which all these things and those of a different sort are managed; one for the life of the whole and the part [*zoen holou kai merou*], not one for the sensation of the whole and the part." This last occurrence is the only one in which, through the opposition between life and sensation, the term *zoè* seems to acquire a less generic meaning.

The verb *zen*, to live, which appears in the *Corpus* fifty-five times, also never has a technical meaning, and when it does not generically designate the "living," it refers to the duration of life or, in the stereotypical form *ouk an dynaito zen*, to the impossibility of surviving in a determinate condition.

The other term for "life" in Greek, *bios* (in the sense that interests us here, that of form of life or qualified human life) appears in the *Corpus* thirty-five times, first of all in the celebrated *incipit* of the *Aphorismi* [LCL 4]: *Ho bios brachys, he de techne makrè* ("Life is short, art is long"). In confirmation of the lack of technicalization of the concept "life" in the medical sphere, the texts of the *Corpus* show, with respect to literary and philosophical texts, a certain indetermination of the opposition *zoè/bios* (cf., for example, *On Breaths*, 4).

1.2. Let us now open Aristotle's *Politics*. Even though it is not concerned with citizens as natural living bodies but with the city as hierarchically supreme community, the concept "life" assumes a technical meaning from its very first pages. It is not necessary that it be defined for a term to have a technical character; it is sufficient that it develops a decisive strategic function in the theory. A summary survey of the meanings of the terms *zoè* and *zen* shows that, even if Aristotle never gives it an axiomatic definition, it is precisely its articulation in the couple "living/ living well," "natural life/politically qualified life," "*zoè/bios*" that allows one to define the sphere of politics. The celebrated definition of the *polis* as "born in view of living [*tou zen*], but existing in view of living well [*tou eu zen*]" (*Politics* 1252b 28–30) has given canonical form to this interweaving of life and politically qualified life, of *zoè* and *bios*, that was to remain decisive in the history of Western politics.

It is the structure of this interweaving that we have sought to define in *Homo Sacer I*.

1.3. As Aristotle never ceases to remind us, men have not united together "only in view of living but rather for living well" (*tou zen monon heneka, alla mallon tou eu zen*). Otherwise, he adds, "there would also be a *polis* of slaves and animals" (ibid., 1280a 30–31), which for him was obviously impossible. The perfect community consequently results from the articulation of two communities: a community of the simply living (*koinonia tes zoes*; 1278b 17) and a political community (*politikè koinonia*; 1278b 25). Even if the first implies a certain "serenity" and a "natural sweetness" (1278b 30), it is in view of the second that the first is constituted ("the *polis* is by nature prior to the family [*oikia*] and to each individual, because the whole is necessarily prior to the parts"; 1253a 19–20).

The threshold that marks the passage from one community to the other is autarchy (*autarkeia*). This concept develops an essential function in Aristotelian politics, which has perhaps not yet received its due attention. Victor Goldschmidt has shown that in Aristotle "autarchy" is not a juridical or economic or political concept but a biological one (Goldschmidt, p. 86). The *polis* is autarchic, whose population has reached the just numeric consistency. An initial examination of the passages of the *Politics* in which Aristotle makes use of this concept seems to confirm this thesis. The term in fact appears in a strategic function already in the above-cited definition of the *polis* at the beginning of the treatise: the *polis* is "a complete community, which has reached the limit of complete autarchy [*pases echousa peras tes autarkeias*], born in view of living but existing in view of living well" (1252b 28–30). The definition is confirmed in the course of the treatise in almost the same words: "a community of living well for both families and aggregations of families, for the sake of a perfect and autarchic life" (1280b33), "a community of families and villages in a perfect and autarchic life" (*zoes teleias kai autarkous*; 1281a 1). But what is an "autarchic life"?

A passage from Book VII specifies in what sense one should understand the term:

> To the size of the *polis* there is a limit, as there is in other things, plants, animals, and implements; for none of these retain their natural power [*dynamin*] when they are too large or too small. . . . In like manner a *polis* when composed of too few is not autarchic—and the *polis* is something autarchic—and when of too many, though autarchic in necessities, like an ethnic community (*ethnos*), but not like a *polis*, being almost incapable of a political organization (*politeia*). For who can be the general of such a vast multitude, or who the herald, unless he have the voice of Stentor? It is necessary, then, so that there may be a *polis*, that it have a multitude (*plethos*, a quantity of population) that is autarchic with respect to the good life in accordance with political commu-

nity. . . . Clearly then, this is the best limit of a *polis*: the greatest extent of the multitude with respect to autarchy of life, which can be taken in at a single view. (1326a 35–1326b 9)

1.4. The concept of autarchy serves to define the measure of population and "life" that permits one to pass from a mere *koinonia zoes* or a purely ethnic community to a political community. Political life is necessarily an "autarchic life." This implies, however, that there is a life that is insufficient for politics and that it must become autarchic to be able to accede to the political community. *That is to say, autarchy, like* stasis, *is a biopolitical operator, which allows or negates the passage from the community of life to the political community, from simple* zoè *to politically qualified life.*

This is all the more problematic, insofar as there are, within the confines of the *polis*, human lives that participate in a community of *zoè* but that are constitutively excluded from the political community. The slave, for example, lives in community of life (*koinonos zoes*; 1260a 40) with the master but not in political community, and the same can be said for the woman. The family is the place that is inhabited by that life, which while being a constitutive part of the city and theoretically capable of autarchy ("the family," writes Aristotle, "is more autarchic than a single individual"; 1261b 11), is constitutively excluded from political life (or, if you like, included through its exclusion).

From this point of view, Goldschmidt's thesis should be specified in the sense that there is a life that, while able to reach biological autarchy, is incapable of acceding to political community and whose existence is nevertheless necessary to the existence of the city. His thesis remains pertinent, however, insofar as it shows that, through the concept of autarchy, the Aristotelian political community preserves a biological character. Autarchy is, in this sense, a signature that betrays the presence in the Greek *polis* of a genuinely biopolitical element.

1.5. A more thorough examination of the meaning of the syntagma "autarchic life" shows, however, that it implies something more than simply the most appropriate numerical size. A passage of the *Nicomachean Ethics*, in which Aristotle inquires about happiness as the supreme good of the human being, in this sense furnishes a decisive indication:

The perfect good seems to be autarchic. Now by the term autarchic we do not mean that which is sufficient for a man by himself, for one who lives a solitary life, but also for parents, children, wife, and in general for his friends and fellow citizens, since man is by nature a political being. But some limit must be set to this; for if we extend our requirement to ancestors and descendants and friends' friends we are in for an infinite series. Let us examine this question, however, on another occasion; the autarchic we now define as that which when isolated makes life desirable and lacking in nothing; and such we think happiness to be; and further we think it most desirable of all things, without anything needing to be added to it. . . . Happiness, then, is something perfect and autarchic, being the end of all actions. (1097b 7–20)

An autarchic life, such as that of the human being as political animal, is thus a life capable of happiness. But this implies that the concept of autarchy moves beyond the strictly biological sphere to acquire an immediately political meaning. And the sense in which one should understand this constitutive connection between autarchic life, happiness, and politics is stated in the passage immediately following, in which Aristotle seeks to define the work (*ergon*) proper to the human being. It cannot be a matter of simple living (*zen*), "because this seems to be common even to plants, but we are seeking what is proper [*idion*] to the human being. Let us exclude, therefore, the life of nutrition and growth. Next there would be sensitive life, but it also seems to be common even to the horse, the ox, and every animal. There remains, then, a life of action [*praktikè*] of a being bestowed with *logos*. . . . [W]e state that what is proper to the human being is a certain life [*zoen tina*], and this is being in act of the soul and actions accompanied by *logos*" (1097b 34–1098a 15).

The caesura that excludes—and at the same time includes—*zoè* from—and within—the political community thus pierces within human life itself, and this division of life has been so determinate for the history of Western humanity that it still decides on the way in which we think not only the political and the social sciences but also the natural sciences and medicine.

א. Autarchic means both "what has reached the just measure" and "politically qualified." In this latter sense, it functions as a signature and not as a concept. That autarchy refers not only to a certain proportion of population but has in itself a political meaning is evident in medieval treatises. In both Marsilius of Padua's *Defensor pacis* and Giles of Viterbo's *De regimine christiano*, the end of political society is precisely autarchic life (*sufficiens vita* or *sufficientia vitae*):

Perfecta communitas, omnem habens terminum per se sufficiente, ut consequens est dicere, facta quidem igitur vivendi gracia, existens autem gracia bene vivendi . . . ;

homines . . . naturaliter sufficientem vitam appetere . . . quod eciam nec solum de ho-
mine confessum est, verum de omni animalium genere [A perfect community possessing every limit of self-sufficiency, as it is consequence to say, having thus come about
for the sake of living, but existing for the sake of living well . . . ; all men . . . naturally
desire a sufficient life . . . this principle is not only granted for man but also for every
kind of animal]. (Marsilius, 1, 1–5)

Understanding what politics is therefore entails understanding what a "self-
sufficient life" is, with all the ambiguities that such a concept, which is at once
biological and political, seems to imply.

1.6. In a previous study (Agamben 1, pp. 21–22/13–14), we have tried to
show how the strategic articulation of the concept of life had its original
place in Aristotle's *De anima*. Here, among the various ways in which the
term "life" is said, Aristotle isolates the most general and separable one.

> It is through living that the animal is distinguished from the inanimate. Liv-
> ing is said in many ways [*pleonachos*], and provided any one alone of these is
> found in a thing, we say that thing is living—namely, thinking or perception
> or local movement and rest, or movement in the sense of nutrition, decay,
> and growth. Hence we think of plants also as living, for they are observed to
> possess in themselves a principle through which they increase or decrease in
> all spatial directions. . . . This principle can be separated from the others, but
> not they from it—in mortal beings at least. The fact is obvious in plants; for
> it is the only psychic power they possess. It is therefore through this principle
> that living belongs to the living. . . . We call the nutritive [*threptikon*] poten-
> tial that part of the soul in which even plants participate. (413a 20ff.)

Following his customary strategy, Aristotle in no way defines what life is:
he limits himself to dividing it thanks to the isolation of the nutritive function, in order then to rearticulate it into a series of distinct and correlative
potentials or faculties (nutrition, sensation, thought). One of the ways in
which life is said is separated from the others in order to constitute in this
way the principle by means of which life can be attributed to a certain being. What has been separated and divided off (in this case, nutritive life) is
precisely what permits one to construct the unity of life as a hierarchical articulation of a series of faculties and functional oppositions, whose ultimate
meaning is not only psychological but immediately political.

א. Aristotle calls "nutritive" (*threptikon*) or "nutritive soul" (*threptikè psychè*)
"the most primary and common potential of the soul, through which all things

have life" (*prote kai koinatote dynamis psyches, kath' hen hyparchei to zen tois apa-sin*; *De anima*, 415a 25). He makes use of the term *phytikon* (vegetative or vegetable) to designate this part of the soul only one time, in the *Nicomachean Ethics*, to distinguish it from the desiring (*epithymetikon*) part and nail down its exclusion from *logos*: "The irrational part of the animal is twofold: the vegetative does not participate in reason in any way, but by contrast the desiring participates in it in some way, insofar as it obeys and complies with reason" (1102b 29–34). But since it is only in plants that the nutritive faculty is separated from the sensitive faculty ("the *threptikon* is separated from the sensitive [*aisthetikon*] in plants [*en tois phytois*]"; *De anima*, 415a 1), ancient commentators took up the habit of designating it with the term *phytikon* (or *phytikè psychè* or *phytikè dynamis*). Thus, in his commentary on the *De anima*, Themistius can write: "the soul has many faculties [*dynameis*] . . . such as that which is called vegetative [*phytiken*], whose operations are causing nourishment, causing growth, and finally generation" (Themistius, p. 44/62). "Vegetative soul" (*phytikè psychè*), by contrast, is found in Alexander of Aphrodisias's *De anima*.

It is significant that Alexander can ask whether the vegetative principle belongs to the soul or simply to nature: the vegetative principle is, in fact, always in act in animals, even during sleep, while the other potentials of the soul are not always in act (Alexander, p. 74/59). "For if the vegetative part belonged to the soul, it would then be impossible to bring the other capacities into act at the same time; for the nutritive is always in act in living things, while none of the other faculties is. . . . [W]e will perform no other activity in respect of our soul, if the faculty of soul is single . . . ."

Through the Latin translations of Greek commentators, the expression "vegetative life" passed into medieval and modern medicine as a technical term. Modern medicine assumes at its foundation an articulation of life whose origin is metaphysical-political and not biological-scientific.

א. The *De anima* is probably the first text in which "life" (*zoè*) takes on a generic sense, distinct from the life of the single living individual, from *a* life. Ivan Illich has defined the modern concept of "life" as a "spectral" concept and a fetish, and he has traced its first appearance to the Gospel passage in which Jesus says: "'I am the Life.' He does not say, "I am a life,' but 'I am Life,' *tout court*" (Illich 2, p. 225; cf. above, Prologue, §7). "The notion of an entitative life," he writes, "which can be professionally and legally protected has been tortuously constructed through a legal-medical-religious-scientific discourse whose roots go far back into theology" (ibid., p. 226). Church and lay institutions are converging today in regarding this spectral notion, which can be applied in the same way to everything and nothing, as the sacred and principal object of their care, as something that can be manipulated and managed and, at the same time, defended and protected.

1.7. What is decisive from our perspective is that this division of life as such immediately has a political meaning. Since *zoè* can achieve autarchy and constitute itself as a political life (*bios politikos*), it is necessary for it to be divided and for one of its articulations to be excluded and, at the same time, included and placed at the negative foundation of the *politeia*. For this reason, in the *Nicomachean Ethics* Aristotle takes care to specify that the political man must be familiar with what concerns the soul and know that there is in it a part—nutritive (or vegetative) life—that does not participate in reason in any way and, being therefore not truly human, remains excluded from happiness and virtue (and thus from politics):

> It is thus necessary that the political man also be familiar with what concerns the soul. . . . We have said that there is a part of it that is deprived of reason and another that by contrast possesses it. Whether these are separated as parts of the body or of anything divisible are, or are distinct by definition but by nature inseparable, like the convex and concave in the circumference of a circle, does not affect the present question. Of the irrational element one division seems to be common [to all the living] and vegetative, namely, the principle of nutrition and growth; for such a faculty of the soul is found in all the beings that are nourished, in embryos as also in complete beings. . . . Now the virtue of such a faculty seems to be common to all beings and not properly human [*anthropine*]; for this part or faculty seems to function most in sleep, while goodness and badness are least manifest in sleep, whence comes the saying that the happy are not better off than the wretched for half their lives. . . . Let us, however, leave the nutritive faculty alone, since it has by its nature no share in human virtue. (1102a 23–1102b 14)

In the *Magna Moralia* this exclusion is confirmed in particular with respect to happiness: "the nutritive soul does not contribute to happiness" (1185a 35).

א. In the *De anima*, Aristotle establishes a striking correspondence between touch and nutritive life, as though to touch there belonged, on the level of sensation, the same primordial role that corresponds to nutrition. After having confirmed that "the nutritive faculty must be found in all beings that grow and decay" (434a 23), he writes, "An animal is a body with a soul in it: every body is tangible [*hapton*] and perceptible by touch [*haphei*]; hence necessarily, if an animal is to survive, its body must have tactile capacity. . . . That is why taste is also a sort of touch; it is relative to nutriment, which is a tangible body . . . and it is clear that without touch it is impossible for an animal to exist" (434b 12–20).

And just as, with respect to the nutritive faculty, sensation and intellect entail a heterogeneous supplement that differentiates the animal and the human from the plant, so too, while touch renders life possible, do "the other senses exist in view of the good" (ibid., 24), and just as it is not possible in mortals to separate the nutritive soul from the others, in the same way "without touch it is not possible for there to be any other sense . . . and, with the loss of touch, animals die" (435b 3–4). The metaphysical-political apparatus that divides and articulates life acts on all levels of the living body.

1.8. At this point we can further specify the articulation between simple life and politically qualified life, *zoè* and *bios*, that we placed at the foundation of Western politics in *Homo Sacer I*. What we can now call the ontological-biopolitical machine of the West is founded on a division of life that, by means of a series of caesurae and thresholds (*zoè/bios*, insufficient life/autarchic life, family/city), takes on a political character that was initially lacking. But it is precisely by means of this articulation of its *zoè* that the human being, uniquely among the living, becomes capable of a political life. The function proper to the machine, that is to say, is an operation on the living that, by "politicizing" its life, renders it "self-sufficient," namely, capable of taking part in the *polis*. What we call politics is above all a special qualification of life, carried out by means of a series of partitions that pass through the very body of *zoè*. But this qualification has no content other than the pure fact of the caesura as such. This means that the concept of life will not truly be thought as long as the biopolitical machine, which has always already captured it within itself by means of a series of divisions and articulations, has not been deactivated. Until then, bare life will weigh on Western politics like an obscure and impenetrable sacral residue.

One can therefore understand the essentially ontologico-political and not only psychological meaning of the division of the parts of the soul (nutritive, sensitive, intellectual faculties) in Book II of *De anima*. From this perspective, the problem of whether the parts of the soul are only logically or also physically-spatially separable, which Aristotle does not fail to dwell upon, seems all the more determinative. While what is proper to the vegetable soul is, in fact, being able to exist independently of the others (as happens in plants), the other parts, at least in mortal beings (the restriction allows one to understand that it was perhaps possible in the gods), cannot be separated from it. "Is each of these faculties," asks Aristotle,

> a soul or a part of the soul? And if a part, a part separable only logically [*logoi*] or a part distinct according to place [*topoi*]? In some cases it is not difficult to answer, while others contain difficulties. Just as in the case of plants that, when divided, are observed to live though separated from one another (thus showing that in their case the soul of each individual plant was actually one, potentially many), so we notice a similar result in other varieties of soul, as in insects that have been cut in two. . . . We have no evidence as yet about intellect or the potential for thought, but it seems to be a different kind of soul, differing as what is eternal from what is perishable; it alone is capable of being separated. All the other parts of the soul, it is evident from what we have said, are, in spite of certain statements to the contrary, incapable of separate existence though, of course, distinguishable by *logos*. (413b 14–29)

Logos can divide what cannot be physically divided, and the consequence that this "logical" division exercises on life is that of rendering possible its politicization. *Politics, as the* ergon *proper to the human, is the practice that is founded on the separation, worked by the* logos, *of otherwise inseparable functions*. Politics here appears as what allows one to treat a human life as if in it sensitive and intellectual life were separable from vegetative life—and thus, since it is impossible in mortals, of legitimately putting it to death. (This is the meaning of the *vitae necisque potestas* that we saw defined sovereign power; cf. Agamben 4, pp. 97–101/87–90).

For this reason, a decisive threshold in the history of Western biopolitics was reached when, in the second half of the twentieth century, through the development of techniques of resuscitation (the Italian expression, *reanimazione*, is significant: in question here are, once again, the soul and life), medicine succeeded in actualizing what Aristotle maintained was impossible, namely, the separation of vegetative life from the other vital functions in the human being. It should not surprise us if, from that moment on, all the fundamental concepts of politics were also again called into question. From a redefinition of life there necessarily follows a redefinition of politics.

ℵ.   It is necessary to reflect on the analogy between being and living in the Aristotelian strategy. The metaphysical-political thesis declares: "To be for the living is to live" (*to de zen tois zosi to einai estin, De anima,* 415b 13). Both being and living, however, "are said in many ways" and are thus always already articulated and divided. Just as the articulation of being allows one to introduce movement into it and to render it finally thinkable, so also the division of life, by removing its unidimensionality, allows one to make it the foundation of politics. To the isolation of a being, "which is said most properly in the first place and above all," there corresponds, on the level of being, the separation of a sphere of life (vegetative life), which functions as *archè*, "by means of which living belongs to the living." In this sense, life is the political declension of being: to the *pleonachos legesthai* of the latter, there corresponds the *pleonachos legesthai* of the former, and to the ontological apparatus, which articulates being and puts it in motion, there corresponds the biopolitical machine, which articulates and politicizes life. And a deactivation of the biopolitical machine necessarily implies a deactivation of the ontological apparatus (and vice versa).

1.9. What allows nutritive life to function as foundation and motor of the bio-political machine is above all its separability from the other spheres of life (while the others cannot be separated from it). But what constitutes its privilege is also what authorizes its exclusion from the city and from everything that defines the human as such.

A more rigorous reading of the section of the *De anima* devoted to the nutritive faculty shows, however, that it contains elements that could allow us to regard it in a completely different way. Just as he is defining the *erga* proper to this faculty, namely, generation and the use of food (*gennesai kai trophei chresthai*; 415a 26), Aristotle seems to establish a striking correspondence between the lowest part of the human soul and the highest, thought (*nous*): "The most natural work of the living . . . is the production of another like itself, an animal producing an animal, a plant a plant, in order that, to the extent possible, it may partake in the eternal and the divine" (415a 27–30). A few pages later, he writes that nourishment "preserves the being" (*sozei ten ousian*) of the living and that the nutritive faculty "is a principle [*archè*] capable of preserving the one that possesses it as such" (416b 15–16). In both Aristotle and the commentators one encounters, moreover, a curious terminological proximity between the nutritive (or vegetative) soul and the intellectual: the intellectual is in fact also "separable" (*choristos*; 430a 18) and, like the intellect, the nutritive principle is also "active" (*poietikon*; 416b 15); even more decisively in Alexander of Aphrodisias, the theorist of the active (or poetic) intellect: "the nutritive principle is *poietikon*" (Alexander, p. 74/59).

In an exemplary essay, Émile Benveniste has called attention to the apparently inexplicable double meaning of the Greek verb *trepho*, which means both "to nourish" and "to thicken, to coagulate a liquid" (for example, *trephein gala*, "to cause milk to curdle"). The difficulty is resolved if one understands that the true meaning of *trepho* is not merely to nourish but rather "to let grow or to favor the natural development of something." There is no contradiction between *trephein gala* ("to nourish the milk," that is, "to let it curdle") and *trephein paidas* ("to nourish children"), because both mean "to let something attain the state toward which it is tending" (Benveniste, p. 349/252).

By all evidence, this is the meaning that the verb and its derivative *threptikon* have in Aristotle, and for this reason he can write that the nutritive soul is a "a principle that preserves the being of the one that possesses it." Preoccupied solely by the necessity to hold firm the political function of the signature of the division of life, the philosopher nonetheless had to exclude nutritive life from the happiness and *aretè* that define the city of men.

Both with and against Aristotle, it is a question, rather, of thinking nutritive life as what allows the living to reach the state toward which it tends, as the *conatus* that drives every being to preserve its being (*sozein ten ousian*). Not only must we learn to think an *aretè* of nutritive life, but *trephein* names in this sense the fundamental virtue of the living, the impulse thanks to which every faculty reaches the state toward which it naturally tends. And its political meaning lies not in its exclusion-inclusion in the city but in the fact that, in letting the heart beat, the lungs respire, and the mind think, it confers unity and sense on every form of life. Up to now we have thought politics as what subsists thanks to the division and articulation of life, as a separation of life from itself that qualifies it on different occasions as human, animal, or vegetable. Now it is a question of instead thinking a politics of form-of-life, of life indivisible from its form.

§ 2   A Life Inseparable from Its Form

2.1. This project started from the observation that the Greeks did not have a single term to express what we understand by the word *life*. They made use of two semantically and morphologically distinct terms: *zoè*, which expressed the simple fact of living common to all living things (animals, human beings, or gods), and *bios*, which signified the form or manner of life proper to an individual or group. In modern languages, in which this opposition gradually disappears from the lexicon (where it is preserved, as in *biology* and *zoology*, it no longer indicates a substantial difference), one sole term—whose opacity grows to an extent proportional to the sacralization of its referent—designates the bare common presupposition that it is always possible to isolate in each of the innumerable forms of life.

With the term *form-of-life*, by contrast, we understand a life that can never be separated from its form, a life in which it is never possible to isolate and keep distinct something like a bare life.

2.2. A life that cannot be separated from its form is a life for which, in its mode of life, its very living is at stake, and, in its living, what is at stake is first of all its mode of life. What does this expression mean? It defines a life—human life—in which singular modes, acts, and processes of living are never simply *facts* but always and above all *possibilities* of life, always and above all potential. And potential, insofar as it is nothing other than the essence or nature of each being, can be suspended and contemplated but never absolutely divided from act. The habit of a potential is the habitual use of it and the form-of-life of this use. The form

of human living is never prescribed by a specific biological vocation nor
assigned by any necessity whatsoever, but even though it is customary,
repeated, and socially obligatory, it always preserves its character as a real
possibility, which is to say that it always puts its very living at stake. That
is, there is not a subject to which a potential belongs, which he can decide
at his will to put into act: form-of-life is a being of potential not only or
not so much because it can do or not do, succeed or fail, lose itself or find
itself, but above all because it is its potential and coincides with it. For
this reason the human being is the only being in whose living happiness
is always at stake, whose life is irredeemably and painfully consigned to
happiness. But this constitutes form-of-life immediately as political life.

2.3. This means that what we call form-of-life is a life in which the
event of anthropogenesis—the becoming human of the human being—
is still happening. Only because what is at stake in form-of-life is the
memory and repetition of this event, can thought reach back archeologically to the very separation between *zoè* and *bios*. This separation was
produced in the anthropogenetic event when, following a transformation
whose study is not the task of the human sciences, language appeared
in living beings and these latter put their very natural life at stake in
language. That is to say, the anthropogenetic event coincides with the
fracture between life and language, between the living being and the
speaking being; but, precisely for this reason, the becoming human of
the human being entails the unceasing experience of this division and, at
the same time, of the just as unceasingly new historical rearticulation of
what has been thus divided. The mystery of the human being is not the
metaphysical one of the conjunction between the living being and language (or reason, or the soul) but the practical and political one of their
separation. If thought, the arts, poetry, and human practices generally
have any interest, it is because they bring about an archeological idling
of the machine and the works of life, language, economy, and society, in
order to carry them back to the anthropogenetic event, in order that in
them the becoming human of the human being will never be achieved
once and for all, will never cease to happen. Politics names the place of
this event, in whatever sphere it is produced.

2.4. The political power that we are familiar with is instead always ultimately founded on the separation of a sphere of bare life from the context

of forms of life. Thus, in the Hobbesian foundation of sovereignty, life in the state of nature is defined solely by its being unconditionally exposed to the threat of death (the unlimited right of all over all), and political life, namely, that which develops under the protection of the Leviathan, is only this same life, exposed to the threat that now rests in the hands of the sovereign alone. The *puissance absolue et perpétuelle*, which defines state power, is in the last instance not founded on a political will but on bare life, which is preserved and protected only to the extent that it is subjected to the sovereign's (or the law's) right of life and death. The state of exception, on which the sovereign always decides, is precisely that state in which bare life, which in the normal situation seems to be rejoined to the multiple social forms of life, is again explicitly called into question as ultimate foundation of political power. The ultimate subject, which it is a question of excepting and at the same time including in the city, is always bare life.

2.5. "The tradition of the oppressed teaches us that the 'state of exception' in which we live is the rule. We must arrive at a concept of history that corresponds to this fact." This diagnosis of Benjamin's, at this point more than fifty years old, has lost none of its contemporaneity. And this is not so much or not only because power today has no form of legitimation other than emergency and everywhere and continually refers to it and, at the same time, secretly works to produce it (how can one not think that a system that can now only function on the basis of an emergency is also interested in maintaining it at any price?). It is also and above all because, in the meantime, bare life, which was the hidden foundation of sovereignty, has everywhere become the dominant form of life. Life, in the state of exception that has become normal, is the bare life that in all spheres separates forms of life from their cohesion into a form-of-life. From the Marxian scission between man and citizen there follows that between bare life, ultimate and opaque bearer of sovereignty, and the multiple forms of life abstractly recodified into juridical-social identities (voter, employee, journalist, student, but also HIV-positive, transvestite, porn star, senior citizen, parent, woman), which all rest on the former. (Having mistaken this bare life separated from its form, in its abjection, for a superior principle—sovereignty or the sacred—is the limit of Bataille's thought, which renders it useless to us.)

2.6. Foucault's thesis according to which "what is at stake today is life" and politics has therefore become biopolitics is, in this sense, substantially accurate. But what is decisive is the way in which one understands the sense of this transformation. What in fact remains uninterrogated in contemporary debates on bioethics and biopolitics is precisely what is above all worthy of interrogation, mainly, the very biological concept of life. This concept—which today appears in the garb of a scientific notion—is in reality a secularized political concept.

Hence the often unnoticed but decisive function of medical-scientific ideology in the system of power and the growing use of scientific pseudoconcepts for ends of political control: the very drawing out of bare life, which sovereign power in certain circumstances could work on forms of life, is now achieved massively and on a daily basis by pseudo-scientific representations of the body, of sickness and health, and by the "medicalization" of ever wider spheres of life and of the individual imagination. Biological life, a secularized form of bare life, which has in common with the latter unspeakability and impenetrability, thus constitutes the real forms of life literally into forms of *survival*, remaining intact in them as the obscure threat that can be suddenly actualized in violence, in extraneousness, in sickness, in an accident. It is the invisible sovereign that watches us behind the idiotic masks of the powerful who, whether they realize it or not, govern us in its name.

2.7. A political life, which is to say, one oriented toward the idea of happiness and cohering in a form-of-life, is thinkable only starting from emancipation from this scission. The question of the possibility of a non-state politics thus necessarily has the form: is it possible today, is there today something like a form-of-life, namely, a life for which, in its living, one has to do with the living itself, a *life of potential*?

We call *thought* the connection that constitutes forms of life into an inseparable context, into form-of-life. By this we do not understand the individual exercise of an organ or psychic faculty but an experience, an *experimentum* that has as its object the potential character of life and human intelligence. Thinking does not mean simply being affected by this or that thing but this or that content of thought in act, but being at the same time affected by one's own receptivity, gaining experience, in every thought, of a pure potential of thought. Thought is, in this sense, always use of oneself, always entails the affection that one receives insofar as one is in contact with a determinate body ("Thought is the being whose nature is that of being in potential . . . when thought has become active in each of the intelligibles . . . it also therefore remains in some way potential, and it is then able to think itself"; Aristotle, *De anima*, 429a–b).

Only if act is never totally separated from potential, only if, in my lived experiences and my acts of understanding [It., *nei mei vissuti e nei miei intesi*], I always have to do with living and understanding in themselves—that is to say, if there is, in this sense, thought—then a form of life can become, in its very facticity and thingliness, *form-of-life*, in which it is never possible to isolate something like a bare life.

2.8. The experience of thought that is here in question is always an experience of a potential and of a common use. Community and potential are identified without remainder, because the inherence of a communitarian principle in every potential is a function of the necessarily potential character of every community. Among beings who were always in act, who were always already this or that thing, this or that identity, and in these had entirely exhausted their potential, there could be no community but only factual coincidences and partitions. We can communicate with others only through what in us, as in others, has remained in potential, and every communication (as Benjamin had intuited for language) is above all a communication not of a common but of a communicability. On the other hand, if there were a unique being, he would be absolutely impotent, and where there is potential, there are always already many (just as, if there is a language, namely, a potential to speak, then there cannot be only one being who speaks it).

For this reason modern political philosophy does not begin with classical thought, which had made of contemplation, of *bios theoreticos*, a separate and solitary activity ("exile of one alone with one alone"), but only with Averroism, namely, with the thought of one sole possible intellect common to all human beings, and most decisively at the point in *De monarchia* at which Dante affirms the inherence of a *multitudo* in the very potential for thought. After having affirmed that "there is some activity specific to humanity as a whole, for which the whole human race in its vast multitude is designed" (Dante 2, 1.3.4), he identifies this operation not simply with thought but with the potential of thought:

> So the highest faculty in a human being is not simply to exist, because the elements too share in the simple fact of existence; nor is it to exist in compound form, for that is found in minerals; nor is it to exist as a living thing, for plants

too share in that; nor is it to exist as a creature with sense perception, for that is also shared by the lower animals; but it is to exist as a creature who apprehends by means of the potential intellect [*esse apprehensivum per intellectum possibile*]; this mode of existence belongs to no creature (whether higher or lower) other than human beings. For while there are indeed other beings who like us are endowed with intellect, nonetheless their intellect is not potential in the way a human being's is, since such beings exist only as intelligences and nothing else, and their very being is simply the act of understanding that their own nature exists; and they are engaged in this without discontinuity [*sine interpolatione*], otherwise they would not be eternal. It is thus clear that the highest potential of humankind is its intellectual potential or faculty. And since that potentiality cannot be fully actualized all at once in any one individual or in any of the particular social groupings, there must needs be a multitude in the human race [*multitudinem esse in humano generi*], through whom the whole of this potential can be actualized [*per quam tota potentia hec actuetur*]. . . . [T]he activity proper to humankind considered as a whole is to constantly actualize the full intellectual potential of humanity, primarily through thought and secondarily through action. (Dante 2, 1.3.6ff., 1.4.1)

2.9. Let us reflect on the constitutive connection that Dante establishes between *multitudo* and the potential of thought as generic potential of humanity (*ultimum de potentia totius humanitatis*). Here multitude is not only a quantitative or numerical concept. As results unmistakably from the fact that it defines the specificity of the human with respect to the animals and angels and from the specification "as a whole," it instead names the *generic form* of existence of the properly human potential, namely, thought. That is to say, it is not a matter of something like the sum of individual actualizations of potential nor— hence the special relevance of the adverb "always" (*semper*)—of a process at the completion of which the potential of humanity will be fully actualized. There is a multitude because there is in singular human beings a potential—that is, a possibility—to think (and not, as in the angels, a thought that can know no interruption—*sine interpolatione*); but precisely for this reason, the existence of the *multitudo* coincides with the generic actualization of the potential to think and, consequently, with politics. If there were only the multiple individual actualizations and their sum, there would not be a politics but only the numerical plurality of activities defined by the variety of particular goals (economic, scientific, religious, etc.). But because the actualization of the generic potential of thought coincides with the existence of a *multitudo,* this latter is immediately political.

Just as according to Averroës the *multitudo,* as generic subject of the potential of thought, is always to be thought in relation to the existence of a singular philosopher who, by means of the phantasms of his imagination, is united with the unique intellect, so also is the potential of thought of which we are speaking always to be put into relation with the singular use of a common potential. For this reason, that is to say, insofar as the unicity of common thought remains linked to the contingency of a singular exercise, it is necessary to consider cautiously the political function of the Internet, of which one speaks so often today. Insofar as it depends on the permanent availability *in actu* of a preconstituted social knowledge, there is lacking in it precisely the experience of *potential* that defines human knowledge with respect to the angelic. What remains caught in the "net," so to speak, is thought without its potential, without the singular experience of its generic actualization.

The *multitudo* is a political concept only insofar as it inheres in the potential of thought as such. And thought does not define one form of life among others in which life and social production are articulated: it is *the unitary potential that constitutes the multiple forms of life into form-of-life.* In the face of state sovereignty, which can affirm itself only by separating bare life from its form in every sphere, it is the potential that ceaselessly reunites life with its form or prevents them from being dissociated. The distinction between the simple, massive inscription of social knowledge in the productive processes, which characterizes the contemporary phase of capitalism, and thought as antagonistic potential and form-of-life, passes through the experience of this cohesion and this inseparability. Thought is form-of-life, life unsegregatable from its form, and wherever there appears the intimacy of this inseparable life, in the materiality of corporeal processes and habitual modes of life not less than in theory, there and there alone is there thought. And it is this thought, this form-of-life that, abandoning bare life to "man" and the "citizen," who provisionally served as clothing for it and represented it with their "rights," must become the guiding concept and the unitary center of coming politics.

§ 3 Living Contemplation

3.1. A genealogy of the idea of life in modernity must begin from the re-valuation and hypostatization of *zoè* that was carried out beginning from the second century of the Christian era in Neoplatonic, Gnostic, and Christian spheres. We do not know the reasons why late-ancient thought arrived at the reversal of the hierarchical relationship between *bios* and *zoè*: what is certain is that, when the second Academy and then Neoplatonism elaborate the theory of the three hypostases (being, life, thought) or when early Christian texts speak of an "eternal life" or even when the couple "life and light" (or "life and *logos*") make their appearance in the *Corpus hermeticum* and in Gnosticism, it is not, as we might have expected, the term *bios* that appears in the foreground but simply *zoè*, the natural life common to all living beings that has, however, in the meantime undergone a complete semantic transformation. A lexical indicator for this phenomenon is the progressive, inexorable decline of the term *bios* in the course of the third century CE and the resulting weakening of the *bios/zoè* opposition. A glance at the *Index Plotinianum* shows that while in the *Enneads*, *bios* is retained in relatively few passages (almost always to indicate the human mode of life), *zoè*, which up to Plotinus was very rare in the sense of form of life, is gradually substituted for *bios* and acquires the entire range of meanings that flow together into the modern term "life" (in this sense, the spread of *zoè* in the vocabulary of intimacy and private life is significant, both as proper name and as an expression of tenderness, as in the modern "my life").

3.2. The most significant document of this transformation of the classical conception of *zoè* are Plotinus's two treatises "On Happiness" (*En-*

nead 1, 4) and "On Contemplation" (3, 8). Here in all likelihood Plotinus
is starting from the passage in the *Sophist* (248e–249a) that attributes to
being "change, life, soul, and thought, since it cannot stay changeless,
solemn, and holy without living or thinking and without understanding"
and from the analogous affirmation, in Book Lambda of the *Metaphysics*
(1072b 27), according to which "life [*zoè*] also belongs to God; for the
actuality of thought is life, and God is that actuality; and God's essential
actuality is the perfect and eternal life [*zoè aristè kai aidios*]." For Plato
and Aristotle it was essentially a matter of attributing life to thought and
of conceiving the life of thought as a property specific to divine being
(and human being, to the extent to which it is capable of "making itself
eternal"). For Plotinus, however, with a radical inversion that constitutes
one of the most characteristic traits of the late-ancient world's vision, it
is not that thought is also living, but life itself, in all its forms (including
animals and plants), is immediately contemplation (*theoria*).

Indeed, Plotinus begins with a gesture of whose novelty he is perfectly
aware, attributing contemplation to all living beings, including plants
(which for Aristotle were the "alogical" beings par excellence) and suddenly announces, apparently in the form of a joke, the thesis of a *physis*
that generates and produces by means of contemplation:

> Suppose we said, playing at first before we set out to be serious, that all things
> aspire to contemplation, and direct their gaze to this end—not only rational
> but irrational living things, and the power of growth in plants, and the earth
> which brings them forth—and that all attain to it as far as possible for them
> in their natural state. . . . Now let us talk about the earth itself, and trees, and
> plants in general, and ask what their contemplation is, and how we can relate
> what the earth makes and produces to its activity of contemplation, and how
> nature, which people say has no power of forming images or reasoning, has
> contemplation in itself and makes what it makes by contemplation. (3, 8, 1)

The first consequence of this "theoretical" or contemplative character of
physis is a transformation of the very idea of natural life (*zoè*), which ceases
to be a sum of heterogeneous functions (psychic life, sensible life, vegetative
life) and is defined from the very start with a strong accent on the unitary
character of every vital phenomenon, as "neither vegetative nor sensitive
nor psychic" but rather as "living contemplation." The Stoics had elaborated the concept of "logical life" (*logikè zoè*) and "logical animal" (*zoon
logikon*) to characterize properly human with respect to that of other living

things. The novelty of this notion, with regard to the classical definition of the human being as an "animal that has *logos*" (*zoon logon echon*) is that *logos* here is not simply added to the vital functions common to the other animals while leaving them unchanged but pervades the entire human *physis*, transforming it from top to bottom so that its impulses, its desires, its sensations, and its passions appear as intimately logical. Plotinus pushes this Stoic idea to the extreme and extends it to some extent to all living things and all forms of life without distinction. Now what is logical and theoretical is life itself, which is articulated, disseminated, and diversified according to the more or less manifest character (*ergastes*, "luminous") of contemplation that is proper to it. The intuition of this profound unity of life in its intimate logical tension toward expression and thought is the most original legacy that the late-ancient world leaves as an inheritance to Christian theology and, by means of the latter, to modernity.

> Contemplation is a movement of nature toward the soul, and of the soul to thought, and contemplations become always more intimate and unified to the contemplators. . . . So this must be something where the two become truly one. But this is living contemplation [*theoria zosa*], not an object of contemplation [*theorema*] like that in something else. For that which is in something else is alive because of that other, not in its own right. If, then, an object of contemplation [*theorema*] and thought [*noema*] is to have life, it must be a life that is not vegetative [*phytikè*] nor sensible [*aisthetikè*], nor psychical. For the other lives are thoughts [*noesis*], but one is a growth-thought, one a sense-thought, and one a soul-thought. How, then, are they thoughts? Because they are *logoi*, languages. And every life is a certain thought [*pasa zoè noesis tis*], but one is dimmer than the other, just as life has degrees of clarity and strength. But this life is more luminous [*enargestera*]; this is first life and first intellect in one. So the first life is thought, and the second life thought in the second degree, and the last life thought in the last degree. All life, then, belongs to this kind and is thought. But perhaps people may speak of different kinds of thought but say that some are thoughts, but others not thoughts at all, because they do not investigate at all what kind of thing life is. But we must bring out this point, at any rate, that again our discussion shows that all beings are contemplations. And if the truest life is the life of thought, then the truest thought lives and contemplation and the object of contemplation are a living and a life and the two together are one. (3, 8, 8)

3.3. The counterpart of this dual unity of life and thought in all their manifestations is a new ontological status of the living thing, which the treatise "On Happiness" thematizes obliquely, making use of categories that seem to come from the traditional vocabulary of political reflection. The central concept of this new ontology is that of form of life (*eidos zoes* or *tes zoes*), whose peculiarity as a technical term in Plotinus's lexicon has escaped the attention of scholars. Plotinus begins by asking whether, once "living well" (*eu zen*, the same term that in Aristotle's *Politics* defines the end of the *polis*) has been identified with being happy (*eudaimonein*), one must then also render the other living beings aside from humans participants in it, for example, birds and plants (in his writings Plotinus betrays a striking predilection for plants, which by contrast generally function in Aristotle as negative paradigms with respect to the human). Those who deny to irrational beings the capacity of living well end up, without realizing it, placing living well in something other than life (for example, in reason). For his part, Plotinus instead declares unreservedly that he situates happiness in life and therefore seeks to think a concept of life and of being in line with this radical thesis. Let us read the passage in question, which constitutes one of the supreme achievements of Plotinus's genius, the ontological implications of which have perhaps not yet been fully grasped:

> Suppose we assume that happiness is to be found in life; then if we make life a term which applies to all living things in exactly the same sense, we allow that all of them are capable of happiness, and that those of them actually live well who possess one and the same thing, something which all living beings are naturally capable of acquiring; we do not on this assumption grant this potential solely to living beings endowed with reason, denying it to the irrational. Life is common [*koinon*] to both, which have in potential the same attitude with respect to happiness, if happiness is to be found in a kind of life. So I think that those who say that happiness is to be found in rational life [*en logikei zoei*] and not in common life [*en koinei zoei*] are unaware that they are really assuming that being happy is not a life at all. They would have to say that the rational potential on which happiness depends is a quality. But their starting point is rational life, and happiness depends on this, namely on another form of life [*perì allo eidos zoes*]. I do not mean "another form" in the sense of a logical distinction, but in the sense in which we Platonists speak of one thing as prior and another as posterior. The term "life" is used in many ways, distinguished according to the rank of the things to which it is applied, first, second, and so on; and thus life and living is a homonymous term that is said in one sense of plants, in another of rational animals, and both differ according to their level of clarity or obscurity; so obviously the same applies to living well. (1, 4, 3)

3.4. Plotinus's new bio-ontology is articulated by means of a critical reinterpretation of the Stoic concept of logical life. Plotinus thinks life, however, not as an undifferentiated substrate (*hypokeimenon*) to which determinate qualities would come to be added (for example, rational or linguistic being) but as an indivisible whole, which he defines as *eidos zoes*, "form of life." That this expression here has a terminological character emerges beyond any doubt from the specification that, in it, *eidos* does not indicate the specific difference of a common genus (for this reason it would be erroneous to translated it with "species"). The specification according to which the term *eidos* is not to be understood as species of a genus but according to the prior and posterior, refers, according to the definition that Aristotle gives in *Metaphysics* 1018b 9ff., only to the greater or lesser proximity to an *archè* (for this reason Plotinus had spoken of "primary" and "secondary life"). "Life" is not a synonym (in which there is an identity for the term and of the definition, which have a common referent) but a homonym, which in each form of life takes on a sense that is differentiated according to its being more or less manifest, more or less luminous. Pressed by the need for a new definition of life, Plotinus profoundly transforms Aristotelian ontology: yes, there is a unique substance, yet this is not a subject that remains behind or beneath its qualities but is always already homonymically shared in a plurality of forms of life, in which life is never separable from its form and, quite to the contrary, is always its mode of being, without for that reason ceasing to be one.

3.5. "If then a human being can have the perfect life, then he will be able to be happy. If not, one would have to attribute happiness to the gods, if among them alone this kind of life is to be found. But since we maintain that this happiness is to be found among human beings we must consider how it is so. What I mean is this: it is obvious from what has been said elsewhere that the human being has perfect life by having not only sensibility, but reasoning and true thought. But there is no human being who does not possess it, in potential or in act, and when he has it in act, we will call him happy. But shall we say that he has this form of life [*eidos tes zoes*], which is perfect, in him as a part of himself? The human being who has it in potential have it as a part, but the happy person is the one who already is happy in act and has passed over into being this (form of life) [*metabebeke pros to autò einai touto*]" (1, 4, 4, 1–15).

The happy life here appears as a life that does not possess its form as a part or a quality but *is* this form, has completely passed into it (this is the sense of *metabaino*). In this new and extreme dimension, the ancient opposition of *bios* and *zoè* definitively loses its sense. Plotinus can thus write at this point, with an intentionally paradoxical expression that takes up and twists one of the key concepts from Aristotle's *Politics*: *autarkes oun ho bios toi outos zoen echonti,* "*bios* is autarchic insofar as it in some way has *zoè*" (ibid., 23). We have seen that Victor Goldschmidt demonstrated that *autarkia* in Aristotle's *Politics* is not a juridical or economic or political concept in the strict sense but first of all biological. That *polis* is autarchic, which has reached the just numerical consistency of its population. Only if it has reached this limit can it pass from simple living to living well. It is this biological-political concept that Plotinus completely transforms, rendering it indiscernible from *bios* and form of life. The two terms *bios* and *zoè*, on the opposition of which Aristotelian politics were founded, now contract into one another in a peremptory gesture that, while irrevocably taking leave of classical politics, points toward an unheard-of politicization of life as such ("*bios* is autarchic insofar as it in some way has *zoè*"). The wager here is that there can be a *bios*, a mode of life, that is defined solely by means of its special and inseparable union with *zoè* and has no other content than the latter (and, reciprocally, that there is a *zoè* that is nothing other than its form, its *bios*). Precisely and solely to the *bios* and *zoè* thus transfigured do there belong the attributes of political life: happiness and autarchy, which in the classical tradition were instead founded on the separation of *bios* and *zoè*. One has a political *bios* who never has his *zoè* as a part, as something separable (that is, as bare life), but is his *zoè*, is completely *form-of-life*.

§ 4 Life Is a Form Generated by Living

4.1. One of the places through which the Plotinian concepts of life and form of life (*eidos zoes*) were transmitted to Christian authors is the *Adversus Arium* of Marius Victorinus, a Roman rhetor and convert to Christianity who exercised a determinant influence on Augustine with his translation of the *Enneads*. Victorinus seeks to think the trinitarian paradigm, which is taking form in those years, through Neoplatonic categories, not only by developing from this perspective the doctrine of the three hypostases (being, life, thought) but also and above all by deepening the unity between being and life that we have seen to define Plotinian bio-ontology. Already Aristotle, in a passage of the *De anima* that was to have a long lineage, had affirmed, albeit cursorily, that "being for the living is to live." Now it is a question, by completely translating the ontological vocabulary into a "bio-logical" vocabulary, of thinking the unity and consubstantiality—and at the same time, the distinction—between Father and Son as unity and articulation of "living" and "life" in God. Mobilizing to the point of excess the artifice and subtlety of his rhetorical art, Victorinus dedicates the entire fourth book of his treatise to this difficult theological problem:

> "He lives" and life [*vivit ac vita*], are they one thing, or the same thing, or are they different things? One? But why the two terms? The same thing? But how so, since it is one thing to be actually, the other thing to be actuality. Are they therefore different? But how would they be different, since in that which lives there is life, and in that which is life, it is necessarily the case that it lives? Indeed, that which lives does not lack life, since then there would be life that does not live. Therefore they are different in one another, and

consequently, in one another, whatever they are, they are two; and if, in some way, they are two, they are not however, two purely and simply, since indeed they are one in the other and that is the case with both of them. Are they therefore the same thing? But the same thing in two is other than itself. This identity is therefore at the same time alterity in each of the two. But if there is an identity, and each of the two is identical to itself, both are identical and one. Indeed, each one being what the other is, neither of the two is double [*geminum*]. Therefore, if each of the two, by the very same thing that he is, is also the other, each one of the two will be one in himself. But since each one of the two is one in himself, it is the same one in the other. . . . Living and life are such that what living consists in is life and what life consists in is living: not that one is duplicated into the other, or that one is with the other—for that would be a union [*copulatio*: for from this, even if the connection were inseparable, there is only a union, not a unity (*unitum est, non unum*)]—no in fact they are such that in the very act that is living is to be life and in the same way, to be life is to live. . . . "He lives" and life are therefore one substance. (Victorinus, pp. 502–504/253–255)

4.2. Nothing shows the new and decisive centrality that the concept of life acquires both in the speculations of dying paganism and in nascent Christian theology as much as the fact that the problem of the consubstantiality between Father and Son is thought in terms of a relation between pure living and the life that is co-originarily generated in it. In a passage that, as has been noted, is perhaps the densest of his entire work, the paradox of this bi-unity is resolved by Victorinus, with an unquestionable revival of the Plotinian concept of *eidos zoes*, in the idea of a "form of life" (*vitae forma, forma viventis*) generated by the very act of living (*vivendo*):

Indeed, life is a habit of living [*vivendi habitus*], and it is a kind of form or state generated by living [*quasi quaedam forma vel status vivendo progenitus*], containing in itself living itself and that being which is life [*id esse quod vita est*], so that both are one substance. For they are not truly one in the other, but they are one redoubled in its own simplicity [*unum suo simplici geminum*], one, in itself because it is from itself [*ex se*] and one which is from itself because the first simplicity has a certain work within itself. . . . For living is being; but being life is a certain mode, that is, the form of living produced by the very one for which it is form [*forma viventis confecta ipso illo cui forma est*]. But the producer, living, never having a beginning—for that which lives from itself has no beginning since it lives always—it follows that life also has no beginning. Indeed as long as the producer has no beginning, that which is produced has not a beginning.

As both are together [*simul,* "at the same time"], they are also consubstantial. But living is God, life is Christ, and in living is life, and in life is living. In this way certainly one is in the other because produced [*confectum*] and producer [*conficiens*] are one in the other: for as the producer is in the product, so also the product is in the producer, especially if they always coexist. Therefore the Father is in the Son and the Son in the Father. And indeed, the producer is producer of a product, and the product, product of a producer. Therefore one is their substance, not one in two or two in one but because, in the very substance in which God is, in this same substance is the Son, that is, in the following way: as God lives, so the Son lives also; in whatever kind of substance the Father is, the Son is in such a substance. (Victorinus, pp. 536–538/271)

It is necessary to reflect on the radical transformation that classical ontology undergoes once being is displaced onto the level of living. Essence and existence, potential and act, material and form are indeterminated and now refer to one another as "living" and "life," that is—according to a syntagma that begins to appear with growing frequency in Latin prose—as *vivere vitam,* "living life." Not only does no hierarchical or genetic superiority belong to form, since it is no longer what gives and defines being, but on the contrary, form is generated and produced in the very act of being—that is, living—and it is only a *forma viventis confecta illo ipso cui forma est* ("the form of living produced by the very one for which it is form"). Just like the Father and the Son, so also essence and existence, potential and act, living and life interpenetrate one another to such an extent that it no longer seems possible to distinguish them. It is significant that Victorinus must configure the relationship between God and the three persons of the Trinity in terms of a modal ontology, according to a paradigm that had found its first formulation among the Stoics. "For living is being; but being life is a certain mode . . ." (*modus quidam*—the correction to *motus* in the *editio princeps* is to be rejected in favor of the reading of the most authoritative manuscript), just as, a little later, Father and Son are defined as "modes" of the one divine substance. And just as mode adds nothing to substance and is only a modification or manner of being, so life adds nothing to living; it is only the form that is generated in it by living: precisely form-of-life, in which living and life become indiscernible on the level of substance and discernible only as manifestation and "appearance":

Therefore, life is produced by living [*conficitur vivendo*], and by existing together it is formed. But this formation is an appearance [*formatio apparentia est*]; but the appearance arose, indeed, from hiddenness, and this arising from hiddenness is birth, the birth of the one who, before coming forth, already existed. (Ibid., p. 544/273–274)

4.3. It is at this point that Victorinus, taking up and pushing to the extreme the Plotinian idea of an *eidos tes zoes* in which *bios* and *zoè*, life of thought and common life enter into a threshold of indistinction, can make use of the syntagma "form of—or of a—life" (*vitae forma*) in a technical sense:

> God is nothing other than living, but the original living, the one whence comes all the living of all the others; he is action itself, existing in acting [*actio ipsa in agendo existens*], in this movement having his own being, which is having either existence or substance, although truly not having it [*habens quamquam ne habens quidem*] but existing itself as that which is originally and universally living [*existens ipsum quod sit principaliter et universaliter vivere*]. But that which is produced from this act is in some way its form is life. Indeed as the *aion* (eon) is produced by the always present act of all things, so it is by living and by the act of living which is always present that life is produced, and as we express it, vitality, which is somehow a form of [or "of a"] life [*vitalitas, hoc est ut vitae forma*], is generated according to its own power and substance. (p. 542)

In God, form of life is so inseparably united to living that here there is no place for anything like a "having"; God does not "have" existence and form but rather, with a grammatical forcing that renders the verb "to exist" transitive, he "exists" his living and, in this way, produces a form that is nothing other than his "vitality" or the form of his life. Once again, the modal paradigm (substance/modes) calls into question the Aristotelian ontology founded on the existence/essence, potential/act oppositions: substance does not "have" but "is" its modes. In every case, in the idea of a "form-of-life," just like existence and essence, so also do *zoè* and *bios*, living and life contract into one another and fall together, allowing a third to appear, whose meaning and implications still remain for us to deliberate.

§ 5 Toward an Ontology of Style

5.1. Let us pursue Victorinus's reflection beyond its theological context. Form-of-life is not something like a subject, which preexists living and gives it substance and reality. On the contrary, it is generated in living; it is "produced by the very one for which it is form" and for that reason does not have any priority, either substantial or transcendental, with respect to living. It is only a manner of being and living, which does not in any way determine the living thing, just as it is in no way determined by it and is nonetheless inseparable from it.

Medieval philosophers were familiar with a term, *maneries*, which they traced back to the verb *manere*, while modern philologists, identifying it with the modern "manner," have it derive from *manus*. A passage of the *Book of Muhammad's Ladder* instead suggests a different etymology. The author of this visionary work, which must have been familiar to Dante, at a certain point witnesses an apparition of a pen, from which "ink issued" (*manabat encaustum*). "And all these things," he writes, "were done in such a manner that they seemed to have been created in that very instant" (*et haec omnia tali manerie facta erant, quod simul videbantur creata fuisse*; Hyatte, p. 126). The etymological juxtaposition *manare/maneries* shows that *maneries* here means "mode of welling up": all these things emanate from the pen in such a way that they seem to have been created in that very instant.

In this sense, form-of-life is a "manner of rising forth," not a being that has this or that property or quality but a being that is its mode of being, which is its welling up and is continually generated by its "manner" of being. (It is in this sense that one is to read the Stoic definition of *ethos* as *pegè biou*, "rising-forth of life.")

5.2. It is in this way that we must understand the relationship between *bios* and *zoè* in form-of-life. At the end of *Homo Sacer I*, form of life was briefly evoked as a *bios* that is only its *zoè*. But what can "living (or being) one's own *zoè*" mean? What can a mode of life be that has for its object only life, which our political tradition has always already separated into bare life? Certainly it will mean living it as something absolutely inseparable, causing *bios* and *zoè* to coincide at every point. But above all, what are we to understand by *zoè* if it cannot be a question of bare life? Our corporeal life, the physiological life that we tend to always already separate and isolate? Here one sees the limit and, at the same time, the abyss that Nietzsche had to have glimpsed when he speaks of "great politics" as physiology. Here the risk is the same one that the biopolitics of modernity has fallen into: to make bare life as such the preeminent object of politics.

Therefore it is necessary above all to neutralize the bipolar *zoè/bios* apparatus. Just as every time we find ourselves confronted with a two-sided machine, here one needs to guard against the temptation of playing one pole off against the other as well as that of simply contracting them onto one another in a new articulation. That is to say, it is a matter of rendering both *bios* and *zoè* inoperative, so that form-of-life can appear as the *tertium* that will become thinkable only starting from this inoperativity, from this coinciding—which is to say, falling together—of *bios* and *zoè*.

5.3. In ancient medicine there is a term—*diaita*—that designates the regime of life, the "diet" of an individual or a group, understood as the harmonic proportion between food (*sitos*) and physical exercise or labor (*ponos*). Thus, in the *Corpus Hippocraticum*, "the human diet" (*diaite anthropine*) is something like the mode of life, variously articulated according to seasons and individuals, best adapted to good health (*pros hygeien orthos*). That is to say, it is a question of a *bios* whose object seems to be solely *zoè*.

Curiously, this medical term also has another technical meaning, which this time refers—as also happens, after all, with our term "diet"—to the political-juridical sphere: *diaita* is that arbitration that decides a suit not according to the letter of the law but according to circumstances and equity (hence, in medieval and modern vocabulary, it has developed the meaning of "a political assembly with decision-making power"). In this sense, the term is opposed to *dike*, which indicates not so much custom or mode of life but imperative rule (Aristotle, *Rhetoric*, 1374b 19: "one must recur rather to *diaita* than to *dike*, because *diaitetes*, the will, looks to the convenient, while *dikastes*, judgment, to the law [*nomos*]").

As often happens, the gap between two meanings of the same term can give rise to instructive considerations. If politics, as we have seen, is founded on an articulation of life (living/living well; life/autarchic life), then it certainly cannot be surprising that the mode of life, the "diet" that secures the good health of human beings, can also assume a political meaning, which, however, concerns not the *nomos* but the governance and regime of life (and it is no accident that the Latin term that translates *diaita*—*regimen*—also preserves the same semantic duplicity: the title *de regimine* is common to both medical and political treatises). On the level of "regime," biological life and political life are indeterminated.

5.4. Theologians distinguish between the life that we live (*vita quam vivimus*), namely, the sum of facts and events that constitute our biography, and the life by means of which we live (*vita qua vivimus*), that which renders life livable and gives to it a sense and a form (it is perhaps what Victorinus calls *vitalitas*). In every existence these two lives appear divided, and yet one can say that every existence is the attempt, often unsuccessful and nevertheless insistently repeated, to realize their coincidence. Indeed, only that life is happy in which the division disappears.

If one leaves to one side projects to reach this happiness on the collective level—from convent rules to phalansteries—the place where the study of the coincidence between the two lives has found its most sophisticated laboratory is the modern novel. Henry James's characters—but it holds for all characters—are in this sense only the experiment in which the life that we live is ceaselessly divided from the life by which we live and, at the same time, just as obstinately seeks to reunite itself with it. Thus, on the one hand, their existence is split into series of faces, perhaps accidental and in any case unassumable, object of the mundane *episteme* par excellence, gossip; on the other hand, it appears as the "beast in the jungle," something that is always waiting in ambush for them in the curves and cruxes of life and will one day inevitably pounce to show "the real truth" about them.

5.5. Sexual life—which appears, for example, in the sexual biographies that Krafft-Ebing collects in his *Psychopathia sexualis* in the same years when James is writing his novels—seems to actualize a threshold that escapes the scission between the two lives. Here the beast in the jungle has always already pounced—or rather, has always already unveiled its phantasmatic nature. These biographies, which are by all appearances miserable and have been transcribed solely to bear witness to their patho-logical and infamous character, testify to an experience in which the life *that* has been lived is identified without remainder with the life *by which* it has been lived. In the life that the anonymous protagonists live what is at stake in every instant is the life by which they live: the latter has been wagered and forgotten without remainder from the beginning in the former, even at the cost of losing all dignity and respectability. The short-sighted summaries of medical taxonomy conceal a sort of archive of the blessed life, whose pathographic seals had each time been broken by desire. (The narcissistic withdrawal of libido into the Ego, by which Freud defines perversion, is only the psychological transcription of the fact that for the subject what is in question in that determined and un-controllable passion is his life, that this life has been entirely put at stake in this certain gesture or in that certain perverse behavior.)

It is striking that to find examples and materials of a life inseparable from its form in our society, one has to rummage through pathographic registers—or, as happened to Foucault for his *Lives of Infamous Men*—in police archives. In this sense, form-of-life is something that does not yet exist in its fullness and can be attested only in places that, under present circumstances, necessarily appear unedifying. In any case, it is a matter of an application of the Benjaminian principle according to which the elements of the final state are hidden in the present, not in the tendencies that appear progressive but in the most insignificant and contemptible.

5.6. There is, however, also a high tradition of inseparable life. In early Christian literature, the proximity between life and *logos* that is in ques-tion in the prologue to the Gospel of John was taken as the model of an inseparable life. "Life itself," one reads in Origen's commentary, "comes into existence after the Word [*epigignetai toi logoi*], being inseparable [*achoristos*] from it after it has come into existence" (Origen, II, 129).

According to the messianic paradigm of "eternal life" (*zoè aionos*), the very relationship between *bios* and *zoè* is transformed in such a way that *zoè* can appear in Clement of Alexandria as the supreme end of *bios*: "Piety toward God is the only truly universal exhortation that clearly concerns *bios* in its entirety, stretched out in every instant toward the supreme end, *zoè*" (Clement, XI). The reversal of the relation between *bios* and *zoè* here allows for a formulation that simply would not have made sense in classical Greek thought and that seems to anticipate modern biopolitics: *zoè* as *telos* of *bios*.

In Victorinus the attempt to think the relationship between Father and Son produces an unheard-of ontology, according to which "every being has an inseparable species [*omne esse inseparabilem speciem habet*], or rather, the species is the substance itself, not because the species is prior to being, but because the species defines being" (Victorinus, p. 234/116). Like living and life, so also being and form here coincide without remainder.

5.7. It is from this perspective that one can read the way in which Franciscan theorists completely rethought the Aristotelian division of souls (or lives), to the point of radically calling into question both the very reality of the division and the hierarchy between vegetative, sensitive, and intellectual soul that Scholasticism had drawn from it. Intellectual life, writes Scotus, contains in itself vegetative and sensitive life not in the sense that the latter, being subordinated to the former, are to be abolished or formally destroyed but, on the contrary, only in the sense of their greater perfection (*Intellectiva continet perfecte et formaliter vegetativam et sensitivam per se et non sub ratione destruente rationem vegetativae et sensitivae, sed sub ratione perfectiori quam illae formae habeantur sine intellectiva*). Richard of Middleton can thus affirm that "the vegetative, sensitive, and intellective are not three forms, but one sole form [*non sunt tres formae, sed una forma*], by means of which there is in the human being a vegetative, sensitive, and intellective being." And beyond the Aristotelian division, the Franciscans elaborate the idea of a "form of corporeity" (*forma corporeitatis*), which is already found perfected in the embryo before the intellectual soul and later coexists with it. This means that there is never anything like a bare life, a life without form that functions as a negative foundation for a superior and more perfect life: corporeal life is always already formed, is always already inseparable from a form.

5.8. How to describe a form-of-life? At the beginning of his *Parallel Lives*, Plutarch evokes an *eidos*, a form that the biographer must know how to pick out beyond the muddle of events. What he seeks to grasp is not, however, a form-of-life but an exemplary trait, something that, in the sphere of action, allows him to unite one life to another in a single paradigm. In general, ancient biography—the lives of philosophers and poets that it has transmitted to us—does not seem interested in describing the real events nor in composing them into a unitary form so much as instead choosing a paradigmatic fact—extravagant and significant— deduced from the work rather than the life. If this singular projection of work over life remains problematic, it is nonetheless possible that precisely the attempt to define a life starting from a work constitutes something like the logical place where ancient biography had a presentiment of a form-of-life.

5.9. Fernand Deligny never sought to recount the life of the autistic children with whom he lived. Instead, he attempted to scrupulously transcribe on tracing paper the routes of their movements and encounters in the form of what he called "lines of drift" (*lignes d'erre*). Placed on top of one another, the tracing papers allow a sort of circular or elliptical ring (*cerne*) to appear, beyond the tangle of lines, which include within themselves not only lines of drift but also the points (*chevêtres*, from *enchevrê-ment*, "entanglement"), strikingly constant, at which the routes cross. "It is clear," he writes, "that the routes—the lines of drift—are transcribed and that the ring area each time appears as the *trace* of *something else* that was not *foreseen* or pre-thought by those doing the tracing nor by those being traced. It is clear that it is a question of the effect of *something* that is not due to language, nor does it refer to the Freudian unconscious" (Deligny, p. 40).

It is possible that this striking tangle, apparently indecipherable, expresses more than any account not only the mute children's form of life but any form of life. In this sense it is an instructive exercise to attempt to mark on the map of the cities where we have lived the itineraries of our movements, which prove to be stubbornly and almost obsessively constant. It is in the tracks of that in which we have lost our life that it is perhaps possible to find our form-of-life. In any case, Deligny seems to attribute to his *lignes d'erre* something like a political meaning that is prelinguistic and yet collective: "It is by observing this ring area that there came to us the project of persisting in transcribing the simple *visible* waiting to see *appear* there a trace of what we write with a capital W, inscribed in us since our *species* had existence, a primordial We that insists on foreshadowing, beyond every will and every power, for *nothing*, immutable, just like, on the opposite pole, ideology" (ibid.).

5.10. I have in my hands the page of a French newspaper that publishes personals ads for people who are seeking to meet a life companion. Curiously, the column is called "modes of life," and it includes, alongside a photo, a brief message that attempts to describe through small, laconic traits something like the form or, more precisely, the mode of life of the advertisement's author (and sometimes of the ideal addressee as well). Under the photograph of a woman seated at a café table, with her serious—indeed, decidedly melancholy—face resting on her left hand, one can read: "Parisian, tall, thin, blonde, and classy, in her fifties, lively, good family, sports: hunting, fishing, golf, horseback riding, skiing, would love to meet serious man, witty, sixty, the same profile, to live happy days together, Paris or country." The portrait of a young brunette who is fixated on a ball suspended in the air is accompanied by this caption: "Young juggler, pretty, feminine, spiritual, seeks young woman 20–30, similar profile to be united in the G-spot!!!" At times, the photograph also tries to present the occupation of the one who is writing, like the one that shows a woman who is throwing a rag into a bucket to clean floors: "50, blonde, green eyes, 1m 60cm, porter, divorced (3 sons, 23, 25 and 29, independent). Physically and morally young, charming, desire to share the simple joys of life with lovable companion 45–55." Other times, the decisive element for characterizing the form of life is the presence of an animal, who appears in the foreground in the photograph alongside its owner: "Gentle Labrador seeks for his mistress (36) a sweet master who is a lover of nature and animals, to swim in happiness in the countryside." Finally, the close-up of a face on which a tear leaves a trace of mascara reads: "Young woman, 25, with a skin-deep sensibility, seeks a tender and spiritual young man, with whom to live a river-romance."

The list could continue, but what is both irritating and moving each time is the attempt—a complete success and, at the same time, an irreparable failure—to communicate a form of life. How indeed can this certain face, this certain life coincide with that italicized list of hobbies and character traits? It is as if something decisive—and, so to speak, unequivocally public and political—has collapsed to such a degree into the idiocy of the private that it is becoming forever unrecognizable.

5.11. In the attempt to define oneself through one's hobbies, there comes to light in all its problematicity the relation between singularity, its tastes, and its inclinations. The most idiosyncratic aspect of everyone, their tastes, the fact that they like coffee granita, the sea at summertime, this certain shape of lips, this certain smell, but also the paintings of the late Titian so much—all this seems to safeguard its secret in the most impenetrable and insignificant way. It is necessary to decisively subtract tastes from the aesthetic dimension and rediscover their ontological character, in order to find in them something like a new ethical territory. It is not a matter of attributes or properties of a subject who judges but of the mode in which each person, in losing himself as subject, constitutes-himself as form-of-life. The secret of taste is what form-of-life must solve, has always already solved and displayed—just as gestures betray and, at the same time, absolve character.

Two theses published in *Tiqqun 2* (*Introduction to Civil War*) figuratively summarize the ontological meaning to "tastes" in their relation to a form-of-life:

> Every body is affected by its form-of-life as if by a clinamen, a leaning, an attraction, a *taste*. A body leans toward whatever leans its way. (§3)

> "My" form-of-life relates not to *what* I am, but to *how* I am what I am. (§5)

If every body is affected by its form-of-life as by a clinamen or a taste, the ethical subject is that subject that constitutes-itself in relation to this clinamen, the subject who bears witness to its tastes, takes responsibility for the mode in which it is affected by its inclinations. Modal ontology, the ontology of the *how*, coincides with an ethics.

5.12. In his letter to Milena of August 10, 1920, Kafka recounts his fleeting encounter with a girl in a hotel. During this encounter, the girl did "in perfect innocence" "something slightly disgusting" and "said something slightly obscene"—and yet Kafka realized in that precise instant that he would never forget it, as if precisely this small gesture and this small word had drawn him irresistibly into that hotel. Ever since then, adds Kafka, for years and years his body "was shaken almost unbearably" by the memory and by the desire for that "very particular, trivial, disgusting thing" (Kafka, p. 147).

The decisive element, what renders this trivial disgusting thing unforgettable, is obviously not the thing in itself (Kafka says that it is "not worth mentioning"); it is not only the girl's abjection but her particular mode of being abject, her bearing witness in some way to her abjection. It is this and only this that renders that abjection perfectly innocent, which is to say, ethical.

It is not justice or beauty that moves us but the mode that each one has of being just or beautiful, of being affected by her beauty or her justice. For this reason even abjection can be innocent, even "something slightly disgusting" can move us.

5.13. A double tendency seems to be inherent to form-of-life. On the one hand, it is a life inseparable from its form, an indissoluble unity in itself, and on the other, it is separable from every thing and every context. This is evident in the classical conception of *theoria*, which is in itself united but separated and separable from every thing, in perpetual flight. This double tension is the risk inherent in form-of-life, which tends to separate itself ascetically into an autonomous sphere, theory. It is necessary instead to think form-of-life as a living of its own mode of being, as inseparable from its context, precisely because it is not in relation but in contact with it.

The same thing happens in sexual life: the more it becomes a form-of-life, the more it seems separable from its context and indifferent to it. Far from being a principle of community, it separates itself to constitute a special community of its own (the castle of Silling in Sade or the California bathhouses for Foucault). The more form-of-life becomes monadic, the more it isolates itself from the other monads. But the monad always already communicates with the others, insofar as it represents them in itself, as in a living mirror.

5.14. The arcanum of politics is in our form-of-life, and yet precisely for this reason we cannot manage to penetrate it. It is so intimate and close that if we seek to grasp it, it leaves us holding only the ungraspable, tedious everyday. It is like the form of the cities or houses where we have lived, which coincide perfectly with the life we have frittered away in them, and perhaps precisely for this reason, it seems suddenly impenetrable to us, while other times, at a stroke, as in revolutionary moments according to Jesi, it is collectively innervated and seems to unveil to us its secret.

5.15. In Western thought, the problem of form-of-life has emerged as an ethical problem (*ethos*, the mode of life of an individual or group) or as an aesthetic problem (the style by which the author leaves his mark on the work). Only if we restore it to the ontological dimension will the problem of style and mode of life be able to find its just formulation. And this can happen only in the form of something like an "ontology of style" or a doctrine that is in a position to respond to the question: "what does it mean that multiple modes modify or express the one substance?"

In the history of philosophy, the place where this problem has been posed is Averroism, as a problem of the conjunction (*copulatio*) between the singular individual and the one intellect. According to Averroës, the mean term that allows this union is the imagination: the singular is joined to the possible or material intellect through the phantasms of its imagination. The conjunction can happen, however, only if the intellect strips the phantasms of their material elements, to the point of producing, in the act of thought, a perfectly bare image, something like an absolute *imago*. This means that the phantasm is what the singular sensible body marks on the intellect to the same extent to which the inverse is true, namely, that it is what the one intellect works and marks in the singular. In the contemplated image, the singular sensible body and the one intellect coincide, which is to say, fall together. The questions "who contemplates the image?" and "what is united to what?" do not have a univocal response. (Averroistic poets, like Cavalcanti and Dante, made love the place of this experience, in which the phantasm contemplated is at once subject and object of love and the intellect knows and loves itself in the image.)

What we call form-of-life corresponds to this ontology of style; it names the mode in which a singularity bears witness to itself in being and being expresses itself in the singular body.

§ 6 Exile of One Alone with One Alone

6.1. At the end of the *Enneads* (VI, 9, 11), in order to define the life of the gods and of "divine and happy men" (namely, philosophers), Plotinus makes use of the formula *phygè monou pros monon*, which remains exemplary as an expression of Neoplatonic mysticism. Bréhier translates it with these words: "Telle est la vie des dieux et des hommes bienheureux: s'affranchir des choses d'ici bas, s'y déplaire, *fuir seul vers lui seul.*"

In 1933, Erik Peterson, who had converted to Catholicism a short time previously, published a study on "The Origin and Meaning of the Formula '*monou pros monon*' in Plotinus." Against the interpretation of Cumont, who had seen in the expression the transposition of a pagan cultic formula, the neo-Roman Catholic theologian, with a gesture that betrays a Protestant sensibility, instead points toward an "old Greek expression" belonging to the vocabulary of intimacy as the origin of the formula. Expressions of the type *monos monoi*, he suggests, are common in Greek to designate a personal, private, or intimate relation. Plotinus did nothing but introduce into this conventional formula "the conceptual meaning of his metaphysics and his mysticism" (Peterson, p. 35). The metaphor "flight of one alone with one alone," which according to Peterson contains in itself both the idea of a bond (*Verbundenheit*) and that of a separation (*Absonderung*), dislocates an expression belonging to the sphere of the private lexicon into that of mystical-philosophical terminology, and in this displacement consists Plotinus's "most proper and original contribution."

6.2. However, the whole question is distorted by the fact that scholars' attention has been concentrated solely on the formula *monou pros monon*, taking for granted the meaning of the term *phygè* that immediately precedes it and of which the formula itself is only a determination. The correct but generic translation with "flight" (or "fleeing") has thus constantly concealed the essential linguistic data, namely, the fact that *phygè* in Greek is a technical term for exile (*phygen pheugein* means "to go into exile," and *phygas* is the exiled person). This is so true that, a few pages before, encountering the substantive *phygè* in the series of three terms by means of which Plotinus describes the distance from the "sources of life," the same translators render it with none other than "exile." Plotinus does not simply transfer a formula from the sphere of intimacy to the metaphysical-philosophical sphere. Much more significant is the fact that he categorizes the divine and happy life of the philosopher above all through a term drawn from the juridico-political lexicon: exile. And yet exile is now no longer the ban of an individual from the city into another plan but that of "one alone with one alone," and the condition of negativity and abandonment that it expresses seems to be inverted into a state of "felicity" (*eudaimonon bios*) and "lightness" (*kouphisthesetai*).

Plotinus's "most proper and original contribution" consists, then, in having united a juridico-political term that means exclusion and exile to a syntagma that expresses intimacy and being together (also in Numenius, in a passage that is often cited as a possible source of Plotinus's formula, we find in place of *phygè* a verb—*omilesai*—that means "to converse" and "to stand together"). The divine life of the philosopher is a paradoxical "separation (or exclusion) into intimacy." At stake in the formula is an exile into intimacy, a ban of the self to the self.

6.3. In defining the condition of the philosopher through the image of exile, Plotinus does nothing but take up an ancient tradition. Not only had Plato made use in the *Phaedo* (67a) of a political metaphor (*apodemia*, emigration, literally the abandonment of the *demos*) to define the separation of the soul from the body, but in the *Theatatus* (176a–b), in a passage that is customarily adduced as a possible source of Plotinus's formula—*phygè de omoiosis theoi kata ton dynaton*—its original political meaning is restored to the term *phygè*: "the assimilation to God is virtually an exile."

Another precedent for the characterization of the philosophical life as exile is found in the passage of the *Politics* in which Aristotle defines the *bios* of the philosopher as "foreign": "Which *bios* is preferable, that which is actualized through doing politics together [*synpoliteuesthai*] and participating in common [*koinonein*] in the *polis*, or instead, that which is foreign [*xenikos*] and untied to the political community?" (1324a 15–16). The contemplative life of the philosopher is here compared to that of a foreigner who, like the exiled, could not participate in political life in the Greek *polis*. That the condition of the *apolis*, of the one who is cut off from all political community, seems particularly disquieting to the Greek (and, precisely for this reason, both superhuman and subhuman) is attested by a choral passage in the *Antigone*, in which Sophocles defines the essence of the *deinos*, the "terrible power" that belongs to man, with the oxymoronic *hypsipolis apolis*, literally: "superpolitical apolitical." And Aristotle was certainly mindful of this passage when, at the beginning of the *Politics*, he affirms for his part that "the one who is stateless by nature and not by chance is either inferior to or stronger than a man" (1253a 4–8).

6.4. In the tradition of Greek philosophy, the exiled and stateless are thus not neutral figures, and only if one restores it to its juridico-political context does Plotinus's formula acquire its full sense. Taking up the juxtaposition between the philosophical life and exile, Plotinus pushes it to the extreme, proposing a new and more enigmatic figure of the ban. The relation of the ban in which bare life is held, which we have identified in *Homo Sacer I* as the fundamental political relationship, is laid claim to and assumed as his own by the philosopher. But in this gesture, it is transformed and inverted into something positive, having been posed as a figure of a new and happy intimacy, of an "alone by oneself" as a cipher of a superior politics. Exile from politics cedes its place to a politics of exile.

In this way, philosophy is presented as an attempt to construct a life at once "superpolitical and apolitical" (*hypsipolis apolis*): separated in the ban from the city, it nevertheless becomes intimate and inseparable from itself, in a non-relation that has the form of an "exile of one alone to one alone." "Alone with one alone" ("alone by oneself") can only mean: to be together beyond every relation. Form-of-life is this ban that no longer has the form of a bond or an exclusion-inclusion of bare life but that of an intimacy without relation.

(It is in this sense that one is to read the gesture in §4.6 of *Homo Sacer I* toward the necessity of no longer thinking the political-social *factum* in the form of a relationship. From the same perspective, developing the idea that the State does not found itself on a social link but on the pro- hibition of its dissolution, §4.3 suggested that dissolution is not to be understood as the dissolution of an existent bond, because the bond itself does not have any other consistency than the purely negative one that it derives from the prohibition of dissolution. Since there is originally nei- ther bond nor relation, this absence of relation is captured in state power in the form of the ban and of prohibition.)

6.5. Developing Aristotle's characterization of the activity of thought as *thigein*, "touching," Giorgio Colli defines "contact" as the "metaphysi- cal interstice" or the moment in which two entities are separated only by a void of representation. "In contact two points are in contact in the limited sense that between them there is nothing: contact is the indica- tion of a representative nothing, which nevertheless is a certain nothing, because what it is not (its representative outline) gives it a spatio-tempo- ral arrangement" (Colli, p. 349). Just as thought at its greatest summit does not represent but "touches" the intelligible, in the same way, in the life of thought as form-of-life, *bios* and *zoè*, form and life are in contact, which is to say, they dwell in a non-relation. And it is in a contact—that is, in a void of representation—and not in a relation that forms-of-life communicate. The "alone by oneself" that defines the structure of every singular form-of-life also defines its community with the others. And it is this *thigein*, this contact that the juridical order and politics seek by all means to capture and represent in a relation. Western politics is, in this sense, constitutively "representative," because it always already has to reformulate contact into the form of a relation. It will therefore be necessary to think politics as an intimacy unmediated by any articulation or representation: human beings, forms-of-life are in contact, but this is unrepresentable because it consists precisely in a representative void, that is, in the deactivation and inoperativity of every representation. To the ontology of non-relation and use there must correspond a non-represen- tative politics.

א. "Alone by oneself" is an expression of intimacy. We are together and very close, but between us there is not an articulation or a relation that unites us. We are united to one another in the form of our being alone. What customarily con- stitutes the sphere of privacy here becomes public and common. For this reason, lovers show themselves nude to one another: I show myself to you as when I am alone with myself; what we share is only our esoterism, our inappropriable zone of non-knowledge. This Inappropriable is the unthinkable; it is what our culture must always exclude and presuppose in order to make it the negative foundation of politics. For this reason the bare body must be covered by clothing to assume a political value: like bare life, so too is nudity something that must be excluded and then captured in order then to reappear only in the form of undressing (the fact that in the *Lager* the deported had to be stripped of all clothing before being eliminated again shows this political significance of nudity).

Ethologists and scholars of behavior are familiar with an exhibition of intimate parts—both among animals and among children and primitives—with an apotropaic and repulsing character. In confirmation of its originary political character, the intimacy that unites here becomes what repulses and separates. This meaning is even more obvious in the gesture of Hecuba, who shows her bare breast to her son Hector to drive him to go to the battlefield: "Hector, my child! Show *aidos* before this!" (Homer, XXII, 82). *Aidos*—translating it as "shame" would be insufficient—is an *intimate* sentiment that makes obligatory a *public* behavior. Nudity here shows its value as threshold between public and private.

6.6. In his course on Hölderlin in the winter semester of 1934–35, Heidegger, taking up an expression of the poet's, calls intimacy (*Innigkeit*) a dwelling that maintains itself in the conflict between two opposites:

> Intimacy does not mean the mere "interiority" [*Innerlichkeit*] of sensation, in the sense of the closing off within oneself of a "lived experience" [*Erlebnis*]. Nor does it mean an intensified degree of "warmth of feeling." Intimacy is also not a word that belongs in the context of the "beautiful soul" and that way of conceiving the world. For Hölderlin, the word carries nothing of the flavor of some dreamy, inactive sentimentality. Quite the contrary: it means, first, supreme force of *Dasein*. Second, this force evinces itself in withstanding the most extreme conflict [*Widersreit*]. . . . (Heidegger 11, p. 117/106)

That is to say, according to Heidegger, intimacy names "a knowing standing [*Innerstehen*] and supporting [*Austragen*] of the essential conflict of that which, in being opposed [*Entgegensetzung*] possesses an original unity" (ibid., p. 119/106).

Heidegger thus calls intimacy the mode in which one must live out the dwelling in the most originary dimension accessible to the human being, the "harmonically opposed." In Heideggerian ontology, this corresponds to the experience of difference as difference. Dwelling in this experience

means maintaining and at the same time negating the opposites, in accordance with a gesture that Heidegger, once again following Hölderlin,
calls *Verleugnung*, from a verb that means "to hide by negating, to re-
nege." Freud had called *Verneinung* an abolition of the repressed, which
in some way gives it expression, yet without carrying it to consciousness.
In an analogous way, *Verleugnung*, leaving unsaid the unsayable in the
said, poetically expresses the secret—namely, the co-belonging of the opposites—without formulating it; it negates it and at the same time maintains it (here there comes to light the problem of the relationship, still
insufficiently investigated, of Heidegger's thought with that of Hegel).

Intimacy as a political concept, which is here in question for us, is situated beyond the Heideggerian perspective. It is not a question of having
an experience of difference as such by holding firm and yet negating the
opposition but of deactivating the opposites and rendering them inoperative. Archeological regression must neither express nor negate, neither
say nor un-say: rather, it reaches a threshold of indiscernibility, in which
the dichotomy diminishes and the opposites coincide—which is to say,
fall together. What then appears is not a chronologically more originary
unity, nor a new and superior unity, but something like a way out. The
threshold of indiscernibility is the center of the ontologico-political machine: if one reaches it and holds oneself there in it, the machine can no
longer function.

§ 7 "That's How We Do It"

7.1. In the *Philosophical Investigations*, Wittgenstein uses the term *Lebensform*, "form of life," five times to explain what a language (*eine Sprache*) is and how one should understand a language game (*Sprachspiel*). "To imagine a language," reads the first occurrence, "means to imagine a form of life" (Wittgenstein 1, §19). Shortly afterward, Wittgenstein specifies that "the word 'language-game' is used here to emphasize the fact that the speaking of language is part of an activity [*Tätigkeit*], or of a form of life [*Lebensform*]" (§23). And that this "activity or form of life" is something different or more profound than recognizing the correctness of a rule or an opinion is stated further on: "What is true or false is what human beings *say*; and it is in their *language* that human beings agree. This agreement is not in opinions [*Meinungen*], but rather in form of life" (§241). Later on, the proximity between language (more precisely: use of language) and form of life is again emphasized: "Can only those hope who can talk? Only those who have mastered the use [*Verwendung*] of a language. That is to say, the manifestations of hope are modifications of a complicated form of life" (p. 183). And the last occurrence suggests that form of life is something like a given that must be assumed as such: "What has to be accepted, the given [*das Hinzunehmende, Gegebene*], is—one might say—forms of life" (p. 238).

7.2. This last occurrence seems to characterize form of life (and the language game with which it is compared) as a sort of limit point at which, in accordance with a typical Wittgensteinian gesture, explanations and justifications seem to stop. "Our mistake," one reads toward the end of

240

the first part of the book, "is to look for an explanation where we ought to regard the facts as originary phenomena [*Urphänomene*]. That is, where we ought to say: this is the language game that is being played" (§654). In the *Remarks on the Foundations of Mathematics* (Wittgenstein 2, pt. 2, §74), the same concept is repeated: "The danger here, I believe, is one of giving a justification of our procedure where there is no such thing as a justification and we ought simply to have said: that's how we do it [*so machen wir's*]." Every investigation and every reflection reaches a limit at which, as in the "originary phenomenon" according to Goethe, the study must halt. But the novelty with respect to the Goethe citation is that this *Urphänomen* is not an object; it is simply a usage and a practice. It does not concern a "what" but only a "how": "that's how we do it." And it is to this "how" that one actually refers in every justification: "What people accept as a justification shows how they think and live" (Wittgenstein 1, §325).

7.3. Some have sought to explain the concept of form of life through that of constitutive rule, namely, of a rule that is not applied to a preexisting reality but constitutes it. Wittgenstein seems to refer to something of the type when he writes that "chess is characterized [*charakterisiert*] by its rules" (Wittgenstein 3, §13) or, even more precisely, "I can't say: that is a pawn and such and such rules hold for [*bestimmen*] this piece. No, it is the rules alone which define [*bestimmen*] this piece: a pawn is the sum of the rules for its moves" (Wittgenstein 4, pp. 327–328/327).

The concept of "constitutive rule," though apparently clear, nevertheless hides a difficulty that one must confront. While customarily one understands by a rule something that is applied to a preexisting reality or activity, in this case the rule constitutes the reality and thus seems to be identified with it. "A pawn is the sum of the rules for its moves": thus, the pawn does not follow the rule but *is* the rule. But what can it mean to "be" its own rule? Here one again finds the same indetermination between rule and life that we have observed in monastic rules: they are not applied to the monk's life but constitute it and define it as such. But precisely for this reason, as the monks had at once understood, the rule is resolved without remainder into a vital praxis, and this coincides at every point with the rule. The "rule-based life" is a "vital rule," and, as in Francis, *regula* and *vita* are perfectly synonymous. Can one say, then, of the monk, as of the pawn in the game of chess, that "it is the sum of the rules for its moves"?

7.4. Those who make use of the concept of "constitutive rule" seem to imply that the rule, while being resolved into the constitution of the game, remains separate from it. But as has been noted, this holds only so long as the game is considered as a formal whole of which the rules describe the structure (or furnish the instructions for use). If we instead consider the game as it is in reality, namely, as a series of "concrete interactive episodes involving actual persons, invested with specific goals, skills, and linguistic and other capacities" (Black, p. 328), if, in a word, we regard the game from the perspective of use and not from that of instructions, then the separation is no longer possible. On the pragmatic level, the game and the rule become indiscernible, and what appears in their becoming indeterminated is a use or a form of life. "How am I able to follow a rule? Once I have exhausted the justifications, I have reached bedrock, and my spade is turned. Then I am inclined to say: 'this is simply what I do'" (Wittgenstein 1, §217).

In the same way, if we regard language from the point of view of grammatical rules, one can see that these define the language as a formal system while remaining distinct from it; but if we regard language in use (namely, as *parole* and not as *langue*), then it is just as true if not more so to say that the rules of grammar are drawn from the linguistic usage of the speakers and are not distinguished from them.

7.5. In reality the oft-invoked distinction between constitutive rule and pragmatic rule has no raison d'être. Every constitutive rule—the bishop moves in this or that way—can be formulated as a pragmatic rule—"one cannot move the bishop except diagonally"—and vice versa. The same happens with grammatical rules: the syntactic rule "in French the subject normally precedes the verb" can be formulated pragmatically as "you cannot say *pars je*; you can only say *je pars*." In truth it is a matter of two different ways of considering the game—or language: one as a formal system that exists in itself (namely, as a *langue*) and another as a use or praxis (namely, as a *parole*).

For this reason it has rightly been asked whether it is possible to transgress a rule of chess, like what constitutes checkmate. One would be tempted to say that transgression, which is impossible on the level of constitutive rules, is possible on the pragmatic level. In reality, the one who transgresses the rule simply ceases playing. Hence the special gravity of the swindler: the one who swindles does not transgress a rule but pretends to keep playing when in reality he has left the game.

7.6. What is really in question in constitutive rules, what they inadequately seek to prove, is something like the process of the autoconstitution of being, namely, the same process that philosophy had expressed in the concept of the *causa sui*. As Spinoza has suitably reminded us, this certainly cannot mean that "before existing it had brought to pass that it was to be, which is absurdity itself and cannot be" (Spinoza 4, II, XVII); instead it means the immanence of being to itself, an internal principle of self-movement and self-modification, because of which every being, as Aristotle says of *physis*, is always on the way to itself. The constitutive rule, like form of life, expresses this auto-hypostatic process, in which the constitutive is and remains immanent to the constituted, is actualized and expressed in it and by means of it, inseparable.

If one reads attentively, Wittgenstein writes as much in one of the rare passages in which he makes use (in English) of the term "to constitute" with respect to the rules of chess:

> What idea do we have of the king of chess, and what is its relation to the rules of chess? . . . Do these rules follow from the idea? No, the rules are not something contained in the idea and got by analyzing it. They constitute it. . . . The rules constitute the "freedom" of the pieces. (Wittgenstein 5, p. 86)

Rules are not separable into something like an idea or a concept of the king (the king is the piece that is moved according to this or that rule): they are immanent to the movements of the king; they express the auto-constitution process of their game. In the autoconstitution of a form of life what is in question is its freedom.

7.7. For this reason Wittgenstein does not consider form of life from the point of view of rules (constitutive or pragmatic as they may be) but from that of use, which is to say, starting from the moment where explanations and justifications are no longer possible. Here one touches a point at which "giving grounds, however, justifying the evidence, comes to and end" (Wittgenstein 6, §204), something like a "foundation" that corresponds to a level that is, so to speak, animal in the human, to his "natural history." As one of the very rare passages where the term "form of life" appears outside the *Philosophical Investigations* says, "Now I would like to regard this certainty, not as something akin to hastiness or superficiality, but as a form of life. . . . But that means I want to conceive it as something that lies beyond being justified or unjustified; as it were, as something animal" (ibid., §§358–359). The animality that is here in question is in no way opposed, according to the tradition of Western philosophy, to the human being as rational and speaking being. Quite the contrary, they are precisely the most human practices—speaking, hoping, recounting—which here reach their ultimate and most proper ground: "Giving orders, asking questions, telling stories, having a chat, are as much a part of our natural history as walking, eating, drinking, playing" (Wittgenstein 1, §25). For this ground impenetrable to explanations, which constitutive rules seek in vain to grasp, Wittgenstein also makes use of the terms "usage, custom, institutions": "This is simply what we do. This is use and custom among us, or a fact of our natural history" (Wittgenstein 2, pt. 1, §63); "To follow a rule, to make a report, to give an order, to play a game of chess, are customs (usages, relations)" (Wittgenstein 1, §199). The opacity of forms of life is of a practical and, in the last analysis, political nature.

§ 8   Work and Inoperativity

8.1. In his course on *L'herméneutique du sujet*, Foucault closely links the theme of truth and that of mode or form of life. Starting from a reflection on Greek Cynicism, he shows that the ethical practice of the self here takes the form not of a doctrine, as in the Platonic tradition, but of a test (*épreuve*), in which the choice of a mode of life becomes in every sense the decisive question. In the lineage of the Cynical model, which makes of the philosopher's life an unceasing challenge and a scandal, Foucault evokes two examples in which the claim of a certain form of life becomes ineludible: the political militant's style of life and, a little later, the life of the artist in modernity, which seems caught in a curious and inextricable circularity. On the one hand, the biography of the artist must testify through its very form to the truth of the work in which it is rooted. On the other hand, by contrast, it is the practice of art and the work that it produces that are to confer on the life itself the seal of authenticity.

Although the problem of the relation between truth and form of life is certainly one of the essential themes of the course, Foucault does not linger further on the at-once exemplary and contradictory status of the condition of the artist in modernity. The coincidence between life and art that is in question here is, from Romanticism to contemporary art, a constant tendency, which has brought about a radical transformation in the mode of conceiving the work of art itself. This bears witness beyond any possible doubt to the fact that we are not dealing with an accidental question. Not only have art and life ended up being indetermined to such an extent that it has often become impossible to distinguish life practice from artistic practice, but starting from the twentieth-century avant-garde, this has had as a consequence a progressive dissolution of the very consistency of the work. The truth criterion of art has been displaced to such a degree into the minds and, very often, into the very bodies of the artist, into his or her physicality, that these latter have no need to exhibit a work except as ashes or as a document of their own vital praxis. The work is life and the life is only work: but in this coincidence, instead of being transformed or falling together, they continue to pursue each other in an endless fugue.

8.2. It is possible that in the paradoxical circularity of the artistic condition there comes to light a difficulty that concerns the very nature of what we call form-of-life. If life is here inseparable from its form, if *zoè* and *bios* are here intimately in contact, how are we to conceive their non-relation, how to think their being given together and simultaneously falling? What confers on form-of-life its truth and, at the same time, its errancy? And what relationship is there between artistic practice and form-of-life?

In traditional societies and, to a lesser extent, still today, every human existence is caught up in a certain praxis or in a certain mode of life—a trade, profession, precarious occupation (or today, increasingly often, in a privative form, unemployment)—that in some way defines it and with which it tends to identify itself more or less completely. For reasons that this is not the place to investigate but that certainly have to do with the privileged status that, beginning in modernity, is attributed to the work of art, artistic praxis has become the place where this identification comes to know a durable crisis, and the relation between the artist as producer and his work becomes problematic. Thus, while in classical Greece the activity of the artist was defined exclusively by his work, and, considered for this reason as *banausos*, he had a status that was, so to speak, residual with respect to the work, in modernity it is the work that comes to constitute in some way an embarrassing residual of the artist's creative activity and genius. It is not surprising, therefore, that contemporary art has achieved the decisive step of substituting the life itself for the work. But at this point, if one does not wish to remain imprisoned in a vicious circle, the problem becomes the entirely paradoxical one of trying to think the artist's form of life in itself, which is precisely what contemporary art attempts but does not seem to be able to achieve.

8.3. What we call form-of-life is not defined by its relation to a praxis (*energeia*) or a work (*ergon*) but by a potential (*dynamis*) and by an inoperativity. A living being, which seeks to define itself and give itself form through its own operation is, in fact, condemned to confuse its own life with its own operation, and vice versa. By contrast, there is form-of-life only where there is contemplation of a potential. Certainly there can only be contemplation of a potential in a work. But in contemplation, the work is deactivated and rendered inoperative, and in this way, restored to possibility, opened to a new possible use. That form of life is truly poetic that, *in its own work*, contemplates its own potential to do and not do and finds peace in it. *The truth that contemporary art never manages to bring to expression is inoperativity, which it seeks at all costs to make into a work.* If artistic practice is the place where one is made to feel most forcefully the urgency and, at the same time, the difficulty of the constitution of a form-of-life, that is because in it there has been preserved the experience of a relation to something that exceeds work and operation and yet remains inseparable from it. A living being can never be defined by its work but only by its inoperativity, which is to say, by the mode in which it maintains itself in relation with a pure potential in a work and constitutes-itself as form-of-life, in which *zoè* and *bios*, life and form, private and public enter into a threshold of indifference and what is in question is no longer life or work but happiness. And the painter, the poet, the thinker—and in general, anyone who practices a *poiesis* and an activity—are not the sovereign subjects of a creative operation and of a work. Rather, they are anonymous living beings who, by always rendering inoperative the works of language, of vision, of bodies, seek to have an experience of themselves and to constitute their life as form-of-life.

And if, as Bréal suggests, the term *ethos* is only the pronominal reflexive root *e* followed by the suffix *-thos* and thus means simply and literally "selfhood," namely, the mode in which each one enters into contact with oneself, then artistic practice, in the sense that we are here seeking to define, belongs above all to ethics and not to aesthetics; it is essentially use-of-oneself. At the point where he constitutes-himself as form-of-life, the artist is no longer the author (in the modern, essentially juridical sense of the term) of the work nor the proprietor of the creative operation. These latter are only something like the subjective remainders and the hypostases that result from the constitution of the form of life. For this reason Benjamin could claim that he did not want to be recognized (*Ich nicht* *erkannt sein will*, Benjamin 3, p. 532), and Foucault, even more categorically, that he did not want to identify himself ("I prefer not to identify myself"; Rabinow, p. 184 [in English in original]). Form-of-life can neither recognize itself nor be recognized, because the contact between life and form and the happiness that are in question in it are situated beyond every possible recognition and every possible work. In this sense, form-of-life is above all the articulation of a zone of irresponsibility, in which the identities and imputations of the juridical order are suspended.

§ 9   The Myth of Er

9.1. At the end of the *Republic*, Plato recounts the myth of Er the Pamphylian, who died in battle and unexpectedly returned to life when his body had already been laid on the funeral pyre to be burned. The report that he makes of his soul's voyage into "a certain daemonic place," where he witnessed the judgment of souls and the spectacle of their reincarnation in a new *bios*, is one of the most extraordinary visions of the hereafter, comparable in liveliness and richness of meaning with the *nekyia* in the *Odyssey* and Dante's *Comedy*. The first part of the account describes the judgment of the souls of the dead: between two adjacent chasms in the earth and two other openings in the heavens, there sit judges (*dikastai*) who,

> having rendered their verdict, ordered the just to go upward to the heavens through the door on the right, with signs of the judgment attached to their chests, and the unjust to travel downward through the opening on the left, with signs of all their deeds on their backs. When Er himself came forward, they told him that he was to be a messenger [*angelon*] to human beings about the things that were there, and that he was to listen to and look at everything that happened in that place. He said that he saw souls departing after judgment through one of the openings in the heavens and one in the earth, while through the other two souls were arriving. From the door in the earth souls came up covered with dust and dirt, and from the door in the heavens souls came down pure [*katharas*]. And the souls who were arriving all the time seemed to have been on long journeys so that they gladly went to the meadow, like a crowd going to a solemn festival [*en penegyrei*], and camped there. The souls who knew each other exchanged greetings, and those who

249

came up from the earth asked those who came down from the heavens about the things there and were in turn questioned by them about the things below. And so they told their stories to one another, the former weeping as they recalled all they had suffered and seen on their journey below earth, which lasted a thousand years, while the latter, who had come from heaven, told about how well they had fared and about the inconceivably fine and beautiful sights [*theas amechanous to kallos*] they had seen. There was much to tell, Glaucon, and it took a long time, but the main point was this: for each in turn of the unjust things they had done and for each in turn of the people they had wronged, they paid the penalty ten times over, once in every century of their journey. Since a century is roughly the length of a human life, this means that they paid a tenfold penalty for each injustice. (614c–615b)

9.2. The most significant part of the myth, at least for us, begins only at this point and concerns the choice that every soul, before reentering the cycle of birth and death, must make of its form of life, of its *bios*. All the souls, after having spent seven days in the meadow, on the eighth day had to go on a journey in order to reach on the fourth day a place from which they can make out

a straight column of life that stretched over the whole of heaven and earth, more like a rainbow than anything else, but brighter and more pure. After another day, they came to the light itself, and there, in the middle of the light, they saw the extremities of the bonds stretching from the heavens, for the light binds [*syndesmon*] the heavens like the cables girding a trireme and holds its entire revolution together. From the extremities hands the spindle [*atrakton*] of Ananke, by means of which all the spheres are turned. Its stem and hook are of adamant, whereas in its whorl [*sphondylos*] adamant is mixed with other kinds of material. The nature of the whorl was this: its shape was like that of an ordinary whorl, but from what Er said, we must understand its structure as follows. It was as if a big whorl had been made hollow by being thoroughly scooped out, with another smaller whorl closely fitted into it, like nested boxes, and there was a third whorl inside the second, and so on, making eight whorls altogether, lying inside one another, with their rims appearing as circles from above, while from the back they formed one continuous whorl around the stem, which was driven through the center of the eighth. The first or outside whorl had the widest circular rim; that of the sixth was second in width; the fourth was third; the eighth was fourth; the seventh was fifth; the fifth was sixth; the third was seventh; and the second was eighth. The firm of the largest was spangled; that of the seventh was brightest; that of the eighth took its color from the seventh's shining on it; the second and fifth were about equal in brightness, more yellow than the others; the third was the whitest in color; the fourth was rather red; and the sixth was second in whiteness. The whole spindle turned at the same speed, but as it turned, the inner circles gently revolved in a direction opposite to that of the whole. Of the whorls themselves, the eighth was the fastest, second came the seventh, sixth, and fifth, all the same speed; it seemed to them that the fourth was third in its speed of revolution; the fourth, third; and the second, fifth. The spindle itself turned on the lap of Ananke. And up above on each of the rims of the circles stood a Siren, who accompanied its revolution, uttering a single sound, one single note. And the concord of the eight notes produced a single harmony. And there were three other beings sitting at equal distances from one another, each on a throne. These were the Fates, the daughters of Ananke: Lachesis, Clotho, and Atropos. They were dressed in white, with garlands on their heads, and they sang to the music of the Sirens. Lachesis sang of the past, Clotho of the present, and Atropos of the future. With her right hand, Clotho touched the outer circumference of the spindle and helped it turn; Atropos with her left hand did the same to the inner ones; and Lachesis with both hands helped motions in turn. (616b–617d)

9.3. After this extraordinary vision, entirely under the sign of necessity and perfect—even if obscure—harmony, there follows, in stark contrast, the description of the choice that souls make of their modes of life. The unfailing rigor of a cosmic machine, which operates through bonds and chains and as a result produces a harmonic order, symbolized by the song of the Sirens and the Moirai, is now replaced by the "at once pitiful, ridiculous, and marvelous" spectacle (619e) of the way in which the souls again enter into the "death-bearing" cycle of birth (617d). If there had previously been bond, destiny, and necessity, here Ananke seems to cede her reign to Tyke, and everything becomes chance, contingency, and luck of the draw. And if the cipher of necessity was the wondrous metallic whorl that regulates the movements of the celestial spheres, that of contingency here has an entirely human and erratic name: *airesis*, "choice":

When the souls arrived at the light, they had to go to Lachesis. There a herald [*prophetes*] arranged them in order, took from the lap of Lachesis a number of lots [*klerous*—the tablet and piece of chalk that each citizen signed and then put in a receptacle for the drawing] and examples of modes of life [*bion paradeigmata*], mounted a high pulpit, and spoke to them: "Here is the message of Lachesis, the maiden daughter of Ananke: 'Ephemeral souls, this is the beginning of another mortal cycle bearing death [*periodou thnetou genous thanatephorou*]. Your daemon will not be assigned to you by lot; you will chose [*airesethe*] your daemon. The one who has the first life will be the first to choose a form of life to which he will then be bound by necessity [*aireistho bion oi synestai ex anankes*]. By contrast, virtue is free [*adespoton*, without a master, unallotted]; each will possess it to a greater or less degree, depending on whether he values or disdains it. The fault [*aitia*] lies with the one who makes the choice; the god is innocent.'" When he had said this, the herald threw the lots among all of them and each picked up [*anairesthai*, the same verb that Plato relates to the hypostases in Book VII of the *Republic*] the one that fell next to him, with the exception of Er, who wasn't allowed to choose. And the lot made it clear to the one who picked it up where in the order he would get to make his choice. After that, the herald placed on the ground before them the examples of modes of life. There were far more of them than there were souls present, and they were of all kinds, for the animals' forms of life [*bious*] were there, as well as all kinds of human forms of life. There were tyrannies among them, some of which lasted throughout life, while others ended halfway through in poverty, exile, and beggary. There were lives of famous men, some of whom were famous for the beauty of their appearance, others for strength or athletic prowess, others still for their high birth and the virtue or excellence of their ancestors. And there were also lives of men who weren't famous for any of these things. And the same for lives of women. But the arrangement of the soul was not included in the model because the soul is inevitably altered by the different lives it chooses. But all the other things were there, mixed with each other and with wealth, poverty, sickness, health, and the states intermediate [*mesoun*] to them. . . . Then our messenger from the other world reported that the herald spoke as follows: "There is a satisfactory life rather than a bad one available even for the one who comes last, provided that he chooses it rationally and lives it seriously. Therefore, let not the first be careless in his choice nor the last discouraged."

Er said that when the herald had told them this, the one who came up first chose the greatest tyranny. In his folly and greed he chose it without adequate examination and didn't notice that, among other evils, he was fated to eat his own children as a part of it. When he examined at leisure the life he had chosen, however, he beat his breast and bemoaned his choice. And ignoring the warning of the herald, he blamed chance [*tyken*], daemons, and everything else for these evils but himself. He was one of those who had come down from heaven, having lived his previous life in a well-ordered city, where he had participated in virtue through habit and without philosophy. Broadly speaking, indeed, most of those who were caught out in this way were souls who had come down from heaven and who were untrained in suffering as a result. The majority of those who had come up from the earth, on the other hand, having suffered themselves and seen others suffer, were in no rush to make their choices. Because of this and because of the chance of the lottery [*dià ten tou klerou tyken*], there was an interchange of goods and evils for most of the souls. However, if someone pursues philosophy in a sound manner when he comes to live here on earth and if the lottery doesn't make him one of the last to choose, then given what Er has reported about the next world, it looks as though not only will he be happy here but his journey from here to there and back again won't be along the rough underground [*chtho-nian*] path but along the smooth heavenly one.

Er said that the way in which souls chose their lives was a sight [*thean*] worth seeing, since it was pitiful, ridiculous, and marvelous [*eleinenkai gel-oian kai thaumasian*] to watch. For the most part, their choice depended upon the habit [*synethian*] of their former life. For example, he said that he saw the soul that had once belonged to Orpheus choosing a swan's life, because he hated the female sex because of his death at their hands and so was unwilling to have a woman conceive and give birth to him. Er saw the soul of Thamyris choosing the life of a nightingale, a swan choosing to change over to a human life, and other musical animals did the same thing. The twentieth soul chose the life of a lion. This was the soul of Ajax, son of Telamon. He avoided human life because he remembered the judgment about the armor. The next soul was that of Agamemnon, whose sufferings also had made him hate the human race, so he changed to the life of an eagle. Atalanta had been assigned a place near the middle, and when she saw great honors being given to a male athlete, she chose his life, unable to pass them by. After her, he saw the soul of Epeius, the son of Panopeus, taking on the nature of a craftswoman. And very close to last, he saw the soul of the ridiculous Theristes clothing itself as a monkey. Now, it chanced that the soul of Odysseus got to make its choice last of all, and since memory of its former sufferings had relieved its love of honor, it went around for a long time, looking for the life of a private individual who did his own work, and with difficulty he found one lying off somewhere neglected by the others. He chose it gladly and said that he'd have made the same choice even if he'd been first. Still other souls changed from animals into human beings, or from one kind of animal into another, with unjust people changing into wild animals, and just people into tame ones, and all sorts of mixtures occurred.

After all the souls had chosen their lives, they went forward to Lachesis in the same order in which they had made their choices, and she assigned to each the daemon it had chosen as guardian of its life and fulfiller of its choice. This daemon first led the soul under the hand of Clotho as it turned the revolving spindle to confirm the fate [*moiran*] that the lottery and its own choice had given it. After receiving her touch, he led the soul to the spinning of Atropos, to make what had been spun irreversible [*ametastropha*]. Then, without turning around, they went from there under the throne of Ananke, and, when all of them had passed through, they traveled to the plane of Lethe in burning, choking, terrible heat, for it was empty of trees and earthly vegetation. And there, beside the river of unheeding, whose water no vessel can hold, they camped, for night was coming on. All of them had to drink a certain measure of this water, but those who weren't saved by reason drank more than that, and as each of them drank, he forgot everything and went to sleep. But around midnight there was a clap of thunder and an earthquake, and they were suddenly carried away from there, this way and that, up to their births, like shooting stars. Er himself was forbidden to drink the water. All the same, he didn't know how he had come back to his body, except that waking up suddenly he saw himself lying on the pyre at dawn. (617b–621b)

9.4. Every reading of the myth of Er must try to define the strategy in which it is inscribed, above all by singling out the problem that Plato is seeking to understand through it. In his commentary, Proclus formulates it in this way: it is a question of "showing the whole of providence, whether of Gods or of daemons, insofar as it concerns the soul, its descent into birth [*genesis*], its being separated from it, and the multiform modes of its behavior." Stated more precisely: the problem that Plato wants to address through the myth is the fact that, with birth, every soul seems to find itself necessarily and irrevocably united to a certain form of life (*bios*), which it abandons at death. The life (*zoè*) of mortals (the soul is the principle of life) is always in a certain *bios*, in a certain mode of life (we could say that it is "thrown" into it), and yet it does not coincide with this latter, nor is it united to it by any substantial connection. The myth explains this factical union—which includes a non-coincidence and a gap and, at the same time, a necessary bond—by means of the idea of a "choice": each soul, on entering into birth, chooses its *bios* and then forgets having done so. From this moment on, it finds itself united to the form of life that it has chosen by a necessary bond (*oi synesthai ex anankes*). For this reason Lachesis can say that "the fault lies with the one who makes the choice; the god is innocent."

That is to say, the myth seems to explain the irreparable union of each soul with a certain form of life in terms that are moral and, in some way, even juridical: there has been a "choice," and there is therefore a responsibility and a fault (*aitia*). To the physics of the first part of the account, which explains necessity in terms of a cosmic machine, there corresponds an *a posteriori* necessity, which results from an ethical choice (for this reason Proclus speaks of a "necessity of result"; Proclus 2, p. 234).

9.5. Karl Reinhardt has shown that in Plato, *mythos* and *logos*, explanation through story and dialectical rigor, are not contradictory but are mutually integrated (Reinhardt, passim). This means that, in our case as well, the myth is a complex figure, which seeks to explain something that *logos* by itself cannot clarify and that therefore demands in its turn an uncommon hermeneutical capacity. The myth of Er thus seems to suggest that the factical union of soul and form of life must be explained as a choice, which therefore introduces into the harmonious necessity of the cosmos something like a moral fault (Porphyry, albeit with great reserve, speaks here of something like a "free will," *to eph' emin*, that which is in our power; Porphyry, *On Free Will*, qtd. in Proclus 2, p. 353). But is it really so? Do the souls really choose their life freely from among the "examples" (*paradeigmata*) that the daughter of necessity, Lachesis (the name simply means: "the one who distributes lots"), puts before them?

First of all we will do well not to let it escape us that the image of cosmic necessity, which takes up the first part of Er's report, not only is not as serene and harmonic as the commentators profess but includes decidedly sinister traits. Plato certainly could not have been ignorant of the fact that the Moirai are inscribed in the lineage of Night, before whom even Zeus shows terror (in Homer, the Moira is defined as "destructive" and "difficult to bear"). The threads that the Moirai spin out are the days of our life, which Atropos (the name means "she who cannot be dissuaded," "the inexorable") suddenly cuts. The Sirens are creatures who are just as sinister, true and proper goddesses of death (Kerényi, p. 58), birds with the strongest of claws. In the *Odyssey*, they dwell on an island full of putrefied bones and desiccated human skins and enchant sailors with their song to make shipwreck there. This is so much the case that to avoid having them cast a gloomy shadow over the cosmic machine, Proclus suggests, obviously without the slightest foundation, that Plato actually meant to refer to the Muses.

But even the singular machine of adamant and other metals chained to the heavens has nothing reassuring about it. If Proclus feels the need to explain that adamant is the symbol of inalterability (Proclus 2, p. 159), this is because he knew perfectly well that in Hesiod, adamant is linked to the third age of the world, that of bronze, a terrible and violent one after the happy age of gold and the less happy age of silver: human beings had arms and houses of bronze then, but their heart, said Hesiod, was adamant. Everything leads one to think that by inserting these and other grim traits (like the "choking, terrible heat" and the desert of Lethe, absolutely barren of every form of life) into the vision of Er, Plato intended to suggest that it was precisely not an image of justice and harmony.

9.6. Let us now look to the souls who, obeying Lachesis's proclamation, choose their forms of life. Just as the machine of necessity was not, in reality, either just or harmonious, in the same way the souls' choice is not properly a free choice. First of all, the order in which the souls must make their choice depends on the way—it is not clear if it is by chance or decided by Lachesis—in which the lots are cast. All the souls pick up the lot that has fallen near them and, according to the order that has befallen them, choose the paradigm of life that the herald has placed on the ground in front of them. If Er defines the spectacle of this choice as "pitiful" and "ridiculous," that is because the souls, as the examples of Orpheus, Thamyris, Ajax son of Telamon, Agamemnon, Atalanta, Ulysses, and Theristes eloquently show, do not choose freely but "according to the habit [*synetheia*, the mode of living] of their former life." For this reason, Porphyry writes that Plato in this way risks "doing away with free will and, more generally, what we call autonomy of choice, if it is true that the souls arrive at their choice in consequence of their prior lives according to preceding cycles and with a character already formed according to what they have loved and· hated" (ibid., p. 349). Even more pertinent is the other objection mentioned by Porphyry, concerning the irrevocable character of the choice, confirmed by the Moirai and by the daemon who will keep watch so that the soul will remain faithful to its choice: "But if all this has been spun, determined by necessity, sanctioned by the Moirai, by Lethe, by Ananke, if a daemon guards the fate and keeps watch so that it is accomplished, of what are we ever masters and in what sense can one say 'virtue is free'?" (p. 350).

To the pseudo-justice of a blind and violent necessity, which seems to make use of souls for its own inscrutable designs, there corresponds the pseudo-freedom of the souls who believe they are choosing but who in this way do nothing but submit to a destiny that has been decided elsewhere. If the game is fixed in this sense, how can judges judge actions that depend on a choice that one is not only not free to revoke but that has, moreover, been worked out as a consequence of past behavior, over which the agent no longer has any power?

9.7. It is necessary to reflect on the "ridiculous" (*geloian*) character of the spectacle (*thea*, the term used by Plato, means "sight" but also "theatrical spectacle") of the choice that the souls make of their *bioi*. That is to say, Er attends a spectacle that, even though it should arouse pity (*eleinen*), actually seems ridiculous to him. If one recalls the preference that Plato seems to accord to comedy, in particular to mime (according to a durable legend, attested by Diogenes Laertius [III, 18] and repeated by Valerius Maximus and Quintilian, he loved the mimes of Sophron so much that he imitated their characters—*ethopoiesai*—and kept them under his pillow at the moment of his death), one could say that Er attends a comic spectacle, in which what was in question was an "ethology," a "description of characters," or a *mimesis biou*, an imitation of form of life ("mime is an imitation of *bios*, which includes both the decent and the indecent"; Keil, p. 491). What in tragedy is presented as the choice of a destiny is actually a comic gesture, the choice of a character. The choice of forms of life, despite the risk (*kindynos*, 618b) that it entails, is thus in the last analysis comical, and in philosophy, which exhibits and describes this ethology, what is in question is an ironic salvation rather than a condemnation of character without appeal. It is in this sense that one should read the passage, precisely at the end of the *Symposium*, in which Socrates convinces Aristophanes and Agathon that the same person ought to compose tragedies and comedies and that "the skillful tragic dramatist should also be a comic poet" (223d).

9.8. What, then, is the sense of the myth that closes the *Republic*, which is to say, a dialogue whose themes are justice and politics? One might say that once the soul, following the decree of necessity, has entered into the cycle of births and has chosen a form of life, all justice—both on its own part and on that of those who must judge him—is impossible. To a blind choice there can only correspond a blind necessity, and vice versa.

And yet there is a passage, which we have up to now omitted to transcribe, in which Plato seems precisely to want to suggest the way of "choosing always and on every occasion the best form of life among those possible." Immediately after having described (618a) how, in Er's report, the modes of life had been mixed before them, some united to riches or poverty, the others to sickness or to health, while others still were intermediate (*mesoun*) among them, Plato adds:

> Now, it seems that it is here, Glaucon, that a human being faces the greatest danger of all. And because of this, each of us must neglect all other subjects and be most concerned to seek out and learn those that will enable him to distinguish the good [*chreston*, literally "usable"] life from the bad and always to choose always and on every occasion the best *bios* among those possible. He should think over all the things that we have mentioned and how they jointly and severally stand with regard to the virtuous life [*pros areten biou*]. That way he will know what the good and bad effects of beauty are when it is mixed with wealth, poverty, and a particular state of the soul. He will know the effects of high or low birth, private life or ruling office, physical strength or weakness, ease or difficulty in learning, and all the things that are either naturally a part of the soul or are acquired, and he will know what they achieve when mixed with one another. And from all this he will be able, by considering the nature of the soul, to reason out which life is better and which worse and to choose accordingly, calling a life worse if it leads the soul to become more unjust, better if it leads the soul to become more just, and ignoring everything else. We have seen that this is the best way to choose, whether in life or death [*zonti te kai teleteusanti*]. Hence we must go down to Hades holding with adamantine determination to the belief that this is so, lest we be dazzled there by wealth and other such evils, rush into a tyranny or some other similar course of action, do many irreparable evils, and suffer even worse ones. And we must always know how to choose the mean form of life [*ton meson bion*] among them and how to avoid either of the extremes [*hyperballonta*], as far as possible, both in this life and in all those beyond it. This is the way that a human being becomes happiest. (618c–619b)

9.9. What does it mean to choose "the mean *bios*"? First of all, a preliminary observation, which concerns the place and time when the choice happens. By writing "whether in life or death" and by specifying a little later "both in this life and in all those beyond it," Plato reveals that what in the myth seemed to concern only the souls of the dead and the not yet born actually refers also and above all to the living. The choice that the myth situates in a "certain daemonic place" takes place also in this life, in which according to the myth souls are always already linked by necessity to a certain form of life. The life of the mean is, that is to say, the virtuous life, and virtue, being adespotic and unassignable, is not one among the various forms of life that souls can choose, but according to Lachesis, each one will have it to a greater or less extent according to whether it loves it or despises it.

If this is true—and it can mean nothing else for virtue to be adespotic—then the "choice" of the life of the mean is not properly a choice but rather a praxis, which by orienting itself in the inextricable mixture of nobility and obscurity, private and public, wealth and poverty, strength and weakness that characterize every *bios*, succeeds in distinguishing and discerning (*diagignoskonta*) the best form of life, namely, that which will render the soul most just. It is necessary to imagine *bios* as a single segment or a single field of forces defined by two opposed extremes (Plato calls them excesses, *ta hyperbollonta*): to choose the mean does not mean to choose a *bios* but, in the *bios* that it has befallen us to choose, to be in a position to neutralize and flee the extremes through virtue. The *mesos bios* cuts every life in half and, in this way, makes use of it and constitutes it into a form-of-life. It is not a *bios* but a certain mode of using and living *bios*.

9.10. It is from this perspective that one must recall that what the herald shows to the souls are not *bioi*, modes of life, but examples (*paradeimata*) of modes of life. Following up on the work of Victor Goldschmidt, we have elsewhere pointed out the peculiar function that the concept of a paradigm, which can refer to both ideas and sensible things, develops in Plato's thought. The example is a singular element that, by deactivating for an instant its empirical givenness, renders intelligible another singularity (or a group of singularities). By proposing paradigms of life and not simply lives to the souls, the herald gives them the possibility of understanding and rendering intelligible each form of life before choosing it, which is precisely what, in contrast with the majority of souls, the virtuous soul succeeds in doing. It is not surprising, then, that in the dialogue in which Plato reflects most extensively on the paradigm, it is never something given but is produced and recognized through a "bringing together," a "putting beside," and a "showing" (*Statesman*, 278b–c). Once again, what the myth presents as a fact (the paradigms of life placed on the ground by the herald) is actually the result of a discernment and a virtuous praxis, which confers on each *bios* an exemplary or paradigmatic character. The *mesos bios* is that form of life that is totally concerned with its own exemplarity (*forma vitae* in the vocabulary of monastic rules means "example of life, exemplary life").

9.11. In his reading of the myth of Er, Porphyry calls attention to the fact that Plato uses the term *bios* in an ambiguous way. That is to say, he means by this term both modes of life in the proper sense and *zoè*. Plato "does not speak of modes of life in the sense of the authors of the treatises *On Modes of Life*, who mention first one mode of life, that of the farmer, then another, that of the statesman, and then still another, the military life." Since, among the numerous modes of life in use among human beings, our free will can choose to abandon one in order to assume another, unprepared readers are surprised that, in the myth, the one who has chosen a *bios* remains bound to it by necessity.

> This is because, according to the Stoics, "mode of life" only has the meaning of rational life [*logikes zoes*], since they mean by this term a certain course [*diexodos*] constituted by actions, reflections, and effects that are produced or undergone. But Plato means by *bios* the lives [*zoas*] of animals as well. Thus for him the *zoè* of a swan is also a *bios*, and that of the lion as lion and that of the nightingale is a *bios* too. And that of men and women are also *bios*. . . . This is, for him, a primary meaning of the term *bios*, but there is another one that refers to accidental traits of these modes of life, a sort of character that is added in a secondary way to the principal sense. Thus for the dog *bios* in the principal sense is the *zoè* of the dog. By contrast, it is accidental to the canine life that it belongs to the species of dogs that hunt or that of bloodhounds or that of dogs who sit next to the table or that of guard dogs: this *bios* is secondary. And if, for animals deprived of free will, this character comes to be added by nature or by the training imposed by their master, it is also given to human beings by nature or by chance to be born of noble parents or to be endowed with physical beauty, and it is clear that this does not depend on our free will. Rather, as to the acquisition of a certain trade, occupation, or knowledge, as to undertaking the political life or public offices or other things of the kind, all this depends on us. . . . (Porphyry, *On Free Will*, qtd. in Proclus 2, p. 351)

This observation, which Porphyry uses solely to distinguish what depends on us from what we cannot change, deserves to be taken up and developed. In Plato, the soul certainly has an essential connection with *zoè* (it "carries life [*pherousa zoen*] into whatever it occupies"; *Phaedo*, 105c). By choosing a certain *bios*, a mode of life, it chooses or has already chosen a *zoè* as well: the life of a man, a woman, a swan, a lion, a nightingale. And yet, just as it cannot be identified with a certain *bios*, neither can it be resolved into a certain *zoè* (the soul "chooses" both, and Plato does not seem to distinguish, as Porphyry professes, between the choice of a *zoè* and that of a *bios* as far as responsibility is concerned).

If the distinction in time between a "before birth," an "after birth," and an "after death" is, as we have seen, only an expedient of the myth, this means that in this life—which constitutes the problem that the myth seeks to render comprehensible—a game is being played between three at once intimate and heterogeneous "partners": the soul, *zoè*, and *bios*. The soul is not (only) *zoè*, natural life, or (only) *bios*, politically qualified life: it is, *in them and between them*, that which, while not co-inciding with them, keeps them united and inseparable and, at the same time, prevents them from coinciding with each other. Among soul, *zoè*, and *bios* there is an intimate contact and an irreducible gap (this is the ul-timate sense of the image of the "choice": what is chosen does not belong to us, and yet in some way it has become ours). And the goal of the myth is not that of furnishing us with a different and better representation of the soul: rather, it is that of stopping representation, in order to exhibit a non-representable.

To comprehend the singular status of the Platonic *psychè*, it will be helpful to compare it with his disciple Aristotle's definition of the soul. Forcing the Platonic connection between soul and *zoè*, Aristotle defines the soul as "the being-at-work [*energeia*] of a body that has *zoè* in poten-tial," and in this way he identifies soul and life in action. On the other hand, having thus resolved the soul into *zoè*, he must then necessarily divide it and articulate it functionally into the vegetative, sensitive, and intellectual soul (or life), in order to then make of it, as we have seen, the presupposition of political existence (which entails a clear distinction and, at the same time, a strategic articulation between *zoè* and *bios*). For this reason there belongs to the vegetative soul a status that in some way recalls that of the Platonic *psychè*: it is separable according to *logos*, while in mortals the others cannot be separated from it.

Let us now return to the aporetic situation of the soul in Plato. While being factically united to a certain *zoè* and a certain *bios*, it remains ir-reducible to them. This irreducibility does not mean that the myth is to be read literally, as if souls existed separately in a certain daemonic or hyperuranian place. The soul moves the body from within and not from without like an adventitious external principle: according to the clear statement of the *Phaedrus* (245c), "every body that moves itself from within [*endothen*] is animate [*empsychon*], because this is the nature of the soul." Hence the striking silence in the myth—over which it seems that the commentators have not sufficiently lingered—on the way in which Er sees and recognizes the souls ("he said that he saw [*idein*] the soul that had once belonged to Orpheus . . ."), as if they were in some way constitutively united to their body or preserved its image. And yet it will be the soul and not the body that is to be judged for the actions committed during life.

The soul, just like form-of-life, is what *in* my *zoè*, *in* my bodily life does not coincide with my *bios*, with my political and social existence, and yet has "chosen" both, practices them both in this certain, unmistakable mode. It is itself, in this sense, the *mesos bios* that, in every *bios* and every *zoè*, adventurously severs, revokes, and realizes the choice that unites them by necessity in this certain life. Form-of-life, the soul, is the infinite complement between life and mode of life, what appears when they mutually neutralize one another and show the void that united them. *Zoè* and *bios*—this is perhaps the lesson of the myth—are neither separate nor coincident: between them, as a void of representation of which it is not possible to say anything except that it is "immortal" and "ungenerated" (*Phaedrus*, 246a), stands the soul, which holds them indissolubly in contact and testifies for them.

§ Epilogue: Toward a Theory of Destituent Potential

1. The archeology of politics that was in question in the "Homo Sacer" project did not propose to critique or correct this or that concept, this or that institution of Western politics. The issue was rather to call into question the place and the very originary structure of politics, in order to try to bring to light the *arcanum imperii* that in some way constituted its foundation and that had remained at the same time fully exposed and tenaciously hidden in it.

The identification of bare life as the prime referent and ultimate stakes of politics was therefore the first act of the study. The originary structure of Western politics consists in an *ex-ceptio*, in an inclusive exclusion of human life in the form of bare life. Let us reflect on the peculiarity of this operation: life is not in itself political—for this reason it must be excluded from the city—and yet it is precisely the *exceptio*, the exclusion-inclusion of this Impolitical, that founds the space of politics.

It is important not to confuse bare life with natural life. Through its division and its capture in the apparatus of the exception, life assumes the form of bare life, which is to say, that of a life that has been cut off and separated from its form. It is in this sense that one must understand the thesis at the end of *Homo Sacer I* according to which "the fundamental activity of sovereign power is the production of bare life as originary political element" (Agamben 4, p. 202/181). And it is this bare life (or "sacred" life, if *sacer* first of all designates a life that can be killed without committing homicide) that functions in the juridico-political machine of the West as a threshold of articulation between *zoè* and *bios*, natural life and politically qualified life. And it will not be possible to think another

263

dimension of politics and life if we have not first succeeded in deactivating the apparatus of the exception of bare life.

2. Yet in the course of the study, the structure of the exception that had been defined with respect to bare life has been revealed more generally to constitute in every sphere the structure of the *archè*, in the juridico-political tradition as much as in ontology. In fact, one cannot understand the dialectic of the foundation that defines Western ontology, from Aristotle on, if one does not understand that it functions as an exception in the sense we have seen. The strategy is always the same: something is divided, excluded, and pushed to the bottom, and precisely through this exclusion, it is included as *archè* and foundation. This holds for life, which in Aristotle's words "is said in many ways"—vegetative life, sensitive life, intellectual life, the first of which is excluded in order to function as foundation for the others—but also for being, which is equally said in many ways, one of which is separated as foundation.

It is possible, however, that the mechanism of the exception is constitutively connected to the event of language that coincides with anthropogenesis. According to the structure of the presupposition that we have already reconstructed above, in happening, language excludes and separates from itself the non-linguistic, and in the same gesture, it includes and captures it as that with which it is always already in relation. That is to say, the *ex-ceptio*, the inclusive exclusion of the real from the *logos* and in the *logos* is the originary structure of the event of language.

3. In *State of Exception*, the juridico-political machine of the West was thus described as a double structure, formed from two heterogeneous and yet intimately coordinated elements: one normative and juridical in the strict sense (*potestas*) and one anomic and extrajuridical (*auctoritas*). The juridico-normative element, in which power in its effective form seems to reside, nevertheless has need of the anomic element for it to be able to apply itself to life. On the other hand, *auctoritas* can affirm itself and have sense only in relation to *potestas*. The state of exception is the apparatus that must ultimately articulate and hold together the two aspects of the juridico-political machine by instituting a threshold of undecidability between anomie and *nomos*, between life and the juridical order, between *auctoritas* and *potestas*. As long as the two elements remain correlated but conceptually, temporally, and personally distinct—as in republican

Rome, in the opposition between senate and people, or in medieval Europe, in that between spiritual power and temporal power—their dialectic can function in some way. But when they tend to coincide in one person alone, when the state of exception, in which they are indeterminated, becomes the rule, then the juridico-political system is transformed into a killing machine.

In *The Kingdom and the Glory*, an analogous structure was brought to light in the relation between rule and governance and between inoperativity and glory. Glory appeared there as an apparatus directed at capturing within the economic-governmental machine the inoperativity of human and divine life that our culture does not seem to be in a position to think and that nevertheless never ceases to be invoked as the ultimate mystery of divinity and power. This inoperativity is so essential for the machine that it must be captured and maintained at all costs at its center in the form of glory and acclamations that, through the media, never cease to carry out their doxological function even today.

In the same way some years earlier in *The Open*, the anthropological machine of the West was defined by the division and articulation within the human being of the human and the animal. And at the end of the book, the project of a deactivation of the machine that governs our conception of the human demanded not the study of new articulations between the animal and the human so much as rather the exposition of the central void, of the gap that separates—in the human being—the human and the animal. That which—once again in the form of the exception—was separated and then articulated together in the machine must be brought back to its division so that an inseparable life, neither animal nor human, can eventually appear.

4. In all these figures the same mechanism is at work: the *archè* is constituted by dividing the factical experience and pushing down to the origin—that is, excluding—one half of it in order then to rearticulate it to the other by including it as foundation. Thus, the city is founded on the division of life into bare life and politically qualified life, the human is defined by the exclusion-inclusion of the animal, the law by the *exceptio* of anomie, governance through the exclusion of inoperativity and its capture in the form of glory.

If the structure of the *archè* of our culture is such, then thought finds itself here confronted with an arduous task. Indeed, it is not a question of thinking, as it has for the most part done up to now, new and more effective articulations of the two elements, playing the two halves of the machine off against one another. Nor is it a matter of archeologically going back to a more originary beginning: philosophical archeology cannot reach a beginning other than the one that may perhaps result from the deactivation of the machine (in this sense first philosophy is always final philosophy).

The fundamental ontological-political problem today is not work but inoperativity, not the frantic and unceasing study of a new operativity but the exhibition of the ceaseless void that the machine of Western culture guards at its center.

5. In modern thought, radical political changes have been thought by means of the concept of a "constituent power." Every constituted power presupposes at its origin a constituent power that, through a process that as a rule has the form of a revolution, brings it into being and guarantees it. If our hypothesis on the structure of the *archè* is correct, if the fundamental ontological problem today is not work but inoperativity, and if this latter can nevertheless be attested only with respect to a work, then access to a different figure of politics cannot take the form of a "constituent power" but rather that of something that we can provisionally call "destituent potential." And if to constituent power there correspond revolutions, revolts, and new constitutions, namely, a violence that puts in place and constitutes a new law, for destituent potential it is necessary to think entirely different strategies, whose definition is the task of the coming politics. A power that has only been knocked down with a constituent violence will resurge in another form, in the unceasing, unwinnable, desolate dialectic between constituent power and constituted power, between the violence that puts the juridical in place and violence that preserves it.

The paradox of constituent power is that as much as jurists more or less decisively underline its heterogeneity, it remains inseparable from constituted power, with which it forms a system. Thus, on the one hand, one affirms that constituent power is situated beyond the State, exists without it, and continues to remain external to the State even after its constitution, while the constituted power that derives from it exists only in the State. But on the other hand, this originary and unlimited power—which can, as such, threaten the stability of the system—necessarily ends up being confiscated and captured in the constituted power to which it has given origin and survives in it only as the power of constitutional revision. Even Sieyès, perhaps the most intransigent theorist of the transcendence of constituent power, in the end must drastically limit its omnipotence, leaving it no other existence than the shadowy one of a *Jury constitutionnaire*, to which is entrusted the task of modifying the text of the constitution, according to definitively established procedures.

Here the paradoxes theologians had to grapple with concerning the problem of divine omnipotence seem to repeat themselves in secularized form. Divine omnipotence implied that God could do anything whatsoever, including destroying the world that he had created or annulling or subverting the providential laws with which he had willed to direct humanity toward salvation. To contain these scandalous consequences of divine omnipotence, theologians distinguished between absolute power and ordained power: *de potentia absoluta*, God can do anything, but *de potentia ordinata*, which is to say, once he has willed something, his power is thereby limited.

Just as absolute power is in reality only the presupposition of ordained power, which the latter needs to guarantee its own unconditional validity, so also can one say that constituent power is what constituted power must presuppose to give itself a foundation and legitimate itself. According to the schema that we have described many times, constituent is that figure of power in which a destituent potential is captured and neutralized, in such a way as to assure that it cannot be turned back against power or the juridical order as such but only against one of its determinate historical figures.

6. For this reason, the third chapter of the first part of *Homo Sacer I* affirmed that the relationship between constituent power and constituted power is just as complex as that which Aristotle establishes between potential and act, and it sought to clarify the relation between the two terms as a relation of ban or abandonment. The problem of constituent power here shows its irreducible ontological implications. Potential and act are only two aspects of the process of the sovereign autoconstitution of Being, in which the act presupposes itself as potential and the latter is maintained in relation with the former through its own suspension, its own being able not to pass into act. And on the other hand, act is only a conservation and a "salvation" (*soteria*)—in other words, an *Aufhebung*—of potential.

For the sovereign ban, which applies to the exception in no longer applying, corresponds to the structure of potential, which maintains itself in relation to act precisely through its ability not to be. Potential (in its double appearance as potential to and potential-not-to) is that through which Being founds itself sovereignly, which is to say, without anything proceeding or determining it, other than its own ability not to be. And an act is sovereign when it realizes itself by simply taking away its own potential-not-to, letting itself be, giving itself to itself. (Agamben 4, p. 54/46)

Hence the difficulty of thinking a purely destituent potential, which is to say, one completely set free from the sovereign relation of the ban that links it to constituted power. The ban here appears as a limit-form of relation, in which being is founded by maintaining itself in relation with something unrelated, which is in reality only a presupposition of itself. And if being is only the being "under the ban"—which is to say, abandoned to itself—of beings, then categories like "letting-be," by which Heidegger sought to escape from the ontological difference, also remain within the relation of the ban.

For this reason the chapter could conclude by proclaiming the project of an ontology and a politics set free from every figure of relation, even from the limit-form of the ban that is the sovereign ban:

Instead one must think the existence of potential without any relation to being in act—not even in the extreme form of the ban and the potential-not-to be—and of the act no longer as fulfillment and manifestation of potential—not even in the form of self-giving and letting be. This implies, however, nothing less than thinking ontology and politics beyond every figure of relation, beyond even the limit-relation that is the sovereign ban. (Ibid., p. 55/47)

Only in this context could it become possible to think a purely destituent potential, that is to say, one that never resolves itself into a constituted power.

א.   It is the secret solidarity between the violence that founds the juridical order and that which conserves it that Benjamin thought in the essay "Critique of Violence," in seeking to define a form of violence that escapes this dialectic: "On the interruption of this cycle maintained by mythic forms of law, on the destitution [*Entsetzung*] of the juridical order together with all the powers on which it depends as they depend on it, finally therefore on the destitution of state violence, a new historical epoch is founded" (Benjamin 4, pp. 108–109/251–252). Only a power that has been rendered inoperative and deposed by means of a violence that does not aim to found a new law is fully neutralized. Benjamin identified this violence—or according to the double meaning of the German term *Gewalt*, "destituent power [It., *potere destituente*]"—in the proletarian general strike, which Sorel opposed to the simply political strike. While the suspension of labor in the political strike is violent, "since it provokes [*veranlasst*, "occasions," "induces"] only an external modification of labor conditions, the second, as a pure means, is non-violent" (ibid., p. 101/246). Indeed, it does not imply the resumption of labor "following external concessions and this or that modification to working conditions" but the decision to take up a labor only if it has been entirely transformed and not imposed by the state, namely, a "subversion that this kind of strike not so much provokes [*veranlasst*] as realizes [*vollzieht*]" (ibid.). In the difference between *veranlassen*, "to induce, to provoke," and *vollziehen*, "to complete, to realize," is expressed the opposition between constituent power, which destroys and re-creates ever new forms of juridical order, without ever definitively deposing it, and destituent violence, which, insofar as it deposes the juridical order once and for all, immediately inaugurates a new reality. "For this reason, the first of these undertakings is lawmaking but the second anarchistic" (ibid.).

At the beginning of the essay, Benjamin defines pure violence through a critique of the taken-for-granted relation between means and ends. While juridical violence is always a means—legitimate or illegitimate—with respect to an end—just or unjust—the criteria of pure or divine violence is not to be sought in its relation to an end but in "the sphere of means, without regard for the ends they serve" (p. 87/236). The problem of violence is not the oft-pursued one of identifying just ends but that of "finding a different kind of violence . . . that was not related to them as means at all but in some different way" (pp. 102–103/247).

What is in question here is the very idea of instrumentality, which beginning with the Scholastic concept of "instrumental cause," we have seen to characterize the modern conception of use and of the sphere of technology. While these latter were defined by an instrument that appears as such only insofar as it is incorporated into the purpose of the principal agent, Benjamin here has in mind a "pure means," namely, a means that appears as such, only insofar as it emancipates itself from every relation to an end. Violence as pure means is never a means with regard to an end: it is attested only as exposition and destitution of the relationship between violence and juridical order, between means and end.

7. A critique of the concept of relation has been indicated in Chapter 2.8 of the second part of the present study, in connection with Augustine's theorem: "Every essence that is called something by way of relationship is also something besides the relationship" (*Omnis essentia quae relative dicitur est etiam aliquid excepto relativo*). For Augustine, it was a question of thinking the relation between unity and trinity in God, namely, of saving the unity of the divine essence without negating its

articulation into three persons. We have shown that Augustine solves this problem by excluding and at the same time including relation in being and being in relation. The formula *excepto relativo* is to be read here according to the logic of the exception: the relative is both excluded and included in being, in the sense that the trinity of persons is captured in the essence-potential of God, in such a way that the latter is still maintained as distinct from the former. In Augustine's words, essence, which is and is said in relation, is something beyond relation. But this means, according to the structure of the sovereign exception that we have defined, that being is a presupposition of relation.

We can therefore define relation as that which constitutes its elements by at the same time presupposing them as unrelated. In this way, relation ceases to be one category among others and acquires a special ontological rank. Both in the Aristotelian potential-act, essence-existence apparatus, and in trinitarian theology, relation inheres in being according to a constitutive ambiguity: being precedes relation and exists beyond it, but it is always already constituted through relation and included in it as its presupposition.

8. It is in Scotus's doctrine of formal being that the ontological rank of relation finds its most coherent expression. On the one hand, he takes up the Augustinian axiom and specifies it in the form *omne enim quod dicitur ad aliquid est aliquid praeter relationem* ("what is said with respect to something is something beyond relation"; *Op. Ox.*, 1, d. 5, q. 1, n. 18; qtd. in Beckmann, p. 206). The correction shows that what is in question for Scotus is the problem of relation as such. If, as he writes, "relation is not included in the concept of the absolute" (ibid.), it follows that the absolute is always already included in the concept of relation. With an apparent reversal of Augustine's theorem, which brings to light the implication that remained hidden in it, he can therefore write that *omne relativum est aliquid excepta relatione* ("every relative is something excepted from the relation"; ibid., 1, d. 26, q. 1, n. 33).

What is decisive, in any case, is that for Scotus relation implies an ontology, or a particular form of being, which he defines, with a formula that will have great success in medieval thought, as *ens debilissimum*: "among all beings relation is a very weak being, because it is only the mode of being of two beings with respect to one another" (*relatio inter omnia entia est ens debilissimum, cum sit sola habitudo duorum*; *Super praed.*, q. 25, n. 10; qtd. in

Beckmann, p. 45). But this lowest form of being—which as such is difficult to know (*ita minime cognoscibile in se*; ibid.)—in reality takes on a constitutive function in Scotus's thought—and starting with him, in the history of philosophy up to Kant—because it coincides with the specific contribution of his philosophical genius, the definition of the formal distinction and of the status of the transcendental.

In the formal distinction, that is to say, Scotus has thought the being of language, which cannot be *realiter* different from the thing that it names; otherwise it could not manifest it and make it known but must have a certain consistency of its own; otherwise it would be confused with the thing. What is distinguished from the thing not *realiter* but *formaliter* is its having a name—the transcendental is language.

9. If a privileged ontological status belongs to relation, it is because the very presupposing structure of language comes to expression in it. What Augustine's theorem affirms is in fact: "all that is said enters into a relation and therefore is also something else before and outside the relation (that is to say, it is an unrelated presupposition)." The fundamental relation—the onto-logical relation—runs between beings and language, between Being and its being said or named. *Logos* is this relation, in which beings and their being said are both identified and differentiated, distant and indistinguishable.

Thinking a purely destituent potential in this sense means interrogating and calling into question the very status of relation, remaining open to the possibility that the ontological relation is not, in fact, a relation. This means engaging in a decisive hand-to-hand confrontation [It., *corpo a corpo*] with the weakest of beings that is language. But precisely because its ontological status is weak, language is the most difficult to know and grasp, as Scotus had intuited. The almost invincible force of language is in its weakness, in its remaining unthought and unsaid in what says and in that of which it is said.

For this reason, philosophy is born in Plato precisely as an attempt to get to the bottom of *logoi*, and as such, it has a political character immediately and from the very start. And for this reason, when with Kant the transcendental ceases to be what thought must get to the bottom of and instead becomes the stronghold in which it takes refuge, then philosophy loses its relation with Being and politics enters into a decisive crisis. A new dimension for politics will be opened only when human beings—

the beings who have *logos* to the same extent that they are possessed by it—have gotten to the bottom of this weakest potential that determines them and tenaciously involves them in an errancy—history—that seems interminable. Only then—but this "then" is not future but always under way—will it be possible to think politics beyond every figure of relation.

10. Just as the tradition of metaphysics has always thought the human being in the form of an articulation between two elements (nature and *logos*, body and soul, animality and humanity), so also has Western political philosophy always thought politics in the figure of the relation between two figures that it is a question of linking together: bare life and power, the household and the city, violence and institutional order, anomie (anarchy) and law, multitude and people. From the perspective of our study, we must instead attempt to think humanity and politics as what results from the disconnection of these elements and investigate not the metaphysical mystery of conjunction but the practical and political one of their disjunction.

Let us define relation as what constitutes its elements by presupposing them, together, as unrelated. Thus, for example, in the couples living being/language, constituent power/constituted power, bare life/law, it is evident that the two elements are always mutually defined and constituted through their oppositional relation, and as such, they cannot preexist it; and yet the relation that unites them presupposes them as unrelated. What we have defined in the course of this study as the ban is the link, at once attractive and repulsive, that links the two poles of the sovereign exception.

We call a potential destituent that is capable of always deposing ontological-political relations in order to cause a contact (in Colli's sense; cf. part III, §6.5 above) to appear between their elements. Contact is not a point of tangency nor a *quid* or a substance in which two elements communicate: it is defined only by an absence of representation, only by a caesura. Where a relation is rendered destitute and interrupted, its elements are in this sense in contact, because the absence of every relation is exhibited between them. Thus, at the point where a destituent potential exhibits the nullity of the bond that pretended to hold them together, bare life and sovereign power, anomie and *nomos*, constituent power and constituted power are shown to be in contact without any relation. But precisely for this reason, what has been divided from itself and captured in the exception—life, anomie, anarchic potential—now appears in its free and intact form.

11. Here the proximity between destituent potential and what in the course of our research we have designated by the term "inoperativity" appears clearly. In both what is in question is the capacity to deactivate something and render it inoperative—a power, a function, a human operation—without simply destroying it but by liberating the potentials that have remained inactive in it in order to allow a different use of them.

An example of a destituent strategy that is neither destructive nor constituent is that of Paul in the face of the law. Paul expresses the relationship between the messiah and the law with the verb *katargein*, which means "render inoperative" (*argos*), "deactivate" (Estienne's *Thesaurus* renders it with *reddo aergon et inefficacem, facio cessare ab opere suo, tollo, aboleo*, "to render *aergon* and ineffective, to cause to cease from its work, to take away, to abolish"). Thus, Paul can write that the messiah "will render inoperative [*katargese*] every power, every authority, and every potential" (1 Corinthians 15:24) and at the same time that "the messiah is the *telos* [namely, end or fulfillment] of the law" (Romans 10:4): here inoperativity and fulfillment perfectly coincide. In another passage, he says of believers that they have been "rendered inoperative [*katargethemen*] with respect to the law" (Romans 7:6). The customary translations of this verb with "destroy, annul" are not correct (the Vulgate renders it more cautiously with *evacuari*), all the more so because Paul affirms in a famous passage that he wants to "hold firm the law" (*nomon istanomen*; Romans 3:31). Luther, with an intuition whose significance would not escape Hegel, translates *katargein* with *aufheben*, which is to say, with a verb that means both "abolish" and "preserve."

In any case, it is certain that for Paul it is not a matter of destroying the law, which is "holy and just," but of deactivating its action with respect to sin, because it is through the law that human beings come to know sin and desire: "I would not have known what it is to desire if the law had not said, 'You shall not desire.' But seizing an opportunity in the commandment, sin rendered operative [*kateirgasato*, "activated"] in me all kinds of desire" (Romans 7:7–8).

It is this operativity of the law that the messianic faith neutralizes and renders inoperative, without for that reason abolishing the law. The law that is "held firm" is a law rendered destitute of its power to command, that is to say, it is no longer a law of commands and works (*nomos ton en-tolon*, Ephesians 2:15; *ton ergon*, Romans 3:27) but of faith (*nomos pisteos*, Romans 3:27). And faith is essentially not a work but an experience of the word ("So faith comes from what is heard, and what is heard comes through the word"; Romans 10:17).

That is to say, the messiah functions in Paul as a destituent potential of the *mitzwoth* that define Jewish identity, without for that reason constituting another identity. The messianic (Paul does not know the term "Christian") does not represent a new and more universal identity but a caesura that passes through every identity—both that of the Jew and that of the Gentile. The "Jew according to the spirit" and "Gentile according to the flesh" do not define a subsequent identity but only the impossibility of every identity of coinciding with itself—namely, their destitution as identities: Jew as non-Jew, Gentile as non-Gentile. (It is probably according to a paradigm of this type that one could think a destitution of the apparatus of citizenship.)

In coherence with these premises, in a decisive passage of 1 Corinthians (7:29–31), Paul defines the form of life of the Christian through the formula *hos me*:

> I mean, brothers and sisters, time has grown short; what remains is so that those who have wives may be as not having, and those who mourn as not mourning, and those who rejoice as not rejoicing, and those who buy as not possessing, and those who use the world as not abusing. For the figure of this world is passing away.

The "as not" is a deposition without abdication. Living in the form of the "as not" means rendering destitute all juridical and social ownership, without this deposition founding a new identity. A form-of-life is, in this sense, that which ceaselessly deposes the social conditions in which it finds itself to live, without negating them, but simply by using them. "If," writes Paul, "at the moment of your call you find yourself in the condition of a slave, do not concern yourself with it: but even if you can become free, make use [*chresai*] rather of your condition as a slave" (1 Corinthians 7:21). "Making use" here names the deponent power of the Christian's form of life, which renders destitute "the figure of this world" (*to schema tou kosmou toutou*).

12. It is this destituent power [It., *potere destituente*] that both the anarchist tradition and twentieth-century thought sought to define without

truly succeeding in it. The destruction of tradition in Heidegger, the deconstruction of the *archè* and the fracture of hegemonies in Schürmann, what (in the footsteps of Foucault) I have called "philosophical archaeology," are all pertinent but insufficient attempts to go back to a historical *a priori* in order to depose it. But a good part of the practice of the artistic avant gardes and political movements of our time can also be seen as the attempt—so often miserably failed—to actualize a destitution of work, which has instead ended up re-creating in every place the museum apparatus and the powers that it pretended to depose, which now appear all the more oppressive insofar as they are deprived of all legitimacy.

Benjamin wrote once that there is nothing more anarchic than the bourgeois order. In the same sense, Passolini has one of the officials of Salò say that the true anarchy is that of power. If this is true, then one can understand why the thought that seeks to think anarchy—as negation of "origin" and "command," *principium* and *princeps*—remains imprisoned in endless aporias and contradictions. Because power is constituted through the inclusive exclusion (*ex-ceptio*) of anarchy, the only possibility of thinking a true anarchy coincides with the lucid exposition of the anarchy internal to power. Anarchy is what becomes thinkable only at the point where we grasp and render destitute the anarchy of power. The same holds for every attempt to think anomie: it becomes accessible only through the exposition and deposition of the anomie that the juridical order has captured within itself in the state of exception. This is also true for thought that seeks to think the unrepresentable—the *demos*—that has been captured in the representative apparatus of modern democracy: only the exposition of the *a-demia* within democracy allows us to bring to appearance the absent people that it pretends to represent.

In all these cases, destitution coincides without remainder with constitution; position has no other consistency than in deposition.

ℵ. The term *archè* in Greek means both "origin" and "command." To this double meaning of the term there corresponds the fact that, in our philosophical and religious traditions alike, origin, what gives a beginning and brings into being, is not only a preamble, which disappears and ceases to act in that to which it has given life, but it is also what commands and governs its growth, development, circulation, and transmission—in a word, history.

In an important book, *The Principle of Anarchy* (1982), Reiner Schürmann sought to deconstruct this apparatus, beginning from an interpretation of Heidegger's thought. Thus, in the later Heidegger he distinguishes being as pure coming to presence and being as principle of historical-epochal economies. In contrast to Proudhon and Bakunin, who did nothing but "displace the origin" by substituting a rational principle for the principle of authority, Heidegger had thought an anarchic principle, in which origin as coming to presence is emancipated from the machine of epochal economies and no longer governs a historical becoming. The limit of Schürmann's interpretation clearly appears in the very (willfully paradoxical) syntagma that furnishes the book's title: the "principle of anarchy." It is not sufficient to separate origin and command, *principium* and *princeps*: as we have shown in *The Kingdom and the Glory*, a king who rules but does not govern is only one of the two poles of the governmental apparatus, and playing off one pole against the other is not sufficient to halt their functioning. Anarchy can never be in the position of a principle: it can only be liberated as a contact, where both *archè* as origin and *archè* as command are exposed in their non-relation and neutralized.

13. In the potential/act apparatus, Aristotle holds together two irreconcilable elements: the contingent—what can be or not be—and the necessary—what cannot not be. According to the mechanism of relation that we have defined, he thinks potential as existing in itself, in the form of a potential-not-to or impotential (*adynamia*), and act as ontologically superior and prior to potential. The paradox—and at the same time, the strength—of the apparatus is that, if one takes it literally, potential can never pass over into the act and the act always already anticipates its own possibility. For this reason Aristotle must think potential as a *hexis*, a "habit," something that one "has," and the passage to the act as an act of will.

All the more complex is the deactivation of the apparatus. What deactivates operativity is certainly an experience of potential, but of a potential that, insofar as it holds its own impotential or potential-not-to firm, exposes itself in its non-relation to the act. A poet is not someone who possesses a potential to make and, at a certain point, decides to put it into action. Having a potential in reality means: being at the mercy of one's own impotential. In this poetic experience, potential and act are no longer in relation but immediately in contact. Dante expresses this special proximity of potential and act when in the *De monarchia* he writes that the whole potential of the multitude stands *sub actu*; "otherwise there would be a separate potential, which is impossible." *Sub actu* here means, according to one of the possible meanings of the preposition *sub*, immediate coincidence in time and space (as in *sub manu*, immediately held in the hand, or *sub die*, immediately, in the same day).

At the point where the apparatus is thus deactivated, potential becomes a form-of-life and a form-of-life is constitutively destituent.

ℵ. Latin grammarians called those verbs deponent (*depositiva* or also *absolutiva* or *supina*) that, similarly to middle-voice verbs (which, in the footsteps of Benveniste, we have analyzed in order to seek in them the paradigm of a different ontology), cannot be said to be properly active or passive: *sedeo* (to sit), *sudo* (to sweat), *dormio* (to sleep), *iaceo* (to lie), *algeo* (to be cold), *sitio* (to be thirsty), *esurio* (to be hungry), *gaudeo* (to be glad). What do middle-voice or deponent verbs "depose"? They do not express an operation but depose it, neutralize it, and render it inoperative, and in this way, they expose it. The subject is not simply, in Benveniste's words, internal to the process, but in having deposed its action, he has exposed himself with it. In form-of-life, activity and passivity coincide. Thus, in the iconographic theme of the deposition—for example, in Titian's deposition at the Louvre—Christ has entirely deposed the glory and regality that, in some way, still belong to him on the cross, and yet precisely and solely in this way, when he is still beyond passion and action, the complete destitution of his regality inaugurates the new age of the redeemed humanity.

14. All living beings are in a form of life, but not all are (or not all are always) a form-of-life. At the point where form-of-life is constituted, it renders destitute and inoperative all singular forms of life. It is only in living a life that it constitutes itself as a form-of-life, as the inoperativity immanent in every life. The constitution of a form-of-life fully coincides, that is to say, with the destitution of the social and biological conditions into which it finds itself thrown. In this sense, form-of-life is the revocation of all factical vocations, which deposes them and brings them into an internal tension in the same gesture in which it maintains itself and dwells in them. It is not a question of thinking a better or more authentic form of life, a superior principle, or an elsewhere that suddenly arrives at forms of life and factical vocations to revoke them and render them inoperative. Inoperativity is not another work that suddenly arrives and works to deactivate and depose them: it coincides completely and constitutively with their destitution, with living a life.

One can therefore understand the essential function that the tradition of Western philosophy has assigned to the contemplative life and to inoperativity: form-of-life, the properly human life is the one that, by

rendering inoperative the specific works and functions of the living being, causes them to idle [It., *girare a vuoto*], so to speak, and in this way
opens them into possibility. Contemplation and inoperativity are in this
sense the metaphysical operators of anthropogenesis, which, in liberating
living human beings from every biological and social destiny and every
predetermined task, render them available for that peculiar absence of
work that we are accustomed to calling "politics" and "art." Politics and
art are not tasks nor simply "works": rather, they name the dimension in
which works—linguistic and bodily, material and immaterial, biological
and social—are deactivated and contemplated as such in order to liberate
the inoperativity that has remained imprisoned in them. And in this consists the greatest good that, according to the philosopher, the human being can hope for: "a joy born from this, that human beings contemplate
themselves and their own potential for acting" (Spinoza 2, III, prop. 53).

ℵ.   At least up to modernity, the political tradition of the West has always
sought to keep operating in every constituted system two heterogeneous powers,
which in some way mutually limited each other. Examples of this are the duality
of *auctoritas* and *potestas* in Rome, that of spiritual power and temporal power in
the Middle Ages, and that of natural law and positive law up to the eighteenth
century. These two powers could act as a reciprocal limit because they were
entirely heterogeneous: the senate, to which *auctoritas* belonged in Rome, was
lacking in the *imperium* to which the people and their supreme magistrates were
entitled; the pope did not have the temporal sword, which remained the exclusive privilege of the sovereign; the unwritten natural law came from a different
source than the written laws of the city. If already in Rome beginning with
Augustus, who had caused the two powers to coincide in his person, and in the
course of the Middle Ages, with the struggles between pope and emperor, one
of the powers had sought to eliminate the others, the modern democracies and
totalitarian states had introduced in various ways one sole principle of political
power, which in this way became unlimited. Whether it is founded, in the last
analysis, on popular sovereignty, on ethnic and racial principles, or on personal
charisma, positive right no longer knows any limits. Democracies maintain constituent power in the form of the power of revision and the control of the con-
stitutionality of laws on the part of a special court, but these are in fact internal
to the system and, in the last analysis, of a procedural nature.

Let us now imagine—something that is not within the scope of this book—in
some way translating into act the action of a destituent potential in a constituted
political system. It would be necessary to think an element that, while remaining
heterogeneous to the system, had the capacity to render decisions destitute, sus-

pend them, and render them inoperative. Plato had in mind something of the kind when at the end of the *Laws* (968c), he mentions as "protector" (*phylake*) of the city a "Nocturnal Council" (*nykterinos syllogos*), which, however, is not an institution in a technical sense because, as Socrates specifies, "it is impossible to lay down the council's activities until it has been established [*prin a kosmethe*] . . . through a long standing together [*metà synousia pollen*]." While the modern State pretends through the state of exception to include within itself the anarchic and anomic element it cannot do without, it is rather a question of displaying its radical heterogeneity in order to let it act as a purely destituent potential.

Bibliography

Where English translations are available, works are cited according to the page number of the original text, followed by the page number of the translation, or else by a standard textual division that is consistent across translations and editions. Translations have frequently been altered for greater conformity with Agamben's usage. Where no English translation is listed, the translations are my own.

All biblical quotations are based on the New Revised Standard Version. All quotations from the works of Aristotle are based on *The Complete Works of Aristotle: The Revised Oxford Translation*, ed. Jonathan Barnes, 2 vols. (Princeton, NJ: Princeton University Press, 1984). All quotations from the works of Plato are based on Plato, *Complete Works*, ed. John M. Cooper and D. S. Hutchinson (Indianapolis, IN: Hackett, 1997). Quotations from these and other ancient texts, however, have been thoroughly revised in light of Agamben's own translations. Transliterations from Greek and Hebrew texts follow those provided by the author in the original Italian edition.

Adorno and Sohn-Rethel: Theodor W. Adorno and Alfred Sohn-Rethel, *Briefwechsel 1936–1969*, ed. Christoph Gödde (Munich: edition text + kritik, 1991).

Agamben 1: Giorgio Agamben, *L'aperto. L'uomo e l'animale* (Turin: Bollati Boringhieri, 2002). English translation: *The Open: Man and Animal*, trans. Kevin Attell (Stanford, CA: Stanford University Press, 2004).

Agamben 2: Giorgio Agamben, *Il Regno e la Gloria. Per una genealogia dell'economia e del governo* (Vicenza: Neri Pozza, 2007). English translation: *The Kingdom and the Glory: For a Theological Genealogy of Economy and Government*, trans. Lorenzo Chiesa and Matteo Mandarini (Stanford, CA: Stanford University Press, 2011).

Agamben 3: Giorgio Agamben, *Nudità* (Rome: Nottetempo, 2009). English translation: *Nudities*, trans. David Kishik and Stefan Pedatella (Stanford, CA: Stanford University Press, 2010).

Agamben 4: Giorgio Agamben, *Homo sacer. Il potere sovrano e la nuda vita* (Turin: Einaudi, 2009). English translation: *Homo Sacer: Sovereign Power and Bare Life*, trans. Daniel Heller-Roazen (Stanford, CA: Stanford University Press, 1998).

Alexander: *Alexandri Aphrodisiensis praeter commentaria scripta minora. De anima liber cum mantissa*, ed. Ivo Bruns (Berolini: Reimer, 1887). English translation: *Supplement to* On the Soul, trans. R. W. Sharples (New York: Bloomsbury, 2014).

Altman: Irwin Altman, "Privacy: A Conceptual Analysis," *Environment and Behavior* 8.1 (1976): 7–29.

Aquinas 1: Thomas Aquinas, *Questiones disputatae de veritate, Questions 10–20*, trans. James V. McGlynn (Chicago: Henry Regnery, 1953).

Aquinas 2: Thomas Aquinas, *The Summa Theologica of St. Thomas Aquinas*, 2nd rev. ed., trans. Fathers of the English Dominican Province (1920). Online edition, 2008: http://www.newadvent.org/summa.

Aquinas 3: Thomas Aquinas, *Questiones disputatae de veritate, Questions 21–29*, trans. Robert W. Schmidt (Chicago: Henry Regnery, 1954).

Aquinas 4: Thomas Aquinas, *Commentary on Aristotle's* Politics, trans. Richard Regan (Indianapolis, IN: Hackett, 2007).

Aquinas 5: Thomas Aquinas, *Summa contra Gentiles, Book Four: Salvation*, trans. Charles J. O'Neill (Notre Dame, IN: University of Notre Dame Press, 1989).

Aquinas 6: Thomas Aquinas, *Expositio super librum Boethii "De hebdomadibus,"* trans. Peter King. Online edition, 2004: individual.utoronto.ca/pking/translations/AQUINAS.Exposition_of_Hebdomads.pdf.

Arendt: Hannah Arendt, *Vita activa, oder von tätigen Leben*, new ed. (Munich: Piper, 1981).

Arpe: Curt Arpe, *Das Ti en einai bei Aristoteles* (Hamburg: Friederichsen, 1938).

Artemidorus: *Artemidori Daldiani Onirocriticon Libri V*, ed. Roger A. Pack (Lipsiae in aedibus B. G. Teunberi, 1963). English translation: Artemidorus, *The Interpretation of Dreams: Oneirocritica*, 2nd ed., trans. Robert J. White (Torrance, CA: Original Books, 1990).

Augustine 1: Augustine, *On Nature and Grace*, ed. Benjamin B. Warfield, trans. Peter Holmes and Robert Ernest Wallis, in *Nicene and Post-Nicene Fathers*, First Series, vol. 5, ed. Philip Schaff (Buffalo, NY: Christian Literature Publishing, 1887).

Augustine 2: Augustine, *On the Trinity*, ed. John E. Rotelle, trans. Edmund Hill (New York: New City Press, 1991).

Barker: Ernest Barker, *The Political Thought of Plato and Aristotle* (New York: Dover, 1918).

Baumstark: Anton Baumstark, *Liturgia romana e liturgia dell'esarcato* (Rome: Liberia pontificia di Federico Pustet, 1904).

Becker: Oskar Becker, *Von der Hinfälligkeit des Schönen und der Abenteuerlich- keith der Künstlers* (1929), in *Dasein und Dawesen. Gesammelte philosophische Schriften* (Pfüllingen: Neske, 1961).

Beckmann: Jan Peter Beckmann, *Die Relation der Identität nach Johannes Duns Scotus* (Bonn: H. Bouvier, 1967).

Bénatouïl: Thomas Bénatouïl, *Faire usage: La pratique du stoïcisme* (Paris: Vrin, 2006).

Benjamin 1: Rolf Tiedemann, ed., *Frankfurter Adorno Blätter*, vol. 4 (Munich: edition text + kritik, 1995). English translation: "Notes toward a Work on the Category of Justice," trans. Peter Fenves, in *The Messianic Reduction: Walter Benjamin and the Shape of Time, by Peter Fenves* (Stanford, CA: Stanford University Press, 2011).

Benjamin 2: Walter Benjamin, *Gesammelte Schriften*, vol. 4.1 (Frankfurt am Main: Suhrkamp, 1980). English translation: *Selected Writings*, vol. 2, pt. 1, ed. Michael William Jennings, Howard Eiland, and Gary Smith, trans. Rodney Livingstone (Cambridge, MA: Harvard University Press, 2005).

Benjamin 3: Walter Benjamin, *Gesammelte Schriften*, vol. 6 (Frankfurt am Main: Suhrkamp, 1985).

Benjamin 4: Walter Benjamin, "Zur Kritik der Gewalt," in *Kairos: Schriften zur Philosophie*, ed. Ralf Konersmann (Frankfurt am Main: Suhrkamp, 2007). English translation: "Critique of Violence," in *Selected Writings: Volume 1, 1913–1926*, ed. Marcus Bullock and Michael W. Jennings (Cambridge, MA: Harvard University Press, 1996).

Benveniste: Émile Benveniste, *Problèmes de linguistique générale*, vol. 1 (Paris: Gallimard, 1966). English translation: *Problems in General Linguistics*, trans. Mary Elizabeth Meek (Coral Gables, FL: University of Miami Press, 1971).

Black: Max Black, "*Lebensform und Sprachspiel* in Wittgenstein's Later Work," in *Wittgenstein and His Impact on Contemporary Thought: Proceedings of the Second International Wittgenstein Symposium, ed.* Elisabeth Leinfellner et al. (Vienna: Holder-Pichler-Tempsky, 1978).

Boehm, A.: Alfred Boehm, *Le vinculum substantiale chez Leibniz: Ses origines historiques* (Paris: Vrin, 1962).

Boehm, R.: Rudolf Boehm, *Das Grundlegende und das Wesentliche: zu Aristoteles' Abhandlung über das Sein und das Seiende (Metaphysik Z)* (The Hague: M. Nijhoff, 1965).

Casel: Odo Casel, "*Actio* in liturgischer Verwendung," *Jahrbuch für Liturgiewis- senschaft* 1 (1921): 34–39.

Cicero 1: Cicero, *De officiis* (Loeb Classical Library), trans. Walter Miller (New York: MacMillan, 1913).

Cicero 2: Cicero, *De finibus bonorum et malorum* (Loeb Classical Library), trans. Clinton Walter Keys (Cambridge, MA: Harvard University Press, 1994).

Clement: Clement of Alexandria, *Exhortation to the Heathen*, trans. William Wilson, in *Ante-Nicene Fathers*, vol. 2, ed. Alexander Roberts, James Donaldson, and A. Cleveland Coxe (Buffalo, NY: Christian Literature Publishing, 1885).

Colli: Giorgio Colli, *La ragione errabonda* (Milan: Adelphi, 1982).

Corpus Hippocraticum: Hippocrates (Loeb Classical Library), 10 vols. (Cambridge, MA: Harvard University Press, 1923–1931).

Courtine: Jean-François Courtine, *Suárez et le système de la métaphysique* (Paris: PUF, 1990).

Dante 1: *The Convivio of Dante Alighieri*, trans. Phillip Henry Wickstool (London: J. M. Dent, 1903). Online edition: https://archive.org/details/convivioofdantea00dantiala.

Dante 2: Dante, *Monarchia*, ed. and trans. Prue Shaw (New York: Cambridge University Press, 1995).

Debord 1: Guy Debord, *Oeuvres cinématographiques complètes, 1952–1978* (Paris: Gallimard, 1994). English translation: *Complete Cinematic Works: Scripts, Stills, Documents*, trans. Ken Knabb (Oakland, CA: AK Press, 2005).

Debord 2: Guy Debord, *Panégyrique*, vol. 2, in *Oeuvres*, ed. Jean-Louis Rançon (Paris: Gallimard, 2006). English translation: *Panegyric: Volumes 1 and 2*, trans. James Brook and John McHale (New York: Verso, 2009).

Debord 3: Guy Debord, *La société du spectacle* (Paris: Buchet-Chastel, 1967). English translation: *Society of the Spectacle* (Detroit, MI: Black & Red, 1997).

Deleuze, Gilles, and Félix Guattari, *What Is Philosophy?*, trans. Hugh Thomlinson and Graham Burchell (New York: Columbia University Press, 1996).

Deligny: Fernand Deligny, *Les enfants et le silence* (Paris: Galilée, 1980).

Digest: Justinian, *Digest*, in *The Civil Law: Including The Twelve Tables, The Institutes of Gaius, The Rules of Ulpian, The Opinions of Paulus, The Enactments of Justinian, and The Constitutions of Leo*, trans. S. P. Scott, 17 vols. (Cincinnati, OH: Central Trust, 1932).

Diogenes Laertius: Diogenes Laertius, *Lives of Eminent Philosophers* (Loeb Classical Library), trans. R. D. Hicks (Cambridge, MA: Harvard University Press, 1972).

Dörrie: Heinrich Dörrie, "*Hypostasis*, Wort- und Bedeutungsgeschichte," in *Nachrichten der Akademie der Wissenschaft in Göttingen*, Phil. Kl., 3 (1955), pp. 35–92; now in Dörrie, *Platonia minora* (Munich: Fink 1976).

Düring: *Der Protreptikos des Aristoteles*, ed. Ingemar Düring (Frankfurt am Main: Klosterman, 1969).

Fehling: Detlev Fehling, *Ethologische Überlegungen auf dem Gebiet der Altertumskunde: phallische Demonstration, Fernsicht, Steinigung* (Munich: C. H. Beck, 1974).

Foucault 1: Michel Foucault, *L'hermeneutique du sujet* (Paris: Gallimard-Seuil, 2001). English translation: *The Hermeneutics of the Subject: Lectures at the Collège de France, 1981–1982*, ed. Frédéric Gros, trans. Graham Burchell (New York: Picador, 2005).

Foucault 2: Michel Foucault, *Dits et écrits (1954–1988)*, vol. 4, *1980–1988* (Paris: Gallimard, 1994). English translation: see Lotringer and Rabinow.

Foucault 3: Michel Foucault, *Histoire de la sexualité 2. L'usage des plaisirs* (Paris: Gallimard, 1984). English translation: *The Use of Pleasure: The History of Sexuality, vol. 2*, trans. Robert Hurley (New York: Vintage, 1990).

Foucault 4: Michel Foucault, "Qu'est-ce qu'un auteur?," in *Dits et écrits (1954–1988)*, vol. 1, *1954–1975* (Paris: Gallimard, 1994). English translation: "What Is an Author?," in *Language, Counter-memory, Practice: Selected Essays and Interviews*, ed. Donald F. Bouchard (Ithaca, NY: Cornell University Press, 1980).

Foucault 5: Michel Foucault, *La courage de la vérité* (Paris: Gallimard, 2009). English translation: *The Courage of Truth: Government of Self and Others II, Lectures at the Collège de France, 1983–1984*, ed. Frédéric Gros, trans. Graham Burchell (New York: Picador, 2011).

Foucault 6: Michel Foucault, *Naissance de la clinique* (Paris: PUF, 1963). English translation: *The Birth of the Clinic: An Archaeology of Medical Perception*, trans. A. M. Sheridan Smith (New York: Vintage, 1994).

Foucault and Le Bitoux: Michel Foucault and Jean Le Bitoux, "The Gay Science," trans. Nicole Morar and Daniel W. Smith, *Critical Inquiry* 37 (Spring 2011): 385–403.

Fremont: Christiane Fremont, *L'être et la relation* (Paris: Vrin, 1981).

Friedmann: Georges Friedmann, *Leibniz et Spinoza* (Paris: Gallimard, 1962).

Galen 1: *Galeni de usu partium libri XVII*, ed. Georgius Helmreich (Amsterdam: Hakkert, 1968). English translation: *On the Usefulness of the Parts of the Body*, ed. and trans. Margaret Tallmadge May, vol. 2 (Ithaca, NY: Cornell University Press, 1968).

Galen 2: Ian Johnston and G. H. R. Horsley, eds. and trans., *Galen: Methods of Medicine* (Loeb Classical Library), 3 vols. (Cambridge, MA: Harvard University Press, 2011).

Goldschmidt: Victor Goldschmidt, *Écrits*, vol. 1, *Études de philosophie ancienne* (Paris: Vrin, 1984).

Gregory Nazianzen: *Orations*, trans. Charles Gordon Browne and James Edward Swallow, in *Nicene and Post-Nicene Fathers*, Second Series, vol. 7, ed. Philip Schaff and Henry Wace (Buffalo, NY: Christian Literature Publishing, 1894).

Gregory of Nyssa: *An Address on Religious Instruction*, in *Christology of the Later Fathers*, ed. Edward R. Hardy (Philadelphia: Westminster, 1954).

Gregory the Great: *The Life of Saint Benedict*, trans. Terrence Kardong (Collegeville, MN: Liturgical Press, 2009).

Hadot 1: Pierre Hadot, "Un dialogue interrompu avec M. Foucault," in *Exercises spirituels et philosophie antique* (Paris: Albin Michel, 2002).

Hadot 2: Pierre Hadot, *Plotin, Porphyre. Études néoplatoniciennes* (Paris: Les Belles Lettres, 1999).

Harper: Kyle Harper, *Slavery in the Late Roman World, AD 275–425* (Cambridge: Cambridge University Press, 2011).

Hegel: Georg Wilhelm Friedrich Hegel, *Phenomenology of Spirit*, trans. A. V. Miller (New York: Oxford University Press, 1977).

Heidegger 1: Martin Heidegger, *Sein und Zeit*, 12th ed. (Tübingen: M. Niemeyer, 1972). English translation: *Being and Time*, trans. John Macquarrie and Edward Robinson (New York: Harper & Row, 1962).

Heidegger 2: Martin Heidegger, *Zur Sache des Denkens* (Tübingen: M. Niemeyer, 1976). English translation: *On Time and Being*, trans. Joan Stambaugh (New York: Harper & Row, 1972).

Heidegger 3: Martin Heidegger, *Holzwege* (Frankfurt am Main: Klostermann, 1950). English translation: *Off the Beaten Track*, ed. and trans. Julian Young and Kenneth Haynes (New York: Cambridge University Press, 2002).

Heidegger 4: Martin Heidegger, "Die Frage nach der Technik," in *Vorträge und Aufsätze* (Stuttgart: Neske, 1954). English translation: "The Question concerning Technology," trans. William Lovitt, in *Basic Writings*, ed. David Farrell Krell, rev. exp. ed. (New York: HarperCollins, 1993).

Heidegger 5: Martin Heidegger, *Die Grundbegriffe der Metaphysik. Welt-Endlichkeit-Einsamkeit* (Gesamtausgabe 29/30) (Frankfurt am Main: Klostermann, 1983). English translation: *The Fundamental Concepts of Metaphysics: World, Finitude, Solitude*, trans. William McNeill and Nicholas Walker (Bloomington: Indiana University Press, 1995).

Heidegger 6: Martin Heidegger, *Parmenides* (Gesamtausgabe 44) (Frankfurt am Main: Klostermann, 1993). English translation: *Parmenides*, trans. André Schuwer and Richard Rojewicz (Bloomington: Indiana University Press, 1992).

Heidegger 7: Martin Heidegger, *Kant und das Problem der Metaphysik* (Frankfurt am Main: Klostermann, 1929). English translation: *Kant and the Problem of Metaphysics*, 5th ed., trans. Richard Taft (Bloomington: Indiana University Press, 1997).

Heidegger 8: Martin Heidegger, *Metaphysische Anfangsgründe der Logik im Ausgang vom Leibniz* (Gesamtausgabe 26) (Frankfurt am Main: Klostermann, 1978). English translation: *Metaphysical Foundations of Logic*, trans. Michael Heim (Bloomington: Indiana University Press, 1984).

Heidegger 9: Martin Heidegger, *Beiträge zur Philosophie* (Gesamtausgabe 65) (Frankfurt am Main: Klostermann, 1989). English translation: *Contributions to Philosophy: Of the Event*, trans. Richard Rojcewicz and Daniela Vallega-Neu (Bloomington: Indiana University Press, 2012).

Heidegger 10: Martin Heidegger, *Wegmarken* (Frankfurt am Main: Klostermann, 1967). English translation: *Pathmarks*, ed. William McNeill (New York: Cambridge University Press, 1998).

Heidegger 11: Martin Heidegger, *Hölderlins Hymnen "Germanien" und "Der Rhein"* (Gesamtausgabe 39) (Frankfurt am Main: Klostermann, 1980). English translation: *Hölderlin's Hymns "Germania" and "The Rhine,"* trans. William McNeill and Julia A. Ireland (Bloomington: Indiana University Press, 2014).

Herrera: Abraham Cohen de Herrera, *Gate of Heaven*, ed. Kenneth Krabbenhoft (New York: Brill, 2002).

Hölderlin: Friedrich Hölderlin, *Sämtliche Werke*, vol. 2, *Gedichte nach 1800*, ed. Friedrich Beissner (Stuttgart: Kohlhammer, 1953).

Homer: *The Iliad*, ed. Bernard Knox, trans. Robert Fagles (New York: Penguin, 1990).

Hugh of Digne: *Expositio Hugonis super regulam fratrum minorum*, in Alessandra Sisto, *Figure del primo Francescanesimo in Provenza. Ugo e Douceline di Digne* (Florence: Olschki, 1971).

Hugh of Saint Victor: *The Didascalicon of Hugh of St. Victor: A Medieval Guide to the Arts*, ed. and trans. Jerome Taylor (New York: Columbia University Press, 1991).

Husserl 1: Edmund Husserl, *Husserliana: Gesammelte Werke*, vol. 14, *Zur Phänomenologie der Intersubjektivität: Texte aus dem Nachlass. 2, 1921–1928* (The Hague: M. Nijhoff, 1973).

Husserl 2: Edmund Husserl, *Husserliana: Gesammelte Werke*, vol. 13, *Zur Phänomenologie der Intersubjektivität: Texte aus dem Nachlass. 1, 1905–1920* (The Hague: M. Nijhoff, 1973).

Hyatte: Reginal Hyatte, ed. and trans., *The Prophet of Islam in Old French: The Romance of Muhammad (1258) and* The Book of Muhammad's Ladder *(1264)* (Leiden, Netherlands: Brill, 1997).

Illich 1: Ivan Illich, *The Rivers North of the Future: The Testament of Ivan Illich*, ed. David Cayley (Toronto: House of Anansi, 2005).

Illich 2: Ivan Illich, *In the Mirror of the Past: Lectures and Addresses, 1978–1990* (New York: Marion Boyars, 1992).

Kafka: Franz Kafka, *Letters to Milena*, trans. Philip Boehm (New York: Schocken, 1990).

Kant: Immanuel Kant, *Critique of Pure Reason*, trans. Werner S. Pluhar (Indianapolis, IN: Hackett, 1996).

Keil: *Grammatici latini*, ed. Henrici Keilii, vol. 1, *Artis grammaticae libri 5* (Lipsiae: in aedibus B. G. Teubnerii, 1955).

Kerényi: Karl Kerényi, *Umgang mit Göttlichem: über Mythologie und Religionsgeschichte* (Göttingen: Vandenhoeck & Ruprecht, 1961).

Koyré: Alexander Koyré, *Études d'histoire de la pensée philosophique* (Paris: A. Colin, 1961).

Leibniz 1: Gottfried Wilhelm Leibniz, *Die philosophischen Schriften*, vol. 2, ed. G. I. Gerhardt (Hildescheim: Olms, 1960). English translation: *The Leibniz-Des Bosses Correspondence*, ed. and trans. Brandon C. Look and Donald Rutherford (New Haven, CT: Yale University Press, 2007).

Leibniz 2: Gottfried Wilhelm Leibniz, *Philosophische Schriften*, ed. Hans Heinz Holz, vol. 1 (Darmstadt: Wissenschaftliche Buchgesellschaft, 1965).

Leibniz 3: Gottfried Wilhelm Leibniz, *Sämtliche Schriften und Briefe*, ed. Deutsche Akademie der Wissenschaft zu Berlin (Leipzig-Berlin: Akademie Verlag, 1923–present).

Levinas 1: Emmanuel Levinas, *De l'évasion* (Fata Morgana: 1982). English translation: *On Escape / De l'évasion*, trans. Bettina Bergo (Stanford, CA: Stanford University Press, 2003).

Levinas 2: Emmanuel Levinas, *De l'existence à l'existant* (Paris: Fontaine, 1947). English translation: *Existence and Existents*, trans. Alphonso Linguis (Boston: Kluwer Academic Publishers, 1988).

Lizzini: Olga Lizzini, *Fluxus (fayd): Indagine sui fondamenti della Metafisica e della Fisica di Avicenna* (Bari: Edizioni di Pagina, 2011).

Lotringer: Michel Foucault, *Foucault Live: Interviews 1961–1984*, ed. Sylvère Lotringer, trans. Lysa Hochroth and John Johnston (New York: Semiotext[e], 1996).

Lucretius: Lucretius, *On the Nature of the Universe*, ed. John Godwin, trans. R. E. Latham (New York: Penguin, 2005).

Maine de Biran: François-Pierre Maine de Biran, *Oeuvres*, vol. 3, *Mémoire sur la décomposition de la pensée, précédé du Mémoire sur les rapports de l'idéologie et des mathématiques*, ed. François Azouvi (Paris: Vrin, 1988).

Marsilius: Marsilius of Padua, *The Defender of the Peace*, ed. and trans. Annabel Brett (New York: Cambridge University Press, 2005).

Montaigne: Michel de Montaigne, *The Complete Essays*, ed. and trans. M. A. Screech (New York: Penguin, 1993).

Origen: Origen of Alexandria, *Commentary on the Gospel according to John, Books 1–10*, trans. Ronald E. Heine (Washington, DC: Catholic University of American Press, 1989).

Peterson: Erik Peterson, "Herkunft und Bedeutung der Monos pro monon-Formel bei Plotin," *Philologus* 88 (1933).

Petrarch: Francesco Petrarch, "The Ascent of Mount Ventoux," in *The Renaissance Philosophy of Man*, ed. E. Cassirer et al. (Chicago: University of Chicago Press, 1948).

Philoponus: *Philoponi in Aristotelis Categorias commentarium*, ed. Adolfus Busse (Berolini: Reimer, 1898).

Picavet: François Picavet, "Hypostases platoniennes et Trinité chrétienne," *Annuaire de l'École pratique des hautes études. Section de science religieuse* (1917–18) : 1–52.

Pliny 1: Pliny, *Letters* (Loeb Classical Library), 2 vols., trans. William Melmoth and W. M. L. Hutchinson (Cambridge, MA: Harvard University Press, 1963).

Pliny 2: Pliny, *The Natural History* (Loeb Classical Library), 10 vols., trans. D. E. Eichholz (Cambridge, MA: Harvard University Press, 1962).

Plotinus: *Enneads* (Loeb Classical Library), 7 vols., trans. A. H. Armstrong (Cambridge, MA: Harvard University Press, 1988).

Pohlenz: Max Pohlenz, *Grundfragen der stoischen Philosophie* (Göttingen: Vandenhoeck & Ruprecht, 1940).

Proclus 1: *The Elements of Theology*, ed. and trans. F. R. Dodds, 2nd ed. (London: Oxford Clarendon Press, 1963).

Proclus 2: Proclus, *Commentaire sur La République*, vol. 3, *Dissertations 15–17, Rép. 10. Index général*, ed. A. J. Festugière (Paris: Librarie Philosophique J. Vrin, 1970).

Rabinow: Michel Foucault, *Ethics: Subjectivity and Truth*, ed. Paul Rabinow (New York: New Press, 1997).

Redard: Georges Redard, *Recherches sur ΧΡΗ, ΧΡΗΣΘΑΙ. Étude sémantique* (Paris: Champion, 1953).

Reinhardt: Karl Reinhardt, *Platons Mythen* (Bonn: Cohen, 1927).

Roguet: Saint Thomas d'Aquin, *Somme théologique. Les sacrements: 3a, Questions 60–65*, ed. A.-M. Roguet (Paris: Cerf, 1999).

Sade: Marquis de Sade, *Juliette*, trans. Austryn Wainhouse (New York: Grove Press, 2007).

Scholem 1: Gershom Scholem, *Origins of the Kabbalah*, trans. Allan Arkush (Princeton, NJ: Princeton University Press, 1991).

Scholem 2: David Biale, "Gershom Scholem's Ten Unhistorical Aphorisms on Kabbalah: Text and Commentary," *Modern Judaism* 5.1 (1985): 67–93.

Schuhl: Pierre-Maxime Schuhl, *Machinisme et philosophie* (Paris: PUF, 1947).

Schürmann: Reiner Schürmann, *Le principe d'anarchie* (Paris: Seuil, 1982).

Seneca: *Ad Lucilium epistulae morales* (Loeb Classical Library), 3 vols., trans. Richard M. Gummere (Cambridge, MA: Harvard University Press, 1962).

Sereni: *The Selected Poetry and Prose of Vittorio Sereni: A Bilingual Edition*, trans. Marcus Perryman and Peter Robinson (Chicago: University of Chicago Press, 2008).

Spinoza 1: Baruch Spinoza, *Compendium grammatices linguae hebraeae*, in *Opera*, vol. 1, ed. Carl Gebhardt (Heidelberg: Carl Winters Universitätsbuchhandlung, 1925).

Spinoza 2: Baruch Spinoza, *The Ethics, The Treatise on the Emendation of the Intellect, and Selected Letters*, ed. Seymour Feldman, trans. Samuel Shirley (Indianapolis, IN: Hackett, 1992).

Spinoza 3: Baruch Spinoza, *Principles of Descartes' Philosophy*, trans. Halbert Hains Britan (Chicago: Open Court, 1905).

Spinoza 4: Baruch Spinoza, *Spinoza's Short Treatise on God, Man, and Human Welfare*, trans. Lydia Gillingham Robinson (Chicago: Open Court, 1909)

Stein: Edith Stein, *On the Problem of Empathy*, trans. Waltraut Stein (Washington, DC: ICS Publications, 1989).

Strycker: Émile de Strycker, "Concepts-clés et terminologie dans les livres II à VII des Topiques," in *Aristotle on Dialectic: The Topics. Proceedings of the Third Symposium Aristotelicum, ed. G. E. L. Owen* (Oxford: Clarendon, 1968).

Suárez 1: *Francisci Suárez e Societate Jesu Opera omnia*, vol. 20 (Paris: Ludovicum Vivès, 1856).

Suárez 2: *Francisci Suárez e Societate Jesu Opera omnia*, vol. 25 (Paris: Ludovicum Vivès, 1861).

Themistius: *Themistii in libros Aristotelis de anima periphrasis*, ed. Ricardus Heinze (Berolini: Reimer, 1900). English translation: *On Aristotle on the Soul*, trans. Robert B. Todd (New York: A & C Black, 2014).

Thomas 1: Yan Thomas, "L' 'usage' et les 'fruits' de l'esclave," *Enquête* 7 (1998): 203–230.

Thomas 2: Yan Thomas, "Le corps de l'esclave et son travail à Rome. Analyse d'une dissociation juridique," in *Corps romains, ed. Philippe Moreau* (Grenoble: J. Millon, 2002).

Tiqqun: "Introduction à la guerre civile," in *Tiqqun* 2 (2001). English translation: *Introduction to Civil War*, trans. Alex Galloway and Jason E. Smith (Los Angeles: Semiotext[e], 2010).

Trapp: Damasus Trapp, "Aegidii Romani de doctrina modorum," *Angelicum* 12 (1935).

Vernant and Vidal-Naquet: Jean-Paul Vernant and Pierre Vidal-Naquet, *Travail et esclavage en Grèce ancienne* (Brussels: Complexe, 1988).

Veyne: Paul Veyne, "Le dernier Foucault," *Critique* 471–472 (1986): 933–941. English translation: "The Final Foucault and His Ethics," trans. Catherine Porter and Arnold I. Davidson, *Critical Inquiry* 20 (Autumn 1993): 1–9.

Victorinus: Marius Victorinus, *Traités théologiques sur la Trinité*, ed. Pierre Hadot, vol. 1, Sources Chrétiennes series (Paris: Les Éditions du Cerf, 1960). English translation: *Theological Treatises on the Trinity*, trans. Mary T. Clark (Washington, DC: Catholic University of America Press, 2002).

Wittgenstein 1: Ludwig Wittgenstein, *Philosophische Untersuchungen/ Philosophical Investigations*, 4th ed., ed. P. M. S. Hacker and Joachim Schulte, trans. G. E. M. Anscombe, P. M. S. Hacker, and Joachim Schulte (New York: Wiley-Blackwell, 2009).

Wittgenstein 2: Ludwig Wittgenstein, *Schriften 6. Bemerkungen über die Grundlagen der Mathematik* (Frankfurt am Main: Suhrkamp, 1974). English translation: *Remarks on the Foundations of Mathematics*, ed. Georg Henrik Wright,

Rush Rhees, G. E. M. Anscombe, trans. G. E. M. Anscombe (Cambridge, MA: MIT Press, 1983).

Wittgenstein 3: Ludwig Wittgenstein, *Schriften 4. Philosophische Grammatik* (Frankfurt am Main: Suhrkamp, 1969). English translation: *Philosophical Grammar*, ed. Rush Rhees, trans. Anthony Kenny (Los Angeles: University of California Press, 1974).

Wittgenstein 4: Ludwig Wittgenstein, *Schriften 2. Philosophische Bemerkungen* (Frankfurt am Main: Suhrkamp, 1970). English translation: *Philosophical Remarks*, trans. Rush Rhees (Chicago: University of Chicago Press, 1980).

Wittgenstein 5: Ludwig Wittgenstein, *Wittgenstein's Lectures, Cambridge 1932–1935* (Oxford: Blackwell, 1979).

Wittgenstein 6: Ludwig Wittgenstein, *On Certainty* (Oxford: Blackwell, 1969).

Wolfson: Harry Austryn Wolfon, *The Philosophy of Spinoza*, vol. 1 (New York: Schocken, 1969).

Xenophon: Xenophon, *Memorabilia, Oeconomicus, Symposium, Apologia* (Loeb Classical Library), trans. E. C. Marchant and E. T. Dodd (Cambridge, MA: Harvard University Press, 1923).

Crossing Aesthetics

Serge Leclaire, *A Child Is Being Killed: On Primary Narcissism and the Death Drive*

Sigmund Freud, *Writings on Art and Literature*

Cornelius Castoriadis, *World in Fragments: Writings on Politics, Society, Psychoanalysis, and the Imagination*

Thomas Keenan, *Fables of Responsibility: Aberrations and Predicaments in Ethics and Politics*

Emmanuel Levinas, *Proper Names*

Alexander García Düttmann, *At Odds with AIDS: Thinking and Talking About a Virus*

Maurice Blanchot, *Friendship*

Jean-Luc Nancy, *The Muses*

Massimo Cacciari, *Posthumous People: Vienna at the Turning Point*

David E. Wellbery, *The Specular Moment: Goethe's Early Lyric and the Beginnings of Romanticism*

Edmond Jabès, *The Little Book of Unsuspected Subversion*

Hans-Jost Frey, *Studies in Poetic Discourse: Mallarmé, Baudelaire, Rimbaud, Hölderlin*

Pierre Bourdieu, *The Rules of Art: Genesis and Structure of the Literary Field*

Nicolas Abraham, *Rhythms: On the Work, Translation, and Psychoanalysis*

Jacques Derrida, *On the Name*

David Wills, *Prosthesis*

Maurice Blanchot, *The Work of Fire*

Jacques Derrida, *Points . . . : Interviews, 1974–1994*

J. Hillis Miller, *Topographies*

Philippe Lacoue-Labarthe, *Musica Ficta (Figures of Wagner)*

Jacques Derrida, *Aporias*

Emmanuel Levinas, *Outside the Subject*